WOMEN IN ASIA AND THE PACIFIC
Towards an East-West Dialogue

WOMEN IN ASIA AND THE PACIFIC
Towards an East-West Dialogue

edited by
Madeleine J. Goodman

The Women's Studies Program
University of Hawaii

This publication has been funded by the
University of Hawaii Foundation

Distributed for the Women's Studies Program
by the University of Hawaii Press:

Order Department
University of Hawaii Press
2840 Kolowalu Street
Honolulu, Hawaii 96822

Library of Congress Cataloging in Publication Data
Main entry under title:

Women in Asia and the Pacific.

1. Women--Cross-cultural studies--Congresses.
2. Feminism--Cross-cultural studies--Congresses.
3. Women--Asia--Congresses. 4. Women--Pacific Area--
Congresses. I. Goodman, Madeleine J., 1945-
II. University of Hawaii at Manoa. Women's Studies Program.

GN479.7.W665 1985   305.4'095   85-10034
ISBN 0-8248-1013-9

Cover design by Billie Ikeda

CONTRIBUTORS

BELINDA AQUINO is an Associate Professor of Political Science
    and Director of the Philippine Studies Program at the
    University of Hawaii.

DONNA BELLORADO is Director of the Educational Equity Center
    for the Pacific in San Francisco.

CAROL J. PIERCE COLFER is a specialist in Women in Development
    at the College of Tropical Agriculture, University of
    Hawaii.

LARENE DESPAIN is an Assistant Professor of English at the
    University of Hawaii.

JEAN BETHKE ELSHTAIN is Professor of Political Science at the
    University of Massachusetts, Amherst.

AGNES ESTIOKO-GRIFFIN is a graduate student in Anthropology at
    the University of the Philippines, Manila.

LENN E. GOODMAN is Professor of Philosophy at the University of
    Hawaii.

MADELEINE J. GOODMAN is Director of the Women's Studies Program
    at the University of Hawaii.

P. BION GRIFFIN is an Associate Professor of Anthropology at
    the University of Hawaii.

JANICE S. HYDE is a doctoral candidate in Anthropology at
    Syracuse University in New York.

MALASHRI LAL is Professor of English at Jesus and Mary College,
    University of Delhi, New Delhi.

MARTHA LOGSDON is an Associate Professor of Political Science
    at Central Michigan University, Mount Pleasant, Michigan.

JANE MARGOLD is an independent researcher and journalist from
    Oakland, California.

JOYCE PETTIGREW is Senior Lecturer in Social Anthropology at
    Queen's University, Belfast, Northern Ireland.

IRENE TINKER is Director of the Equity Policy Center in
    Washington, D.C.

Contents

For many Women's Studies scholars in the 1970s feminist scholarship held an exclusively Western and theoretical orientation with the straightforward objective of exploring and exposing androcentric biases in the basic disciplines of the Humanities, the Natural and Social Sciences. The "universality of male dominance" often became an ideological bug-bear, while the "status of women" became a categorical catch-all to denominate the interests of all women as a unified under-class with respect to society as a whole. The perspectives which fired much of the initial content of Women's Studies research and provided much of the thrust toward the development of Women's Studies courses and curricula in virtually every major Western university in turn became subject to evaluation and criticism as the field of Women's Studies broadened and matured.

Shortcomings of the prevailing trends in feminist scholarship could be identified in its concentration on invidious distinctions between the sexes and its disinclination to view gender and gender-equity in any but economic and political terms. The androgynous ideal projected in many of the feminist revisionist prescriptions, can be seen in retrospect to have been extracted at a heavy cost: the willing immolation of those distinctive attributes of maleness and femaleness--skills, values, styles and modes of expression in which so much of human identity, culture, history and biologically speaking, even futurity are invested.

Even as patriarchal stereotypes of women were revealed and exploded, other insidious images and iconographies of ideal womanhood were devised. The woman of the future was exhorted to free herself from the overburdening demands of the family by monetarizing aspects of her role as wife, mother and homemaker or by bartering for equivalent worth in reciprocal services within the family. This overly mechanistic contractual view of marriage and the family was criticized by Betty Friedan and others as unduly militant and hostile, at cross purposes with the general aim of depolarizing male and female roles within the family. Only a veneer of cooperation could be achieved through contractual obligations to perform equal shares of every domestic chore and child care activity. By fitting the family to an industrial model, male and female roles were reduced to interchangeable components, trivializing their value in non-materialistic terms. By treating familial relations legalistically many would be defenders of women's rights sacrificed for themselves and were ready to see others sacrifice the informal reciprocity and intimacy of family relations in exchange for the very impersonality and adversariship feminist leaders had rightly criticized in the workplace and the public arena. In the name of building individual identity many were prepared to weaken or jettison the family which has been historically both a focus and a fosterer of individual identity for women as well as men.

Scholars such as Jessie Bernard warned of the need to protect traditional aspects of women's social and familial roles which have value as parts of personal gender identity and women's cultural heritage. For many women there seemed no means of achieving the feminist egalitarian ideal of womanhood without alienation from the traditionally female valued traits of nurturance and domestic competence. Some rejected feminist objectives which they saw as destructive of their position within the family and of the values they had appropriated as expressive of their identities. For others, personal fulfillment was redefined in narrowly atomistic economic terms. And for the sake of an ideal equality to be realized by rather nebulously imagined means among generations of women yet unborn, the actual welfare of living children, spouses and the sacrificers themselves was heroically offered up. In both cases women were ideological victims, deceived by a false dichotomy between a stereotypically unfair caricature of women's past and an irresponsibly narrow, didactic and unkindly vision of women's future.

In seeking status as leaders and spokespersons of a universal feminist movement that could claim to represent the interests of all women everywhere and could claim to draw upon the immense power and resources of women throughout the world, many radical feminist leaders forgot the essentially marginal character of radical programs and aims. They claimed the eclat of an elite vanguard whose ideas drew public interest and intellectual scrutiny by virtue of their disparateness from established folkways and attracted media attention often in proportion to their extremity or even impracticality. Simultaneously they claimed to speak for the human majority, universal womankind.

Radical feminist leaders often hold Marxism, lesbianism, abortion accessibility, even promulgation of hatred and fear of men to be feminist articles of faith, non-negotiable, constitutive demands of feminism. Such leaders and others who have marched under their banners or linked themselves with their movement's name have been repeatedly disappointed by suburban housewives' disavowal of identification with "bra-burning libbers" and dismayed at the demurrals of poor women and Black women particularly, who do not always share the feminist "leaders" visions as to ends or as to means. Yet many of the women who do not follow the radical feminist intellectual elite can fairly be described as feminists. Most favor clearly indentifiable women's rights and interests. Most support political, economic and social modes of equity, although they may not define equity in terms of the abolition of all gender differences.

The participation of large numbers of women in the anti-abortion and anti-ERA movements was not hailed by radical feminists as marking a new chapter in the development of women's political participation. The same ambivalence which long prevented militant feminist organizations from finding common ground with the home-makers who seemingly should have been these leaders' natural constituency, as it were their rank and file, prevented them from welcoming women's political manifestation of their values and principles of conscience unless those principles and values conformed to an already established pattern and measure. Yet the active resistance of many women to items of the feminist agenda which had been presented as unquestionably feminist causes, unproblematically progressive and universally to be supported by all women, above all by the poor and oppressed, affords an experience which feminist theorists and thinkers of all persuasions would do well to ponder.

Is a universal feminist issue one on which all women can agree? Can it be an issue which divides women? Or are we to assume that when women disagree that can only be because some of them have been brainwashed or bought? When Black women express caution about emasculating Black men, should feminists assume that Black women are wrong or expressing a problem unique to the Black community? Surely feminism can learn from diversity. Black women's boldness in articulating an objection to what was becoming a platitudinous contempt for the male sex among some radical feminists may lend balance and wisdom to feminist thinking.

The persistent strength, resiliancy, even resurgence of traditional values in industrial societies is clear evidence that no narrowly conceived feminist program is adequate to the needs of a majority, let alone the totality of women's interests or intentions. To some, for whom feminism is a clearly laid out campaign, any disparity between the preconceived feminist agenda and the aspirations of all women is simply expressive of the need for further efforts at "education." For others, more liberally or more empirically minded, who suppose that women themselves could chiefly formulate the feminist agenda, the disparity leads to a questioning not only of the sources of intellectual, moral, and spiritual power behind the traditionalism of traditional groups but also of the content of the feminist agenda itself. Is there broader, more universal ground on which we all or nearly all can meet?

In the industrial countries the strength of traditional values has already long provided grounds for the questioning and probing of feminist assumptions, the testing of feminist models, the development of feminist values and ideals. When we turn to the Third World largely composed of traditional societies, where the disparity between elites and their constituents is often far greater and more complex than the sufficiently baffling disparity would be feminist leaders experience in the industrial nations, the testing of feminist models and assumptions and the generalizability of proposed theories and solutions is at its most severe.

Third World reactions to the women's movement have included Marxist constructions which subsume feminist issues under the umbrella of purportedly larger international political struggles and cultural nationalist rejections of feminism as yet one more neo-colonial fabrication. Exported along with other trappings of "modern" or bourgeois living, the women's movement is often presented both by Marxists and by defenders of traditions as one more diversion, diverting energies of women from more essential social enterprises and activities. But these political and often opportunistic objections are overshadowed by the general resistance of the large majority of women who fear alienation from the protection of the traditional family setting and structure. Feminist options of

5

single parenthood, self-supporting careers, living alone, are not only beyond the realm of current practice but also seemingly dislocating in the absence of social institutions and industrial facilities to accommodate such life styles. They also seem undesirable, empty and lonely. In cultures where personal identity is deeply funded into communal and familial identity, the individualism which underlies much of Western feminism seems not only foreign but perverse and destructive. It is not the case, as a twentieth century follower of Mill might have supposed, that merely to know individualism is to adopt it. Many women of traditional societies or of traditional background within Western societies regard individualism, perhaps unfairly caricatured, as an aberration to be combatted and overcome.

If feminism is to be accepted by many Third World women it must prove itself compatible with their values and beneficial to their economic and social wellbeing as they choose to define it. Objectively the tenability of feminist proposals as human projects on a global scale rests on cultural, intellectual and social developments which in all fairness cannot be expected to include developments within the conception of feminism itself, to take account of the wisdom and experience of women and men of many cultures. Similarly, feminist programs cannot be expected to be achieved in the absence of an infrastructure of institutions, formal and informal, by which those programs are made feasible, or to which those programs are adapted.

Historically, proposals to abolish the family or radically curtail its influence, have remained utopian, partly because the goals pursued in such enterprises have been deemed secondary in the order of priorities of those societies in which such essays were attempted to the higher value assigned to the maintenance of the family as a functioning human institution. If the maintenance of the family is assigned precedence to most other values for whose sake social planners might intend to subvert it, perhaps the feminist goals of equity and dignity for women should be sought within and through the family rather than through a captious and quixotic tilting with so powerfully grounded a set of human values as those the family represents. Similarly, if it is felt that the activity of the extended family in traditional societies fosters dependency, infra-familial oppression and exploitation, and extra-familial nepotism and corruption, social planners, including feminists would do well to reckon with the positive functions such an institution achieves. The extended family, clan or caste, do function in traditional societies. The abolition of such networks, if accomplished, would create dislocations which would often worsen the lot of women, since adequate functional replacements for the discarded institutions have not yet been developed. Moreover, no such social reorganization is to be achieved merely at the stroke of a pen. Traditional institutions are resilient and adaptive. One can expect them to be defended, often fiercely, in the interest of the functions they perform, by means of strategies, both ancient and modern, and with the use of every device of technology and politics which their defenders can deploy.

In the articulation and elaboration of new roles for women which will be unfolding in the coming century the work of feminist thinking will be critical. The thinking which will emerge most constructively in this regard will not arise from a set of preconceived nostrums, sloganeering panaceas, ready made remedies or atavistic reactions, but will define itself through dialogue, self-criticism, openness to diverse experience, drawing upon the resources of history, culture, imagination and the sciences. In this constructive thinking Women's Studies research will make a central contribution. Such research, to be effective, cannot be merely doctrinaire, a ritual chanting of pre-established formulae, whether Marxist, nationalist, radical feminist or traditionalistic. Rather its strength will come from clearly conceptualized and articulated insight into women's conditions, problems, capabilities and aspirations. The full resources of the arts and sciences--of literary criticism, cultural and biological anthropology, history, philosophy, the social sciences, the planning, helping and healing arts--will be necessary to create the knowledge by which women's situation will be rethought and improved.

This enterprise is neither a colonial nor a parochial endeavor. It is not furthered by the paternalistic equation of modernity with the projects and problematics of Western culture. Nor is it furthered by the obscurantist chauvinism of the romantic claim that only indigenes are competent to speak to the social issues affecting their own countries. The methodologies of every discipline and mode of articulating human insight are as pertinent, necessary and accessible to the hands of one investigator as to the hands of another. National origin, cultural outlook, gender or class are not the issue. Only competence in thinking, skill in methodology, aptness of perception, openness to criticism, replicability, testing and probing will determine which contributions are real contributions and which remain rhetorical dead letters and aborted experiments.

In this volume are collected twelve preliminary contributions to the dialogue by which the authors hope to expand feminist discourse and debate to an intercultural plane. Included are theoretical and practical studies representing the disciplines of political theory and political science, biophilosophy, anthropology, sociology and literature. Each essay draws upon a distinctive body of literature and experience, and each makes a distinctive contribution to synthetic thinking about problems posed for women of widely varying cultural backgrounds. While each author articulates individual values and perspectives, none is simply riding on a hobby horse of data and analysis to a pre-determined destination. In intellectual terms, that would mean riding in place. Rather the analysis of each paper, proceeding by different methodological routes and drawing upon different bodies of articulated experience, contributes to a larger synthesis in which the situation of women and the possibilities and responsibilities of feminism may be more adequately conceived and so ameliorated.

In Part I, which is devoted to theory and criticism, the authors take a fresh look at the development of gender identity, the boundaries and implications of gender roles, and the interaction of the social constructions of gender with invidious notions of race and ethnic identity. Notions of gender and ethnic background are central to all human self-definition and the categorizations they express are fundamental operators in human intercourse and activity. Rectification of the assumptions attached to such predicates by wrongful appropriations of the authority of science is fundamental to all feministically oriented research, whether theoretical or applied.

Jean Bethke Elshtain examines two prominent feminist models of gender development, Dorothy Dinnerstein's in The Mermaid and the Minotaur and Nancy Chodorow's in The Reproduction of Mothering. Elshtain rejects Dinnerstein's Freudian version of human gender development as excessively deterministic. She criticizes it for making exclusive maternal rearing during early childhood the cause of defensive and nature-assaulting male behavior, and of the continued subjugation of women as sexually and reproductively exploited menials. Elshtain argues against Chodorow's functionalist analysis of the family as an instrument of society's sex-gender system, and against her determination that gender differences themselves are the root cause of social inequality. Elshtain builds her own alternate account based on the self-defining ability of the body-subject and the importance of sex and gender distinctions to the essential character of human culture. She argues that the appropriation of gender is a crucial part of the active (not merely passively determined) development of the person, the subjective recognition of corporeality within the evolving stages of psycho-sexual maturation, leading to the prospect of gender distinctions but not necessarily to gender inequality.

Agnes Estioko-Griffin and P. Bion Griffin provide evidence for Elshtain's thesis in their report of 3 years of field work among a tropical foraging society in a remote area of the northern Philippines. The Griffins describe a society where boundaries of traditional gender roles are flexible, but where gender role distinctions are nevertheless maintained. Agta women, like Agta men, hunt. They hunt together with men and in all women groups. They bring back substantial quantities of large game, the major and preferred protein source in Agta diets. Agta women are also conscientious and concerned mothers, but their maternal role does not preclude their serious involvement in hunting which is traditionally presented in feminist and anti-feminist anthropological accounts as an exclusively male activity. The Griffins' findings give us important insights into the fluidity of gender roles and cast doubt on the traditional correlation of biological capabilities with social functions and the gender marked division of labor.

The third chapter considers the projection of sexual fantasies, wishes and fears upon racial stereotypes, a central feature of that disturbing area of thought which lies at the interface between sexism and racism. This chapter is a result of the collaborative researches of a biological scientist and an ethical philosopher, the editor of this volume and her philosopher husband who are currently engaged in an extended study of the structural and methodological factors which foster the persistence of sexual racism within the discourse of human biological sciences.

A practical impact of the manifestation of the fantasies of
sexual racism within science is exerted by the effects upon
population policy of two related stereotypes: The idea that
peoples of the less developed world are over-sexual and hence
over-fertile and the idea that the intellect of such peoples is
inadequate to form responsible judgments about the strategy and
tactics of family planning. Disseminated through the public
relations efforts of population planners, who export the
invidious assumptions of racially biased soi disant scientific
appraisals, these two assumptions serve as foundations of
governmental and non-governmental policies which treat the
reproductive choices of individuals viewed as "other" in a
manner which denies respect to their human subjecthood. Such
campaigns, which draw much of their intellectual authority from
a bias-infected mode of scientific discourse, have a
particularly damaging effect upon the lives of women. For they
involve withholding information about the dangerous side
effects of injectable contraceptives, coercing contraception,
abortion and sterilization, or in the extreme, promoting the
intentional mass starvation of entire populations on the basis
of an argument that life (as invidiously pictured among the
"others") is of insufficient quality to be worthy of
proliferation or even preservation, and that members of such
groups who are incapable of making the appropriate
determinations for themselves--or culpably unwilling to make
them--should be aided to them by the sanctions, controlled
information, and policy decisions of those who understand the
global situation more adequately.

Closing this section, Irene Tinker raises in a practical
context an issue dealt with more speculatively in earlier
chapters, the question of the relevance and applicability of
feminist models and goals in the context of developing nations
and traditional cultures. She explores the conflict between
the egalitarian and individualistic ideals of the American

women's movement and the pragmatic approach of the specialists in the emerging field of Women in Development, professionals who work to provide economic and social advancement for women in developing countries without unduly disrupting local cultural values or combatting the structures represented in many traditional roles. Tinker contends that insistence on the primacy of individual rights over those of the family and community is an expression of ethnocentrism in the American women's movement which requires re-examination in light of alternative value systems and the experience of other countries and cultures.

Part II concerns itself with practical and experiential dimensions of the lives of women from the Pacific and South Asia as analyzed in terms of feminist values. The chapters include studies addressing feminist issues in Micronesia, Indonesia, China, and India. A comparative study considers of the interaction of feminist and nationalist political movements in the Philippines, Vietnam and Indonesia.

Jane Margold investigates women's political participation and influence in two Pacific Island countries, the Republic of Palau and the state of Ponape, of the Federated States of Micronesia. Her interviews yield evidence of connections between matrilineal land inheritance and the related sense of duty to the extended family on the one hand and sources of power and prestige for women in Palau. In Ponape, by contrast, the absence of women's land ownership and a role structure which affords women limited access to educational and economic opportunities are linked to more restricted political influence and uncertain attitudes about women's political participation.

Janice Hyde examines the effectiveness of mahila mandals, or "ladies circles," as an instrumentality of vocational education, health and home improvement activities among rural women in India. A vestige community development project of the 1950s, mahila mandals have been called irrelevant to the needs of women in subsistence agricultural economies, inappropriate to the complex age and kin structure of rural families, and even disruptive of well established social and economic reciprocities among traditional women. The mahila mandal is not in fact effective as the basis of economically productive cooperative enterprises, but it has exhibited some success as a vehicle of shared community interests and concerns.

Carol Colfer presents a quantitative approach to the documentation of women's political and economic roles in two neighboring communities, Long Ampung and Long Segar, in Indonesia. She shows that women's agricultural work is critical to the Dayak economy. In Long Ampung women's economic contributions are equivalent to men's wage earnings; whereas in Long Segar greater proximity to market centers creates greater emphasis on male wage labor, with a greater share in economic decision making shifting towards the men in the family. Colfer warns of the loss of prestige and political influence for women in societies undergoing rapid transitions to cash economies.

Joyce Pettigrew describes the personal and familial consequences of the mini-laparotomy tubectomy operation which is a mainstay of family planning programs in rural India. Case studies reveal the physical hardship the operation brings to women who are already undernourished, overworked and inadequately provided with post-operative care and recuperative help. The data speak for themselves as an indictment of a governmental policy to reduce birth rates using methods which disproportionately burden women and the rural poor, through the virtual exclusion of non-surgical methods which would be more responsive to the women's self-perceived needs and express desires.

The chapter contributed by Martha Logsdon, examines gender roles as portrayed in officially sanctioned elementary school texts in Indonesia. She finds that the texts reflect traditional Western middle-class values in portraying women exclusively in domestic situations. These depictions are at odds with Indonesian women's actual active economic roles as entrepreneurs but seem to express cultural goals of the national current political leadership.

LaRene Despain writes a personal account of her two years as an English language teacher in China. She chronicles the conflict many talented women there express between personal ambitions and the constraints of the Chinese socialist morality. These conflicts exacerbate the struggle between traditional, familial attitudes and personal values as to marriage and careers.

Using the techniques of literary analysis, Malashri Lal projects the impact of feminism in India by visualizing Indian women's situations through the eyes of three contemporary women novelists. The existential and cultural situations brought to life in these literary treatments lead her to conclude that necessary change must take place slowly and surely within the haveli to be acceptable to Indian women.

In the final chapter, Belinda Aquino surveys feminist movements within several Southeast Asian countries. She traces a vigorous strain of indigenous feminism which has weathered both external political influences and internal political struggles with its distinctive nature undeflected. She contends that while Southeast Asian feminism must be seen as part of broader social and political movements, the association does not imply any obscuring or demeaning of feminist goals.

The project of discovering the scope of application for feminist discourse within societies whose cultures are distinct from that in which the new and growing feminism of the industrial world has developed will require a sustained and responsive dialogue among feminists of many persuasions and backgrounds. Both feminism and the cultures it addresses will be altered by such a dialogue, but it is naive to expect that either feminism or traditional culture will be altered beyond recognition. Sensitivity to the universal human concerns which will be articulated as the dialogue progresses will strengthen both feminism and the cultures of the industrial and developing nations. Dogmatism, politicization, the endeavor to exploit feminism as a rhetorical vehicle and political hobby horse will only put the movement identified with such sloganeering out of touch with the very majority it seeks to lead.

The present essays represent just one effort to contribute to the needed dialogue. They will be successful, not if they are "definitive" but if they encourage further studies and explorations, disputes and an attendant broadening of awareness and heightening of sensibilities to the diversity of women's perspectives and situations, and the need for catholicity in any program which would address the global condition of women. They form in no case a final word but in each case a partial contribution to a continuing discourse which each contributor is confident is of moment to the universal human condition.

The contributions to this volume, with the exception of the chapters by Janice Hyde and Joyce Pettigrew, grew out of conference presentations at the international conference Concepts and Strategies: Women's Studies in Different Cultural Contexts held on November 15-17, 1982 at the East-West Center in Honolulu, under the auspices of the Women's Studies Program of the University of Hawaii.

PART I

Theory and Criticism

FEMINIST ACCOUNTS OF GENDER DEVELOPMENT: A CRITIQUE

Many of the most important feminist theorists of gender development propose a symmetrical social world in place of the world we now inhabit. They describe the present as "asymmetrical" and condemn our social arrangements as systematically deranged. This derangement, on their view, flows in a direct line from "universal" child-rearing practices to political, economic and social structures on the grand scale. That is, the thinkers I shall take up assert that their arguments are compelling because they have demonstrated a tight connection between the particular nature of private sexual and social arrangements and public outcomes, both by way of explanation as to what is wrong and by way of prescription for what must be changed. Why our--the human species--gender arrangements are so badly botched at present, and how they can be transformed to attain the new world of gender symmetry is a matter I propose to explore with a skeptical eye. The ideal symmetrical world is construed as a social universe in which the sexes have identical commitments to, involvements with, and interest in child-rearing (often called reproduction) and careers (often called production). This "symmetry" holds across the board, even into the world of sexual fantasy for the Total Symmetrist. I shall argue that symmetry may work to eliminate sex-based differences but would do little to eradicate sex-based injustice.

I shall lead into my subject by noting an important distinction, taken for granted as the backdrop to the explanatory frameworks I shall explicate and criticize, between biological sex and social gender. Though one cannot altogether sever biological maleness and femaleness from the social creation and meaning of norms of masculinity and femininity and the distinctive parts men and women play in the human story, the accounts I shall take up propound a vary sharp cleavage between the two. That is, whether one has a female body or a male body is given very little theoretical weight in the over-all scheme of things. The explanatory emphasis is placed on a tight fusion of "psychological" and "social" considerations with embodiment a kind of dependent "biological variable" or some general feature of a human condition. Maleness and femaleness are of vital importance only because we now organize social life around these markers though we need not in the future. This assumption is largely unquestioned and unargued in the texts under consideration.

The essay is divided into three main parts. First, I shall make some general comments on psychoanalytic theory and what it offers to social theory if it is construed as an interpretive enterprise. Second, I shall submit two widely discussed and disseminated feminist accounts of gender development to a critique on a number of levels, involving theoretical and political considerations. In view of the daunting problems posed by <u>any</u> appropriation of psychoanalysis for social explanation, and in view of the explicit political aims of feminist gender theorists, theoretical and political arguments are invited and required. Third, I shall suggest an alternative in the sense of providing a series of intimations of a different approach. I shall not propose some new, tautly drawn theoretical frame but, instead, draw out some of the markers that my alternative account, if plausible, requires that we "attend to" in some serious way.

Psychoanalytic Theory and Feminism

Freud was critical of the search for a <u>Weltanschauung</u>, "an intellectual construction which solves all the problems of our existence uniformly on the basis of one overriding hypothesis, which, accordingly, leaves no question unanswered and in which everything that interests us finds its place."[1] Psychoanalysis, he insisted, could not serve--or should not--as the basis of such a systematic theory. It could explain some things but not everything. His "peculiar" science, moreover, could not be a predictive science. That is, one could not deploy psychoanalysis to construct a set of causal laws, as some feminist gender theorists do, along the lines of 'If x, then ineluctably y'.

To be sure, Freud is at times more sanguine about what psychoanalytic theory can do for us. He attacks pretensions of the Weltanschauung sort, but like Marx, he also clings to the hope that a unity of scientific explanation might be achieved. But the main body of his work, particularly the case histories, undercuts any attempt to merge the Geisteswissenschaften with natural scientific explanation.[2] For Freud could not do without purposive accounts; and his theory, at its best, grinds things fine, allowing us to enter a complex world at its most concrete and particular level. Psychoanalysis as Freud conceived it is preeminently a theory of the psychodynamic self, the night traveler who wakes in wonder or terror, the rational irrationalist, the romantic hero or heroine, the vulnerable child, the builder, destroyer, giver, taker, the authoritarian, anarchist--the self, attempting to carve out a liveable life, in history, between the intractable pole of necessity and the ephemeral dream of possibility. There is an expressive subject, crucially self-defining, active--no mere social 'product'--who inhabits his pages. It is this subject which psychoanalytic discourse helps to constitute, and it is this subject who interprets and is interpreted. The essential task of psychoanalytic theory, what it is best equipped to do, given its subject, is to probe human meanings, individual and social.

Freud's devotion to a scientific method did not blind him to a somewhat rueful recognition that his peculiar science could not be contained within a language which failed to make essential reference to the human being as such. Given this recognition, he could not, and did not, claim that he had promulgated a set of laws with the power to predict. What could be done, he insisted, with such potent concepts and constructs as projection, displacement, regression, repression, identification, and the rest, was to forge explanations having the form of post-hoc reconstructions of a particular individual's psychic history. If the account was detailed and "thick" enough, it might have broader applicability on another level to understanding human psychic life in more general terms. Freud made no claim that he had got things wie es eigentlich gewesen. Instead, the psychoanalytic dialogue aimed at the active construction of explanations that made sense to analyst and analysand; the better interpretation was one that could account for more details than an alternative.[3]

Freud's case histories retain their freshness because he never explained away or abstracted from the rich intrapsychic world of his subject. Before others became devoted to the idea, Freud practiced the art of "thick description", the commitment to present human contexts as tangled webs of meaning, open, hidden, or veiled. Well executed, the theorist's explanation should take the reader or critic "into the heart of that of which it is the interpretation."[4] In Freud's case this was the densely "populated" world of the human mind.

One sign of the strength of Freud's accounts is that they allow for (though he might not wish it) multiple interpretations. One can read the case of Dora, for example, and, using the "thick description" Freud provides emerge with an interpretation that varies from his own. Psychoanalysis, at its best, admits of such diversity of interpretation.

Notwithstanding Freud's occasional reductive statements and scientistic hopes, his method and his own account of that method locate psychoanalysis firmly in the human sciences. Within psychoanalytic theory, language, non-linguistic expression, and action in general all become subject to analysis and interpretation--not in isolation from one another but in a constant dialogue that is constitutive of the theory as well as of the psychoanalytic subject. Within a gradually emerging framework, the psychoanalytic thinker moves, through interpretation, to link minute details to higher level conceptual abstractions.[5]

Following through on this interpretive imperative for human studies, if what is to be explained is gender development and the identity of human beings, an adequate interpretative approach should help us to "get inside" the worlds in and through which gender and identity emerge--the psycho-sexual worlds of children and the social worlds of families.

If we are to follow Freud's counsel at least three central aspects must be taken into account in the study of sex differences--the biological, the psychological, and the cultural. Freud argued against the naive belief that biological maleness or femaleness simply determines psychological maleness or femaleness and this, in turn, determines the social roles of the two sexes. But while these aspects of sexual identity are not <u>so</u> tightly bound to one another that no space remains for variation, all human beings, Freud insists, need to situate themselves sexually. Most try to construct a unifying experience out of the diverse components of their sexual identities. We have a form of experimental access to the world of constituted sexual identities through interpretations of how and why some individuals get de-railed in their efforts to forge an identity. Through this interpretive process critical

reflections can be made on those social arrangements that
sustain or constrain in particular ways to particular ends.[6]

Two Models of Gender

Our understanding of human beings and their social worlds
will vary dramatically depending on whether we approach those
beings and their worlds with great lumbering earth moving
equipment, formal models designed to excavate some underlying
causal context of which social participants are said to be
unaware, or whether we embrace a mode of theoretical reflection
that finds human self-understanding in the heart of its
interpretations. The latter yields a different theory. I
shall argue that it secretes or sustains a different politics.
Embracing rather than earth moving makes the interpretive
theorist's life complex. She cannot stalk about making
proclamations about the world and the folks who inhabit it
without making a serious effort to explore and to enter
empathically into their contexts and meanings. Her theoretical
commitments must be grasped with a certain humility as she
confronts the richness of even a single human life.

The political implications will become clearer as my
analysis takes shape. For now I simply indicate that an
interpretive approach to theory must take seriously the assent
or dissent of human beings to social change undertaken
ostensibly in their behalf. Just how such "assent" or
"dissent" is articulated is a controversial point, but
minimally I would urge we keep in mind an imperative along
these lines: a public debate of a certain sort must precede
and be a concomitant of social changes that will profoundly
affect human beings, their children, and their communities.

My reason for raising the flag on this question now will
emerge with particular force as I take up two distinctive
gender theories. Each is couched in categories and claims that
are imposed over the diversity of ways of life. As a result,

cultures, including our own, are shrunk down to too few points of order, drained of their inner meaning to the human subjects who inhabit them. The human story, in these texts, is much less interesting than we know it to have been and to be. And the politics each text either affirms explicitly or sustains implicitly is troubling in its treatment of social change--who is to undertake it and to what ends. The appraisal that follows traverses the terrain between theoretical argument--are the arguments convincing and why?--and political ends--what politics flows from the theory and has the author gerrymandered the discussion in order to focus attention only on the most favorable possible outcomes of her agenda for change?[7] Remember: if any of these arguments is to be compelling there must be a concretely specified connection between private arrangements and public outcomes, both by way of diagnosis and by way of prescription. This is a requirement gender theorists force upon the critic, for each insists that she has explained where the problem lies, has seen what must be done to put things right, and has foreseen what the effects of the demanded transformation must be.

I have are two texts in mind: Dorothy Dinnerstein's The Mermaid and the Minotaur and Nancy Chodorow's The Reproduction of Mothering. Each involves a different appropriation of psychoanalysis for purposes of feminist social thought. Yet each locates the ultimate, underlying causal context for human malaise in the "universal fact" that it is women who mother. I shall argue that this thesis cannot bear the explanatory and political weight these authors place upon it.

Dorothy Dinnerstein's The Mermaid and the Minotaur should be located within the wider project of such cultural, left-wing Freudians as Norman O. Brown and Herbert Marcuse. Dinnerstein begins her discussion with what she calls the "normal psychopathology" of the human race, a starting point that I shall challenge below. Her description of our current condition is extreme in its language. Characteristic terms include "intolerable," "diseased," "malignant," "maiming," "pathological," "poisoned." At one point, motherhood is termed "monstrous, atavistic."[8] Her argument is grounded in the Kleinian concept of "splitting" as a basic process in human mental life. Splitting is pervasive but can be gotten over if we, finally, will it.[9] Dinnerstein places the greatest explanatory weight on the oral stage and preverbal development. Our species-wide pathology, she argues, is rooted there and we can be redeemed only by "the project of sexual liberty" whereby we shall achieve "true spontaneity" and "full humanity." But first we must undo what is now invariably done--inducing "fertile adults to do their unwitting work for posterity" through a series of "bribes" rooted in our asymmetrical sexual relations.[10] We need "more efficient societal arrangements," arrangements not so draining on "adult female energy."

It is always difficult to attempt what Dinnerstein has attempted--to take theoretical account of what happens to human beings before they become language users. My disagreement with Dinnerstein is not that she has made this attempt but that she has created a privileged epistemological position, a foundational imperative that is overriding. Let me explain. Preverbal development with female-mothering, she insists, leads to a vast array of specific evils. Her argument runs along these lines: (1) The "normal" condition of the human species is psychopathological--maladaptive and life-threatening, (2) This malaise has its roots in our gender arrangement, (3) These gender arrangements are "asymmetrical," leading to specific paranoid and other defenses around gender, (4) The central marker of this asymmetry is the fact that "for virtually every living person it is a woman" who provides the first and most important "contact with humanity and with nature." From this, Dinnerstein concludes that female monopoly of child care makes the human race collectively deranged; we are all, we mother-raised humans, maimed. Dinnerstein foresees the end of civilization, and soon, if something is not done to "break the female monopoly."

Linger for a moment over two of Dinnerstein's key presuppositions. First, the notion of "normal" psychopathology. Every social theorist of critical intent offers some characterization of a transformed human condition as a contrast model indicative of what social life might become once certain changes are made. Marx's concept of "alienation," for example, comprises both a condemnation of the distortion of humanity that emerges under conditions of exploitation and oppression and holds forth the promise of a more complete, even transcendent human possibility once those conditions have been destroyed. Dinnerstein's argument along these lines invokes an apocalyptic vision of the present and a utopian vision of the future. But she makes the case for our present collective pathology only by blurring a number of important distinctions or washing away several vital concerns. If, for example, we are all "normally" deranged what are we to make of those souls who cannot function at all in the world, victims of persistent and destructive delusions or fixations of one sort or another--are they simply more "normal" than the rest of us? Or, if we are all in the grips of a shared, universal psychopathology, how is it possible for anyone to glimpse the merest intimation of what a normal, non-psychopathological human condition might be? If we have always been deranged, perhaps that is the human condition. Dinnerstein's notion of "normal" psychology is parasitic upon some absolute but tacit standard of psychic health thus far not approached by any known human society anywhere at any time. Where does this standard come from if all we have ever known is psychopathological? Dinnerstein intimates her awareness of a problem here when she writes in a note that the "mitigation of our trouble could come about...only if it were emotionally possible for mother-raised women and mother-raised men to take part freely and equally in what are now male affairs. And, unhappily,...this is just what mother-raised men and women cannot do."[11]   So how do we get to the new world?

A second key presupposition of privileged standing in Dinnerstein's system is the conviction that psychic splitting in the preverbal stage is the key to our collective psychopathology. Indeed, this splitting is our collective disorder. The oral stage and preverbality set a powerful, but unrecognized, causal context for all else in human life. One effect of this portion of her argument is to erode the benefit human studies are receiving from non-designative accounts of language use as that which makes human beings potentially and irrepressibly self-defining and self-creating. If the critical stage is one when we do not use language, there is no crucial benefit to be gained from language use. We have no freedom or deliberative power but are mere mechanisms to be manipulated. Dinnerstein plays into the hands of those who reduce language use and its importance to a matter of some putative correspondence between words and states of affairs. Although Dinnerstein does not share this reductive view of language, by eviscerating the possibility that human beings, through language, may "talk" their way into or out of alternative ways of being and acting, she joins hands with those thinkers to whom the notion of deliberative change is meaningless and who underplay or ignore humans as speaking subjects.

A second dimension of the causal context Dinnerstein privileges is, as I indicated, the notion of splitting itself. I cannot here enter into a full-fledged theoretical debate drawing on the vast clinical literature on this subject. But what seems to be going on in The Mermaid and the Minotaur is the framing of a deterministic case in which splitting is not only presented as a psychic mechanism of defense but accounted fully with ready made readings of its meaning and content. Dinnerstein presumes a direct line from intrapsychic splitting on gendered terms to the structural arrangements in the social and political world. Everything is tidily severed and gendered. I do not find the tautly drawn homology of structures persuasive and I shall have more to say on the structure of the argument. But, first, a few words on psychic splitting may be helpful for those unfamiliar with the concept and its use in psychoanalytic discourse.

An early notion of splitting was formulated by Janet and characterized by Freud, in An Autobiographical Study, in these words: "According to Janet's view a hysterical woman was a wretched creature who, on account of constitutional weakness, was unable to hold her mental acts together, and it was for this reason that she fell victim to a splitting of her mind and to a restriction of the field of her consciousness."[12] Freud's views grew richer and more complex than Janet's with the emergence of the structural theory of mind, and the concept of splitting was not as central to Freud's theory as to that of later thinkers, most importantly Melanie Klein.

In applications of the concept of splitting the problems and richness of the thesis go hand-in-hand. For splitting is used to refer to a host of "manifest behaviors" or activities "whose nature evokes hypotheses concerning either an underlying rent in the process of awareness or alternatively the simultaneous experience of contradictory, mutually exclusive events within awareness."[13] Perhaps Freud did not make the concept a centerpiece in his theory because he had no vision of real or possible psychic wholeness as some unified totality that can or, from time to time, must, defensively "split." Freud's "self" was (in his terms) a "'normal' fictitious ego." Splitting assumes more theoretical importance if one has, in the back of one's mind a vision of a healed and whole, unified self.

Within the psychoanalytic literature, some thinkers construe splitting in essentially negative terms, stressing defense and the vicissitudes of internalization. Others argue that splitting may be a non-defensive dimension of the way in which the infant mind must work simply to organize itself and participate in experience.[14] In this latter view splitting can take on defensive functions, but the mechanism has limited theoretical use in analyses of pathological mechanisms of defense.

Without attempting here to sort out these theoretical debates, we can observe that it is because splitting is given so privileged a status in Dinnerstein's theory that psychopathology emerges as an ordinary, not an extraordinary phenomenon.[15] The relation between "infantile normative" and "adult pathological" splitting is problematic and puzzling. But for Dinnerstein there is a conduit between the two. And this allows her to connect pre-verbal development to the totality of social structures, arrangements, and practices.

Let me explain. Dinnerstein observes rightly that "...the private and public sides of our sexual arrangements are not separable, and neither one is secondary to the other." But she goes on to insist that every aspect of these arrangements is traceable to "a single childhood condition" and to claim that both our private and public arrangements "will melt away when that condition is abolished,"[16] that condition, remember, being the fact that it is women who mother and psychic splitting of infants which follows. To evaluate these claims, one must take the full measure of the malaise Dinnerstein locates in gender based distinctions (asymmetries, in her language) in the first place. She presumes a world in which psychological imperatives, flowing from female mothering, result in women who depend "lopsidedly on participation in the public domain because they are stymied by love."[17] This outcome is inexorable, putting "women into the pattern of complementarity between male and female personality that emerges from female-dominated early childhood."[18] Asymmetry invites/causes male privilege and demands/requires female oppression (the "universal exploitation of women"). Why? Because female power in the preverbal stage is so overpowering for male and female infants, that mother-raised humans will never be able to see "female authority as wholly legitimate."[19] One senses just enough truth here that one is reluctant to discount the argument entirely--on some level it "makes sense." But the "moment of truth" is just that--a "moment," an important and provocative insight but not the whole ball of wax.

One problematic aspect in the account is the way Dinnerstein's discourse constitutes the infant as a powerfully sensual being with tumultuous feelings. Fine, but she omits the fact that this infant has a mind that grows rapidly more complex in its functioning. And this same infant, rather early on, becomes a sophisticated and inventive language user. (This despite the fact that otherwise sensible and rational adults often aim to shrivel the child's expressivist spark down to manageable proportions.)* Children rapidly become case studies of psychopathology in her text, and adults are just a bigger version of the same.

---

*It would stretch the point to claim that Freud treated the human capacity for language in some explicit way. Yet he did create the "talking cure" and the psychoanalytic encounter involves a dialogue of a certain kind. What is interesting about Freud's treatment of infantile sexuality is how often he tried to see the construction of sexuality from the child's eye point of view. (See especially "On the Sexual Theories of Children", Vol. IX, Standard Edition and "On the Sexual Enlightenment of Children", ibid.) In these essays Freud at his most compassionate and provocative best comes through. He argues that we must take serious account of the understandings of which children are capable at different stages of development, remaining aware of how the child is struggling to make "independent discovery" of conceptual categories through

Dinnerstein construes humans as nearly completely "infantile." There is no indication that children, or adults have minds pursuant of aims not ultimately or "really" reducible to infantile drives, desires, or wishes. I know, of course, that a child lurks within each one of us, threatening to erupt, disrupt, or fall-apart. But that is not all we are. To reduce male activity to the wholly defensive and destructive history-making of naughty boys and female activity to the sexual or "reproductive" activities of a universal class of maternal menials is to 'psychologize' in a reductive way.

Let me elaborate. Dinnerstein describes the public world as combined history-making and "nature-assaulting." Women, embodying nature, have been excluded from history-making but have also refrained from nature-killing. Men, in murdering nature, are in the first and last instance getting back at their mothers. (All-in-all, it seems rather a good thing that Dinnerstein's women have been exempted from the thoroughly nasty business of history-making though, of course, they are complicit.)

I accept the idea that in this culture at this time aspects of male and female self-definition may be defensive in relation to one another; that human beings, at least some of the time, over-define themselves as "real men" or "true women" in relation to their internalized images of the opposite sex. To the extent that this is the case, we could aim to enhance our

---

his or her own observations. Not surprisingly, this epistemic drive focuses around the two earliest "grand problems" of life--(1) the distinction between the sexes and (2) where babies come from. Freud argues that each of the child's more complex "sexual theories" contains an important psychic and developmental truth and that children should not be crudely rebuffed by know-it-all rational adults who "on a single occasion" disclose "the truth" to the child "in turgid and solemn language". Indeed, Freud compares the sexual theories of children, and the fragments of truth each contains, to adult philosophers trying to solve the problems of the universe.

ability to secure our male-female identities in ways that are less defensive in relation to one another. This is an important and plausible project. But it is not Dinnerstein's project. She accepts no limits on human freedom once the thorny matter of gender asymmetry is ironed out. There is irony here for comparable hubris is condemned when Dinnerstein turns to her characterizations of male plunder and war against nature—to male refusal to recognize limits on the control of nature. Men, in history, both deny and destroy nature; women, outside history, help to perpetuate this male nastiness by continuing to play out their maternal-menial part.

Our appraisal of Dinnerstein's argument can be enhanced by exploring the background to her deployment of a binary opposition: nature versus culture. In a recent, essay, "Natural Facts: a historical perspective on science and sexuality," Ludmilla Jordanova traces the modern, self conscious version of the assumption of a dichotomy between nature and culture to the rationalizing discourse of eighteenth-century science.[20] By documenting the entry of the categories of "nature" and "culture" into Western rationalism, Jordanova challenges accounts that begin their analyses on the basis of this dichotomy as in a sense, pre-given. The nature/culture split entered feminist discourse with Simone de Beauvoir's The Second Sex. Abstracting from the complexity of women's history and social life as lived, de Beauvoir located men squarely in the realm of Transcendence as Beings-for-themselves and women in the bog of Immanence as Beings-in-themselves. De Beauvoir's model offered an unambiguous linkage from nature/culture; woman/man; to oppressed/oppressor. It made "women...the bearers of ignorance and men of knowledge," rather a baffling notion to set as the basis of feminist discourse.[21] In de Beauvoir's argument, men and men alone are declared the agents of reason and bearers of culture; women, the flip side of the coin, outside civilization, in nature, are inessential to culture though they are a necessary condition for the reproduction of human life, a process de Beauvoir does not find a task of culture.

Although Dinnerstein's use of the dichotomy is not so harsh in its devaluation of women's traditional sphere as de Beauvoir's, she repeats the notion that women are oppressed and victimized because they are located in "nature." Yet anthropologists and social historians have repeatedly shown that there are "no simple scales on which men and women can be ranged."[22] The upshot is this: rather than countering a categorical rigidity that has plagued our understanding of past and present social life, Dinnerstein retains it. Jordanova makes a telling point when she states that "one of the problems with the current promiscuous use of the nature/culture dichotomy in relation to gender is that it has taken the claims of Western science at face value, and so lapsed into a biologism which it is the responsibility of the social sciences, including history and anthropology, to combat."[23]

Given the fact that she carves up the social universe along the lines of a nature/culture dichotomy, Dinnerstein proposes, as the solution to our ills, a break in the female monopoly of early child care. Only this will defuse female linkage with nature and female oppression by culture. She calls for men and women to have homogeneous commitments to, and involvement with, "mothering" and participation in the public world in full parity. Were this done, our public and private arrangements would be transformed. Children would no longer be split psychopathologically. This outcome requires, in her view, two sorts of pre-conditions: the first is "psychological" (just described) and the second, not political, in her terms, but technological. This technological precondition is characterized as "the practical possibility of making parenthood genuinely optional, the concrete feasibility of adult work life flexible enough so that men and women can take equal part in both domestic and public life"--something, she insists, that is "already available", just as restructuring of child-rearing, if we have the will for it, is ready-to-hand.

But on this road to sex-quality something curious has happened: important considerations involving the structure of our political and economic life are shrunk down to a set of "technological" considerations. In this manner Dinnerstein reflects a dimension of the current order she otherwise deplores--the tendency to reduce vital human issues to technical problems amenable to technological resolution. Surely the public conditions she requires for her solution to asymmetrical disorders are profoundly and inescapably political. But she has no way to handle these issues because she has neither a political analysis of the present, nor a political vision of the future. There is no space in her order for political debate and action; indeed, it is difficult to see how any human dialogue at all is possible given her therapeutic insistence that our current utterances are symptomatic of our collective derangement.

Because Dinnerstein evades how it is, politically, we shall get to the world of gender symmetry save through willing it, given that the "technological" prerequisites for it currently exist, her vision encounters no points of friction. Her argument is alternately despairing of the present and naive in its evocation of a liberated future, if we can but.... Ironically, one political block to her project is the self-understandings of many women, a self-understanding tied to their care of the young. Dinnerstein can discount this self-understanding as one of the defensive aspects of femininity flowing from centuries of enforced domesticity. But this will not quite do, for one caveat in her argument is her insistence that women have certain qualities of mind, emotion, and purpose that are more virtuous than those of men in that they are not given over to nature-killing. There is a bind:

35

these female qualities, not "innate," seem to emerge given, not in spite of, our present asymmetry. For women, identifying with Mother (Nature) have no need to plunder and rape her.

Women, it seems, stay as "sweet as they are" even as they gain full public power. In the process of achieving history-making parity they will not take on the previously denied to them nasty and aggressive male qualities. All the nastiness, in fact, evaporates in Dinnerstein's future. Somehow we can "integrate" or heal destructive splitting and in the future, once we are no longer exclusively mother-reared, there will be no need for integration as destructive splits will not get a chance to develop into full-blown psychopathologies. In the first instance (now), integration seems impossible: in the second, unnecessary. What seeps through Dinnerstein's pages is the evangelical sexual liberationism Foucault has so powerfully criticized in The History of Sexuality, Vol. I. Dinnerstein's project fuses the promise of destroying old repressions, fulfilling immediate desires, and ushering in both total justice and "wholeness."

I shall move now to a very different account of gender development in Nancy Chodorow's The Reproduction of Mothering. Chodorow draws heavily upon a model of the relationship between the family and the larger society developed in the functionalist sociology of Talcott Parsons in two essays written in 1942 and 1943.[24] Her model, with Parsons, presupposes a stable congruity or "fit" between the modern industrialized economy, the capitalist order, and the nuclear family--a tie-up questioned by the new family history. But in this scheme family functions are given and change with changes in the mode of production or over-all structure of social purposes and patterns of action. Male and female roles are "asymmetrical," a term first deployed by Parsons. Gender roles revolve around the division between what Parsons called the instrumental adaptive father and the nurturant, expressive mother. This division was seen as necessary to the ends of maintaining the equilibrium of society. The family, in functionalist terms, becomes one substructural buttress in a pattern of systems maintenance; the family is construed primarily in instrumental terms. Functionalists hold to a unilinear theory of history which, in the words of Lawrence Stone, "ignores the ups and downs of social and intellectual change, the lack of uniformity in the direction of trends, and the failures of the various trends to synchronize in the way they ought if the paradigm is to fit. Above all, by sweeping broadly across the vast spectrum of highly distinctive national cultures, status groups and classes, these theories reduce the enormous diversity of social experience to a uniformity which has never existed in real life."[25] Chodorow shares these aspects of the functionalist project. Now, in most cases, a functionalist perspective yields a politics supportive of any given status quo constituted in functionalist terms. Chodorow, however, from the same over-all perspective, wishes to see a gender revolution. I shall consider whether this can be done convincingly or not given her own analysis of the current situation.

Human subjects are constituted by Chodorow's discourse as over-socialized beings stuck in a rigid "sex-gender system and sexual asymmetry."[26] Chodorow argues that sexuality itself, sexual desires and fantasies, including the "libidinization" of various zones as well as the emergence of gender identity, is a "social product." Children learn early to "manipulate and transform drives" in order to attain personal contact, to achieve "object relations." Chodorow's own version of psychoanalytic discourse involves the soldering of "object relations theory" to functionalist sociology. The human subject as a desiring, fantasizing, importantly self-defining agent is nowhere to be found. Children are molded into "gendered members of society."[27]

37

Chodorow's account, like Dinnerstein's, involves a few key premises leading to an analytic conclusion that is, simultaneously, a political agenda. The ordering goes like this: (1) The normal pattern of human gender development leads to the construction and reproduction of male dominance and would, independent of any other factors. (2) Our gender arrangements are asymmetrical, that is, systematically skewed and disordered. (3) This derangement generates male dominance and female subordination because psychologists "have demonstrated unequivocally that the very fact of being mothered by a woman generates in men conflicts over masculinity, a psychology of male dominance, and a need to be superior to women,"[28] pointing to the inescapable: it is women's mothering which guarantees continued male dominance and female subordination.*

The sex-gender system, then, in Chodorow's terms, is "a fundamental determining and constituting element" of society; it is "socially constructed, subject to historical change and development, and organized in such a way that it is systematically reproduced."[29] Given this tautly drawn system, Chodorow has difficulty accounting for change. Nor can she take serious account of human being as reflective and

---

*Her argument suggests a counter-factual, namely, that men not mothered by a woman or women exclusively will experience no need to be superior to women and will less likely be warped by a psychology of male dominance. Whether this is so or not is a matter for exploration on many levels. But there is compelling anthropological evidence which suggests that the male psychology Chodorow finds caused inevitably by female mothering is not as universal as she claims; moreover, many men in our own society, mothered by women, have no apparent need to bully women nor to dominate them. (Remember, for Chodorow's argument to hold, a psychology of male dominance, internalized in each mother-reared male and structured in social arrangements must be present. For the psychology is foundational--it undergirds social structure and arrangements.)

active; instead, we are reactive, shaped by external forces, primarily the "object relations" of family life.[30]

Chodorow's children identify--more or less consciously--not so much with real, particular mothers and fathers as with role-players. Identification is a "conscious phenomenon". By over-rationalizing this process, Chodorow bleaches out the importance of cross-sex identification which cannot be explained by a conscious social-learning model she otherwise rejects. That is, she presumes identification has occurred when children "learn their gender" and "then identify...with the appropriate parent." She overlooks evidence on the importance of the individual's identifications with beings of the opposite sex, with public heroes and villains, with characters in film and fiction, with ideas and hopes, etc. We never get out of the familial knot in her world. Our identifications are what Parsons claimed they were forty years ago: girls become nurturant and expressive like "mommy"; boys become instrumental and adaptive like "daddy." One gets no sense of diverse families in a variety of social settings, no thick description of the inner worlds of intimate human life, nor the complexities of infant life. Most problematically, despite occasional mention in footnotes that it is "quality" that counts, her overall argument squeezes out the central importance of quality of parenting to the development of the human person.[31]

Here it is worth pondering Chodorow's attempt to unravel what she calls heterosexual knots and to smooth out gender asymmetries. By asymmetry she, with Dinnerstein, means men and women playing different parts in the social world and having a predominant interest in, even effective control over, different activities on the basis of gender identity. This would not seem to be an evil simpliciter unless these differences were invariably and necessarily the basis for inequities or for distinctions always drawn up invidiously to favor one group, to downgrade the other. But by defining "asymmetry" as male dominance/female oppression, Chodorow construes social reality in a way that downgrades women's contributions and magnifies those of men. That is, she winds up sharing the "devaluation of domesticity which is the hallmark of the very sexist society she deplores."[32]

Rather than challenging the terms of the male dominant society on the basis of its respective valuation of men's and women's worlds, Chodorow attacks gender differences themselves, seeing them as the foundational root of social injustice. It follows that the radically de-gendered society becomes a prerequisite for social equality. This tendency to conflate difference with domination, leaves Chodorow little choice but to embrace the feminist future as a picture of a social world in which sexual differences are blurred or are no longer interesting. One critic, Zelda Bronstein, argues that Chodorow's call for a non-oppositional social world in which "all good ends are reconcilable" places her squarely within a tributary of mainstream liberalism.[33]

There are several ways to raise questions about Chodorow's call for symmetry as the necessary, if not sufficient, precondition for social justice. One is to take a look at anthropological evidence about male and female power and authority in societies different from our own. The anthropologist, Peggy Reeves Sanday, studied some 150 societies for which detailed ethnographies are currently available. She concludes that the only "symmetry" of which we know anything--by which she means a rough parity of power and authority between males and females--appears to be grounded in sex differences, not the blurring or denial of those differences. Sanday's conclusions are particularly interesting because she began her research with the presumption, shared by Chodorow, that women are universally subordinated, men dominant.[34] To her initial consternation, Sanday found that evidence drawn from other ways of life pointed to something more complex. Not only was it not the case that men were the universal culture-creating, dominant sex, women, the nature-stuck subordinate sex, but there were many societies in which women wielded, or had wielded, great authority and power. In such societies, women had access to powerful symbols and myths. Often women as bearers of children and nurturers of plant life occupied central positions in the realm of social authority.

Gender identity leading to the two sexes predominating in different spheres of social life lay at the basis of some societies featuring rough integration between the sexes, as well as other societies that were genuinely separate but equal. In both cases the power to give life--woman's power--was as highly valued as the power to take it away--male power. But paradoxically, male power was the source of male weakness, since the male warrior is expendable. Men were the vulnerable sex. Conceptual distinctions demarcating femaleness from maleness, Sanday argues, are universally evident and, moreover, are necessary if human beings are to create cultural forms, are to order their worlds in some coherent way.[35]

Finding the view that male dominance is everywhere universal to be peculiar as feminist argumentation, Sanday concludes that this presumption--a Western bias--flows from our tendency to equate dominance with official public roles. For example: Karen Sacks adds that to view male and female authority in societies like the Iroquois, where women wielded great power, as unequal rather than different reflects precisely this "state bias in Western anthropological interpretation of prestate politics."[36] If one tries to 'see' societies within their own terms, Sanday concludes, one often finds female economic and political power or authority flowing as a right due the female sex, particularly where a "magico-religious association between maternity and fertility of the soil" links women "with social continuity and social good." In certain West African dual-sex systems, for example, the power and invincibility of womanhood emerges with startling force. "Whether the male chief is big or small," said the woman of a West African solidarity group, "what matters is that he was given birth by a woman."[37] Dozens of societies, it appears, were--and are--worlds in which sex differences invite parity and complementary balance and neither sex is wholly dominant over the other, though each prevails in particular areas of social life.

Other male-female arrangements unpacked by Sandy feature formal male authority balanced, or chastened, by actual female power. This gender balance-of-power is maintained by culturally sanctioned stratagems, including myths of male dominance though males do not actually dominate. In peasant societies, for example, the appearance of male dominance provides an umbrella beneath which women exercise actual power over key sectors of community life, areas where men are not allowed to interfere. (This was certainly my experience growing up on a farm in rural Colorado.) In this world of complex asymmetry, power and authority between the sexes is balanced.

Sanday concludes that arguments calling for sexual symmetry, understood as a world in which males and females have decisions over the same activities and exercise power in identical ways makes little sense. No society has ever existed in which the sexes gave equal energy to exactly the same activities and decisions, nor does such a society seem plausible. This vision of symmetry conflates equality with sameness and it strikes a responsive chord, Sanday insists, only if "one has no knowledge of the many societies which attach supernatural importance to the creation of life."[38]

The thesis of universal male dominance/female subordination does not stand up to historical and anthropological investigation. There are many societies in which women are the central civilizing influence and men are associated with decivilizing forces. Sanday's study suggests that secular male dominance is more likely to occur in societies in which an imbalance has congealed between male and female-linked activities. The way to combat such destructive cleavage is not, it appears, to call for a fusing of male and female activities and spheres such that no vital distinctions remain to expand the actual and symbolic importance and vitality of female-linked activities and systems of meaning. In light of Sanday's findings, the only symmetry for which we have real evidence has not arisen on the basis of gender blurring, but has been grounded in sex differences. This suggests a very different feminist task from that of the symmetrist. The implications are troubling and complex and I cannot spell them out here. But I do wish to turn to one additional piece of contemporary evidence that calls symmetrical presumptions into question.

The work of Diana Grossman Kahn challenges the Chodorow image of parents cloning same-sex children to live in an unchanging world.[39] According to Kahn, Chodorow's argument washes out the complexities of cross-sex identifications. In a series of studies involving over 100 college women, juniors and seniors, with whom she conducted open-ended interviews, Kahn found that daughters were not "locked into" some automatically second-rate model if their mothers were "traditional wives and mothers." Indeed, such mothers were described, with few exceptions, as strong, active, loving and supportive. Most important, for feminist considerations, were the roles of fathers as mentors to daughters. The research literature on what are called "achieving women," including feminists, both nineteenth century and contemporary activists, show the encouragement of fathers to be particularly important. Kahn found that fathers made their own "unique contribution" to the development of their daughters. Only two of her subjects reported fathers who clearly downgraded their capacities compared with those of their brothers. After evaluating the quality of actual individual lives and and experiences, Kahn concludes that mothers and fathers play importantly complementary, not identical or symmetrical roles. Kahn also challenges what emerges as a doctrinal given in Dinnerstein and Chodorow. That is the notion that men, by definition, are deficient in their capacities for intimacy. Kahn concludes that this formulation is one-sided and polemical. It makes intimacy the special sphere of women, a realm somehow regarded as privileged, even while the situation that ostensibly brings women's capacity for creating intimacy is regularly condemned.

Clearly, the ball is now in my court. Given my disagreement with these accounts of "sex-gender systems," and my calls for sexual symmetry, what is my alternative? Perhaps it is worth putting forth the following questions: What is the point of social explanation? Is it to try to figure out what is going on just now, what is happening with, and to, us? Is it to assay how to organize the social world in order to help ease its burdens for those men, women, and children who inhabit it and who try, often against daunting odds, at least most of the time, to be decent, to care for others, to be responsible? Or is our end point, if all goes well, the implementation of a blueprint for social change as foreordained by some theoretical vanguard? If alterations in family life emerge as importantly decent in themselves, and as desired by social participants, that is one thing. But if radical change in human intimate life is called for in order to attain other ends, to remake the world in conformity with some overarching Weltanschauung, that is quite another.

American feminists are, for the most part, trying to make their case through scholarship and textual study and interpretation. We tend to be clustered in colleges and universities; we are middle-class or upper-middle class academics. The two texts on which I have spent the most exegetical time, Dinnerstein's and Chodorow's, do not challenge liberal or radical middle-class academics as much as confirm a way of life towards which many of us were moving anyway. In a sense, their theories help to buttress and sustain practices that were, and are, becoming more common for this social group of "dual career" professionals. I do not mean to suggest that that is all that is going on but it is interesting that a new sort of normative ideal for how families "ought" to be doing things, of the proper way to rear children, etc., is argued in these texts. But the proposed standard or ideal is available (if people "choose it") only to persons in social situations similar to those of the authors. The ideal is not within reach of the vast majority, given the organization of work-life, demographic patterns, etc., even if they would so "choose." It is not, for many, the way they want to organize home and family, mothering, "parenting," and so on. Just as individuals have long been measured against a therapeutic standard of "normalcy" and found wanting, so families can increasingly be measured against a standard of what the (educated, upper middle class) feminist family ought to be and found similarly wanting.

Rather than resurrecting some new standard of family measurement, an alternative project might involve looking at the various ways to be familial that this society currently sustains: How do people in rural Georgia, an ethnic neighborhood of a large city, a mountain community, a seaport in the Northeast, a medium size midwestern town, a California religious cult, an Indian reservation, etc., grow up, live their lives, see their masculine/feminine/human identities, rear their children? What are their hopes, fears, dreams? If we moved in this direction, we could avoid the notion that the vast majority are helpless products of social conditioning who do not know their own minds, a sorry state from which the reconstructors have somehow escaped.

An Alternative Account

In setting down the markers of an alternative, I will indicate those imperatives I believe an alternative must account for, or, better, take account of. First, a compelling alternative to the gender theorists I have criticized would recognize the importance of construing the human subject, child and adult, as importantly self-defining. This need not mean that one ignores the developmentally early, or the primordial at all. But it does mean recognition of the historic struggles women waged against their received identities around the question of what might be called personal "authorship," the view of the person as the "author" of her own story and the responsible liver of her own life. Rigid functionalist models, or reductive psychosexual images are self-defeating. To the extent that social explanation eliminates the self-understanding of social participants, and such explanation and ideology gain acceptance and adherence, we, paradoxically, promote a set of presumptions that have historically been arrayed against female "personhood."

A second feature of an alternative account, tied to the first, would be to frame that account, in part, from what might be called the standpoint of the child. Featuring the child as body-subject, we could see his or her world as a complex web of social relations and meanings alive with competing possibilities. Getting inside a child's world means construing child development and the emergence of gender identity as a dynamic discourse, the history of the "I" ("das Ich"), framed with reference to what I am not ("Ich bin nichts"). This dialectic of human development involves complex negations and affirmations. The child is no passive recipient of this process but the active constructor of various possibilities.

The child's inner discourse of the I/not-I is powerfully structured within the ordering dialogue of child and mother. Louise J. Kaplan has traced the child's dialogues of "oneness and separateness," the coming-towards and the pushing-aways that are punctuation points of a process that, in Kaplan's words, "insures our humanity."[40] The evidence of what happens when things go wrong, when children suffer the diseases of non-attachment and neglect, is overpowering proof of the child's needs for constancy in the form of specific, adult others. The child does not become a language-defining "I" until around thirty months of age, yet well before that she has been interpreting the meaning of space and time, exploring what Kaplan calls the "choreography" of mother and child, carrying on an active dialogue involving mutual excitement, games, and responses. Kaplan demonstrates that the babe in arms is no passive bit of human clay but "an artist," helping "to create the world which holds him,"[41] with a repertoire of "grunts, sighs, coos, postures, droopy-eyed looks, alert looks, finger grabs, head turnings and mouthings, and a set of cries and fretting sounds that give a mother some idea of how she should hold him and interpret the world to him."[42]

The baby is the educator of its own body. She experiments with what it can do. She tests what it cannot. She assays how it all fits together. She locates it in the world.[43] This self-motivation, if all goes well, grows more powerful. The child's capacities for translating bodily-minded imperatives; her growing emotional complexity; her burgeoning capacity to comprehend and create meaning--all paint a picture of a being having agency, not an indeterminate piece of formless fleshy stuff awaiting molding by the organized forces of society. Another important point, lost in most gender accounts, is the fact that adults-as-parents are not unchanged by the discourse of childhood. Each child, a being unique and like no other, calls forth a variety of responses from her parents. Every child-parent dialogue is distinctive and, in subdued or more dramatic ways, may transform all participants.

Just a few other bits of evidence on the child as subject: Rosalind Gould has detailed the ways in which "fantasy activities have a vital place in the child's development, in expanding horizons of thoughts and feelings, and as a potential means of achieving some internal distance from affective dilemmas."[44] Gould shows that the child's "internal well-springs and external world experiences intermingle or oscillate in various ways in fantasy expressions, to the enrichment of both sources of knowledge."[45] Myra Bluebond-Langner, in her account of dying children, convincingly documents the two-way nature of the socialization process often seen as unilinear, flowing from adult shapers to infant shapes. Not so, argues Bluebond-Langner, for such rigid models fail to grasp "the shifting, unfolding, creative aspects of all human behavior," thereby failing to really see children and their world.[46] Her months spent with terminally ill children provide poignant and powerful evidence that children are willful, purposive beings who possess selves; who interpret their own actions, incorporating their self-interpretations and their perceptions of interpretations of others as a way to obtain a view of themselves, others, and objects in the world; who initiate action so as to affect the views others have of them and they have of themselves; who are capable of initiating action to affect the behavior of others towards them; and who attach meaning to themselves, others, and objects, moving from one social world to another and acting appropriately in each.[47]

Finally, in an account at once playful and powerful, Gareth B. Matthews, a philosopher, assays the child as a philosopher. It turns out that "for many young members of the human race, philosophical thinking--including, on occasion, subtle and ingenious reasoning--is as natural as making music and playing games, and quite as much a part of being human."[48] More provocatively, he argues that adults, in their treatment of "childish" questions, should refuse to play the therapist. Instead, parents and teachers should accept a child's inquiries on the level on which they are couched, rather than scouring every utterance for hints at repressed content. He writes, "Even when one suspects that the comment or question carries considerable emotional freight, addressing the question, rather than treating it simply as an emotional symptom, may be part of showing proper respect for the child as a full-fledged human being."[49] His argument here is not that dramatic symptoms should be ignored but that children's expressions of strong views, or children's questions, should not be reductively treated as necessarily symptomatic, thereby abstracting from the child's serious intellectual concerns and development.

A critic might reply at this juncture that he was persuaded by the evidence that children are active agents within a richer social world than the one conveyed in sex-gender system accounts. But, he might then continue, your alternative thus far seems to turn solely on the self-definitional 'moment' of social theory. That is, he might go on, you have made the case for the child as an importantly self-creating subject. But this, in itself, offers no explanation of how it is that gender uniformities do emerge, of why it is biological males wind up as 'men'; biological females become 'women.' A child may understand many things but the stages of her own psycho-sexual development, in some compelling theoretical form, is not one of them. We cannot turn exclusively to the child for this, so how do I propose to explain social gender identity?

I would begin like this. We can assert certain things with surety in advance of any particular, concrete investigation of gender development in specific families and cultural systems. We know, for example, that development will involve the complex emergence of a body-subject within a social matrix. We also

49

know that the human infant comes biologically "prepared" for all sorts of things; there is something like an inner developmental clock that, all other things being equal, will come into play at roughly similar times for human infants. I refer here to myelinization of the nervous system, motor development, and the like. We know that babies are self-motivatedly embodied from the start and act in and upon their worlds on the basis of powerful imperatives which translate, very quickly, into complex social feelings, emotions, needs, demands and desires. We know that young children are extraordinarily preoccupied with their own bodies, though what they can or are allowed to do with those bodies varies from culture to culture. We know that it is impossible to rush this age-specific developmental picture: a child before a certain age doesn't use language, not because her parents haven't taught her but because she literally cannot, given the structure of mouth and tongue, cognitive capacities, etc. There are biological capacities and limits, when one is dealing with human infants and children. But this biology, this embodiment, is expressive of meaning and constitutive of self. Writes Merleau-Ponty, in an essay on "Body as Expression and Speech":

> It is through my body that I understand other people, just as it is through my body that I perceive "things." The meaning of a gesture thus "understood" is not behind it, it is intermingled with the structure of the world outlined by the gesture, and which I take up on my own account. It is arrayed all over the gesture itself--as, in perceptual experience, the significance of the fireplace does not lie beyond the perceptible spectacle, namely the fireplace itself as my eyes and movements discover it in the world.[50]

An alternative, beginning from the body-subject, would also trail in its wake another presumption--the organization of humanity, on conceptual and symbolic levels, into two distinct sexes (with more or less blurring on the boundaries) as an essential aspect of human cultural life. Males and females, to be sure, share in the most basic general characteristics; yet they differ along recognizable and distinctive lines and all cultures acknowledge this difference in some way. To insist on the importance of the sex distinction along a range of cultural meaning is not to surreptitiously smuggle in a sex-gender system geared against women. To say, "my body, myself" will either be a male or female body,[*] or that I will try to create some sense of maleness or femaleness given my embodiment, does not lock me into rigid stereotypes of "masculine"/"feminine."

To accept the sex distinction as ineliminable and important, then, does not mean to acquiesce in received notions of maleness and femaleness without question. To demonstrate that bodily identity is a feature of personal identity, meaning that such identity will also be a sexed identity, requires a dynamic, developmental account of the human subject. I have traced out such an account elsewhere, one which owes much to Freud's theory of human development as dynamically embodied <u>and</u> social, for we are body-subjects in a social universe.[51] The human body registers itself through a complex inner-outer dialectic in which we make internal representations to ourselves of our bodies,[52] and through which, in a sense, we insert ourselves into the world. From her first moments, the infant experiences her body as a source of pleasure and unpleasure that seems to go beyond the mere registering of sensation. Embodiment implicates her in the active construction of an inner and outer world, in part through the taking in of the body's surfaces as part of "external" reality. So far as we can judge, the human infant, at birth,

---

[*]Keeping in mind the relatively rare phenomenon of intersexuality.

does not have the cognitive nor the neurological structure ororganization necessary to differentiate neatly inner from outer, external from internal. What the infant can do is to incorporate with eyes, ears, mouth and touch a world complicatedly inner/outer. Slowly the "I" is built up, in part through complex representations of the child's body, in part through inner representations of the bodies of others with whom the child is involved in exquisitely social relations from the start.

Our corporeality bears powerful imperatives for knowledge and being. A child can neither physically negate nor somehow "transcend" the manner in which his or her body registers itself within the successive stages of psycho-sexual maturation. The body evokes and mediates ways of knowing. "Whether it is a question of another's body or my own, I have no means of knowing the human body other than that of living it," writes Merleau-Ponty, "which means taking up on my own account the drama which is being played out in it, and losing myself in it. I am my body, at least wholly to the extent that I possess experience, and yet at the same time my body is as it were a 'natural' subject, a provisional sketch of my total being. Thus, experience of one's own body runs counter to the reflective procedure which detaches subject and object from each other, and which gives us only the thought about the body, or the body as an idea, and not the experience of the body or the body in reality."[53]

Our most original, primitive experiences with the world cannot be understood save as an embodied engagement with the world. At the beginning the child has no sense of one gender or another. But male and female bodies from the beginning will surely register themselves somewhat differently. One result of the child's early sexual research is the discovery of two types of embodied beings, though she remains uncertain as to the full importance of this distinction. She does 'know,' however, that these are important matters for they involve strange sensations and spur her curiosity. To live in this embodied social world is not, necessarily, to inhabit one in which differential evaluations are placed on gender identity, always to the detriment of the female.

My claim that bodily identity is necessarily a gendered identity and one feature of personal-social identity, neither presupposes nor entails social and political inequality between the sexes. Although sex distinctions in some societies, including our own, have served as justifications for sex inequality, they need not thus serve. Moreover, the burden of anthropological evidence suggests that sex distinctions have formed the basis for systems of parity of power and authority between men and women. Indeed, the claim that sexual "symmetry" is the only sure and secure psychological foundation on which to build equality displaces a political focus upon structures of social, economic and political equality in favor of advancing claims about the transformation of human personality.

Several modest conclusions suggest themselves. The first is that we need to pay more attention to the actual surroundings or contexts of mothering in contemporary society. Perhaps it is an often impoverished surrounding, stripped of supportive community and kin, that makes mothering a frequently onerous burden. Although neither Dinnerstein nor Chodorow provide us with a picture of family life they assume that the family is both oppressive and patriarchal. Perhaps, as well, it is time feminist theorists began to question their own most frequently deployed categories (oppression and patriarchy are two) to see what they conceal as well as what they reveal. For if we continue to locate the family as the first and foremost breeding ground of sexist privilege we will be unable to account for the ways in which women, historically, have been empowered by their authority in the private sphere and used it as a base for social identity and action <u>in</u> the world.

Our situation, the modern human condition, is fraught with ambivalence and the interplay of competing and confluent social and political currents and forces. We must acknowledge that ambivalence and think of how our theories can come to grips with the actual complexities of our lives. We all, for example, favor strengthening the capacities of human beings to live out long-term ties and commitments to one another. Such relations are based upon, and are infused with, values counter to those that prevail on the market or in narrow, instrumentalist world views. This prompts Zelda Bronstein to claim that marriage and the family are "the last institutional intermediary which still stands as a buffer between increasingly impotent individuals and the organized forces of domination."[54] I would put the matter less defensively but I agree that we must find some way to engage the family as a theoretical challenge and a political problem without, at the same time, impugning the ideal of these social relations. With all the many abuses of which we have become conscious (of children, of spouses, most particularly battered wives) we sometimes forget that for the vast majority of individuals the family involves an effort to hold onto meaning and purpose in a social world in which other public and private institutions have been drained of much of their previous legitimacy and normative meaning.

Second, in part because families and intimacy cannot bear the full burden of meaning, purpose, and sociality, we need a vision of politics, a theory of the political community including an ideal of the citizen as one who shares in the deliberate efforts of human beings to order and direct their collective affairs. The thinkers I have criticized offer little here, for politics gets absorbed within psychologized or sociological categories. That feminist theorists have paid scant attention to what the Greeks called "the political," to commonalities and the possibility for a _res publica_ is itself symptomatic of the depoliticization of our era. For we do not simply enter the world as gendered beings but as beings with another possible identity--a public one--for we are citizens. Prescriptions to mend what is wrong with us that see us only as producers or reproducers, as role-players, as abstract "history-makers" or equally abstract "maternalists" wash out this critical aspect of our (possible) identities. Clearly, a major rescue effort will be required for us to reclaim our public identity as constitutive of our beings in some vital way. Here, just possibly, the many neighborhood and community women, often poor, under-educated, and (by our standards) unenlightened, who are fighting for their streets, their children, for safe places to play and live may show us, or remind us, that citizenship is still possible.

Jean Bethke Elshtain
University of Massachusetts

1. Sigmund Freud, "The Question of a Weltanschauung," in New Introductory Lectures, Standard Edition (Vol. XXII, 158-182).

2. Two important critiques include Charles Taylor, "Interpretation and the Sciences of Many," Review of Metaphysics (Vol. 26, 1971, 4-51), and, also by Taylor, "Neutrality in Political Science," in Philosophy, Politics and Society, ed. Peter Laslett and W.G. Runciman (New York, 1967, 25-57).

3. Sigmund Freud, "Constructions in Analysis," Standard Edition (Vol. XXIII, 355-270).

4. Clifford Geertz, The Interpretation of Cultures (New York, 1973), p. 18.

5. See Marie Jahoda, Freud and the Dilemmas of Psychology (London, 1977), and Jean Bethke Elshtain, Public Man, Private Woman: Women in Social and Political Thought (Princeton, 1981).

6. I have drawn on an unpublished essay by Charles Taylor, "Social Theory as Practice."

7. It may be possible that good arguments do not necessarily make for good politics, nor that bad arguments necessarily make for bad politics. Most of the time, however, one's assessment of a thinker's arguments and her politics must be of a piece because the thinker herself has forged such a tight link between the two that they cannot be separated. Even if such a link hasn't been forged, I am persuaded this separation cannot, finally, be made in any tidy way.

8. Dorothy Dinnerstein, The Mermaid and the Minotaur (New York, 1977), p. 77. Dinnerstein's appropriation of Freud, of psychoanalytic theory in general, is highly selective. For example, Freud's metapsychological papers, case studies, major theoretical renderings are all ignored. Only Civilization and Its Discontents and The Future of an Illusion are mentioned.

9. Ibid., p. 33.

10. Ibid., p. 13.

11. Ibid., p. 49.

12. Sigmund Freud, "An Autobiographical Study," Standard Edition (Vol. XX, 7-70), pp. 30-31.

13. Jeffrey Lustman, M.D., "On Splitting," The Psychoanalytic Study of the Child (Vol. 32, 1977, 119-145), p. 119.

14. Ibid., p. 122.

15. Ibid., p. 130. "It may be that splitting, by permitting oscillating expression of polar clusters of mental context, provides the requisite psychic 'stimulation' through which sustained boundary phenomena initially emerge."

16. Dinnerstein, The Mermaid and the Minotaur, p. 159.

17. Ibid., p. 70.

18. Ibid., p. 210

19. Ibid., p. 179. In this Dinnerstein is importantly wrong, as I argue below.

20. L.J. Jordanova, "Natural facts: a historical perspective on science and sexuality," in Carol P. MacCormack and Marilyn Strathern, eds., Nature, Culture and Gender (Cambridge, 1980, 42-69), p. 64. Earlier variants on this theme occur, for example, in the Greek distinction between physis and nomes. See the discussion in Elshtain, Public Man, Private Woman, pp. 7-14.

21. Ibid., p. 43.

22. Ibid., p. 65.

23. Ibid., p. 67.

24. Talcott Parsons, "Age and Sex in the Social Structure of the United States" (1942) in Essays in Sociological Theory (New York, 1964); and Talcott Parsons, "The Kinship System of the Contemporary United States" (1943) in above.

25. Lawrence Stone, The Family, Sex and Marriage: In England 1500-1800 (New York, 1979), p. 416.

26. Nancy Chodorow, The Reproduction of Mothering: Psychoanalysis and the Sociology of Gender (Berkeley: University of California Press, 1978), p. 9.

27. Ibid., p. 39.

28. Chodorow, Reproduction of Mothering, p. 214.

29. Ibid., p. 8. Chodorow draws uncritically on Gayle Rubin's essay, "The Traffic in Women: Notes on the 'Political Economy of Sex's,' in Rayna R. Reiter, Toward an Anthropology of Women (New York, 1975), borrowing Rubin's claim, one seriously contested by most anthropologists, including feminists, that women's relegation to domesticity makes them "less social, less cultural, as well as less powerful than men." Rubin adopts the notion that women, everywhere, have been "goods" to exchange. Given that we no longer require this exchange, we can do away with the organization of sex/gender. Within her functionalist rendering, a conclusion emerges, namely, "eradicating gender hierarchy (or gender itself); the dream she finds most compelling is a "genderless (though not sexless) society, in which one's sexual anatomy is irrelevant to who one is...." (204) (emphasis mine).

30. Though Chodorow also discounts biology as important in any deep way to her account in her book, she later acknowledges that "biological variables" are something feminists must be open to, for we are, after all "embodied creatures" and there is "certainly some biological basis, or influence...," etc. (See Judith Lorber, Rose Laub Coser, Alice S. Rossi and Nancy Chodorow, "On The Reproduction of Mothering: A Methodological Debate," Signs: Journal of Women in Culture and Society (Vol. 6, No. 3, 1981), 482-515. But biological "variables" is precisely what I am not concerned with, for their incorporation only leads to social science notions of "interaction" and "multiple causality" and that boring lot. To call the

body-subject a "variable" is baffling indeed, for the fact that we are never-not-our-bodies and never in the world save as body-subjects seems a rather more basic and ungetoverable reality than to strip our bodies down to size as but one "variable," among others. Variables don't grow up, grow ill, make love, grow old, and die. This paring the body down to size is not radical at all; it is typical of academic social science and a throw-back to plain, old-fashioned dualism. Cf. Jean Bethke Elshtain, "Against Androgyny," Telos (No. 47, Spring, 1981, 5-22).

31. The much-maligned Bowlby remains compelling in his stress on quality of care, though we could, surely, counter the notion that this must be an exclusively female activity. See John Bowlby, Child Care and the Growth of Love (Baltimore, 1965), p. 13, where Bowlby states that the "quality of parental care is what is of vital importance."

32. Zelda Bronstein, "Psychoanalysis Without the Father," Humanities in Society (Vol. 3, No. 3, Spring 1980, 199-212), p. 200.

33. Ibid., p. 207.

34. Peggy Reeves Sanday, Male Power and Female Dominance (Cambridge: 1981), passim.

35. See Mary Douglas, Purity and Danger (London, 1966), passim.

36. Sanday, Male Power and Female Dominance, p. 133.

37. Ibid., p. 155.

38. Ibid., p. 176.

39. Diana Grossman Kahn, "Fathers as Mentors to Daughters," Radcliffe Institute Working Paper, 1981, pp. 1-35 and "Daughters Comment on the Lesson of Their Mothers' Lives," Radcliffe Institute Working Paper, 1980.

40. Louise J. Kaplan, Oneness and Separateness: From Infant to Individual (New York, 1978), p. 27. Another important consideration, omitted from feminist gender theorists, is the thought and practice of mothering, or, better, their ways of thinking and acting tied to, or flowing from, engaging in mothering practices, in which mothers engage. Mothers' concerns for their children, the meaning of mothering to mother-subjects themselves, in all its complexity and conflict, must be taken up with cogent empathy and theoretical clarity.

41. Kaplan, Oneness and Separateness, p. 51.

42. Ibid., p. 195.

43. One compelling feminist complaint has been that female children were restricted in early experimentation with their bodies, in "doing" things physical.

44. Rosalind Gould, Child Studies Through Fantasy: Cognitive-Affective Patterns in Development (New York, 1972), p. 273.

45. Ibid., p. 274.

46. Myra Bluebond-Langner, The Private Worlds of Dying Children (Princeton, 1978) p. 5.

47. Ibid., p. 121.

48. Gareth B. Matthews, Philosophy and the Young Child (Cambridge, MA.: 1980), p. 36.

49. Ibid., p. 86.

50. Merleau-Ponty, The Essential Writings of Merleau-Ponty, ed. Alden L. Fisher (New York: Harcourt, Brace and World, 1969), p. 198.

51. See Elshtain, "Against Androgyny." I would also take fuller account of the work of Richard Wollheim, Bernard Williams, and Merleau-Ponty on Identity.

52. Sigmund Freud, "The Ego and the Id," Standard Edition (Vol. XIX, 3-68). Cf. Richard Wollheim, "The Mind and the Mind's Image of Itself," in On Art and the Mind (Cambridge, MA.: 1974), p. 53.

53. Merleau-Ponty, Essential Writings, p. 213.

54. Bronstein, "Psychoanalysis Without the Father," p. 207.

WOMEN HUNTERS: THE IMPLICATIONS FOR PLEISTOCENE
PREHISTORY AND CONTEMPORARY ETHNOGRAPHY

Sexual division of labor among today's foraging societies is generally and often strongly portrayed as one of men hunting and women gathering.[1] Shellfish, fish, and insects are the females' protein contribution; men favor big and often dangerous game. Because women are universally the child bearers and nurturers, they are widely assumed to be unable to take part in high risk hunting. In many anthropological models, women are assumed to exploit resources close to home, undertaking most domestic and maintenance activities. Child care is pictured as dominating the structure of women's daily lives. Among well known foragers, the !Kung San of Botswana and Namibia exemplify this traditional view.[2]

Naomi   Quinn,   in   her   important   review   paper, "Anthropological Studies of Women's Status," succinctly states the problem of women as non-hunters. She writes:

> Most   writers   agree   that   hunting   is
> incompatible with pregnancy, carrying small
> infants, and child care, although they are
> not always agreed as to whether it is the
> actual   physical   exertion   which   hunting
> demands, the danger it involves, or the long
> distance travel it engenders which is most
> critical to this incompatibility.[3]

We have been presented with a remarkable and timely opportunity; the practice of Agta female participation in hunting allows us to examine the conditions indicated by Quinn, and to attempt a few further insights into the origins and variations of sexual division of labor. That women among some Agta groups hunt was first observed in 1972.[4] Two periods of long-term field work explored Agta adaptation and especially subsistence-settlement systems. Between June 1974 and June

61

1976 the authors worked about fifteen months among the Agta, returning again in October 1980.[5] Field work terminated in June 1982. The second trip focused directly on the problem discussed in this paper: how women hunt and rear children and how hunting fits into the whole Agta adaptative system.

The problem under investigation over the last three years was introduced in an article titled "Woman the Hunter."[6] At around the same time that this article was written two of our colleagues at the University of Hawaii began to approach the same question from the theoretical side. In an early version of their text, The Sexes in the Human Population, Madeleine and Lenn Goodman hypothesized the possibility of women's hunting during the human evolutionary past. In the recent printing of that book they argue that our findings with the Agta confirm the feasibility of a more pluralistic model of human evolution, less dependent on the stereotypic image of passive and sedentary females, nomadic and aggressive males, and less tied to the bizarre notion that male and female human evolution took place under radically different conditions of selection pressure.[7]

Support for the traditional model of man the hunter, woman the gatherer centers on the assumption of the unworkability of the hunter role from women. For this reason a requisite of our research has been the gathering and analysis of quantitative data, leading to an evaluation of women's contributions as hunters in Agta society and the material feasibility of their hunting role. These data have been collected by the authors and are currently being analyzed at the University of Hawaii under the direction of Madeleine Goodman with the assistance of John Grove, and in collaboration with the authors. We are studying proportions of body fat and other anthropomorphic data, fertility, lactation, and their relationships to subsistence activities, childcare and other pertinent variables.

The Agta

Northeastern Luzon, in the Philippines, is a region dominated by a low but rugged chain of mountains--the Sierra Madre. On the eastern coast, the Pacific Ocean meets a topography of coral beaches, granite sea cliffs, and, in spots, living and uplifted dead coral beds. The western foothills of the mountains slope into the dry Cagayan valley, now deforested and occupied by rice farmers. Agta live scattered throughout the Sierra Madre, ranging east-west along the many rivers that penetrate the mountains from the ocean and from the Cagayan valley. The people we studied for the present research live in two provinces of the northern Sierra Madre, Isabela and Cagayan.

The Agta are foragers who live in small groups of extended joint families, camped along rivers and streams. As foragers, they must organize themselves into clusters or units of people fitted to the exploitation of the diversified flora and fauna in the region, and to variation in environmental conditions. The structure that enables effective adjustment among the Agta is the extended joint family. It is the unit of daily cooperation, inter-dependence, and identification with territory. This key unit also fits into a larger structure, the dialect group, and can subdivide into nuclear families.

A dialect group is made up of Agta sharing a similar language and having interlocking ties of kinship and marriage. The dialect group never works together nor is everybody in it related, but it does provide a social network within which most Agta of the group may move. Likewise, the nuclear family is not a viable separate unit, but joins others, all by kinship connections, in establishing both residence and subsistence systems.

The organization of the extended joint family, the basic unit of subsistence and of residence, is one of nuclear families joined through primary ties of kinship, especially through the core sibling unit. In other words, Agta residential clusters are often organized by the co-residence of brothers and sisters (or combinations thereof), their respective spouses, and members of ascending and descending generations. Some preferences seems to be given, at least among Isabela Agta, for the female sibling tie as the organizing principle.[8] But in general, a very flexible structure exists. Since in-marrying spouses usually desire part-time residence with their own siblings and other kin, nuclear families are frequently hiving off one group and joining another, often many kilometers away, but usually within the range of the same dialect group. Fluctuation in group membership varies according to availability of food resources, obligation to kin, demand for adults' services, and the mood of the individuals. Departures from one group to visit another because of social friction or affection may be brief (a few days) or permanent (more than one year).

Residential clusters are usually fewer and larger in the wet season, which lasts from early November through February. During the wet season, the northeast monsoon brings heavy rains, swollen rivers, and difficult movement. Sporadic typhoons are most likely early in the season. The wet season becomes a time of intense social intercourse, and is a time of relatives joining together for fellowship and cooperation in food getting.

During the dry season, March through October, the larger extended joint family is in flux. Seldom do the larger aggregates appear. Instead, one to three nuclear families move, in various combinations, into remote locations up the rivers and into the mountains, hunting, fishing, collecting, and simply getting away from "the crowd." Closeness of kinship, the passions of the day, and subsistence activities all influence which families travel with which.

The Agta are primarily hunters of medium-size game, wild pig and deer. Smaller game such as monkey, palm civet, and monitor lizard are seldom sought but killed when encountered. Birds are shot by youths.

Several considerations are relevant concerning pig and deer as game animals. Both are forest dwellers, but pass through a variety of environmental zones, ranging from the mid-elevation portions of the mountains through the alluvial terraces of rivers into the agricultural fields of Agta and non-Agta farmers. Both pigs and deer are influenced by the forest's productivity of foods, by weather, and by hunting pressure.

Agta residential locations are determined in part by game characteristics. The actual organization of hunting strategies and tactics, especially the type of hunt and the nature of the personnel involved, are all influenced by characteristics of the game populations at the time. Game and weather conditions permitting, Agta choose hunting over other activities, except riverine fishing at the peak of the dry season.

Fishing is a major activity among those Agta whose river resources have not been depleted by loggers and farmers. Only the dry months, with clear, warm water, are productive enough to neglect hunting. During rainy spells the muddy, flooded and dangerous waters preclude the usual Agta spearfishing. Nets may be occasionally used; line fishing on the coast is favored when nylon lines and metal fishhooks are available. Spearfishing in the ocean is possible in days of calm water, but the dangers of spear loss and of attack by marine predators discourage the frequent selection of this option.

Collection of wild plant and animal resources is a daily part of Agta adaptation. Wild plant foods do not make up a major part of the diet of Agta, but are significant supplements, as in honey. Fruit, wild greens, and roots enter the diet when the forest is provident or when scarcity of domesticated cereal grains and roots (sweet potato and cassava) forces forest gathering. Wild faunal resource collection is more sporadic than that of flora, and is limited largely to

crustaceans and mollusks, found in streams and on the reefs
fringing the coastline. Agta vary from place to place in their
emphasis on such food. In Cagayan, for example, collection in
the rainy season months is preferred. Agta seldom if ever
collect shellfish when game has been killed. Meat is clearly
the preferred food.

Agta cannot be correctly termed strictly hunters-gatherers,
since they are now, and have been most of this century,
experimenting with horticulture. They are incipient farmers as
well as traders. Agta have known the basics of plant
cultivation for at least several decades, but in remote regions
are only now beginning serious attempts to raise root crops,
corn, and rice. Generally they are most successful in
locations distant from non-Agta farmers, who invariably steal
Agta land and crops.

The most important crops, in the sense of year round
production and predictability, are cassava and sweet potato.
These are easy to grow, demand little care, and may be
harvested when needed. Rice and corn are grown by many Agta,
but the plots are small and often modest in harvest. Clearing
of forest cover is a late wet season activity, and planting
occurs as the dry season appears and burning of dried, downed
trees and shrubs is possible.

While horticulture is not new, it is a new emphasis or
attempt to adjust to new environmental demands. As non-Agta
farmers expand into Agta territory, take land, affect game
populations, and help create new desires and dependencies, Agta
are choosing to grow domesticated plant crops. Their success
is minimal, but the overall adjustments in the subsistence
system are considerable. In any account of the organization of
men's and women's activities, consideration of present cultural
change is important.

Both men and women participate, although differently, in
all subsistence activities. To the Agta the economic roles of

both sexes are not rigidly defined. Every able-bodied Agta woman or man is capable of accomplishing any of the tasks necessary for the group's subsistence. In this paper, however, we examine only the relationships of women as hunters and as child bearers and nurturers of the young.

The material in this case concerns, the Agta who have established base camp at the cover of the Nanadukan river and where we resided much of the time between October 1980 and June 1982. This river was until late 1982 remote and difficult to reach, since the logging roads and bridges were still south and beyond the difficult and dangerous Malibu river. The family members at the cove numbered as many as fifty at one wet season count and as few as six or seven in drier months.

Women and Hunting

Agta women at and around Nanadukan certainly hunt. The patterns of women's participation in hunting are not, however, identical with that of men. All men hunt, but some are more successful than others. Not all women hunt; the frequency of participation varies greatly among those who hunt. Greater disparity in frequency of hunting and in success rate is found among women than among men.

Hunting itself is not a simple or one tactic system. All hunting is structured by environmental conditions, Agta personnel available and resource needs of the group. The first consideration is ease and likelihood of successful procurement of animal protein. Unless fishing is deemed especially provident, parties will hunt wild pig and deer.

Three general strategies of hunting are known, but tactics vary from day to day. First, small teams of hunters, or a single hunter, may stalk game, either slowly walking about looking for spoor or hoping to jump an animal or ambush it. Second, driving game with dogs is a common strategy. Usually more than one hunter is necessary, although one person with an especially capable team of dogs will suffice. Teams of two hunters are common. Large groups of men and women are thought to follow different tactics, but do utilize strategies based on dogs. As we shall see below, women hunters most commonly participate in game drives and use dogs. A third strategy is to trap wild pig and deer. Agta do not as a rule favor trapping; the people living in more remote regions neglect the practice, and only sporadically trap. Two types of trapping are known. Both involve hidden devices to catch game as it passes along trails, generally to or from water. Some Isabela Agta use a spring mounted spear which, when a trip line is touched, casts horizontally across the path at the torso height of the animal. Cagayan Agta claim not to use the spear trap, but prefer a snare device. Like the spear trap, a spring under great tension releases a restraining mechanism. A loop of cord, lying over the trigger, is designed to catch and close around the lower leg of the animal and to pull upward. The animal is held until the hunter arrives to kill it. For a variety of reasons, we believe that trapping is an introduced non-Agta strategy, and we have never seen women engage in the activity except to check traps.

All men and some women hunt with bows and arrows. In the few cases where guns are used, only men have been seen to carry them. Some women prefer using knives instead of bows. In such cases, once dogs have cornered an animal, the hunter rushes in to stab the prey. The long knife is either thrust directly into the pig's or deer's chest or is bound to a sapling and used as a spear. The later technique is most likely when the animal is large and dangerous.

Team organization in hunting is suited to the needs of the residence groups and to the personnel available. A variety of constraints may immediately affect the tactics chosen and membership of the hunting party. While men frequently hunt alone or travel in all male parties to the hunting location, thereafter splitting up, women seldom (but have been seen to) travel alone in the forest. A woman is most often in the company of other women or her husband or male relative. Some middle aged women prefer the company of a teenaged female, who seldom carries a bow but may act in the kill, using a knife. The girl usually helps carry back the carcass. When men and women hunt together, in large numbers, women tend to interact most closely with each other, thereby avoiding gossip concerning the outcome of chance encounters in the forest. The same is true of the men. In some cases, however, spouses work together as teams.

Butchering of game and distribution of meat are under the control of the hunter, whether a woman or a man. A small animal, just enough for domestic consumption, is divided equally among all nuclear families in the camp. If a bigger animal is killed, both husband and wife decide which parts and how much should be set aside to be sold or exchanged to trade partners. Even if the wife were not a hunter, the husband does not have the sole control over the distribution or exchange of meat and other goods inside or outside the camp.

In the following chart, we present data concerning hunting frequency and success among the Agta at Nanadukan. These data are extracted from field notes taken during 185 days of observation, and have been selected to cross-cut the seasons, since hunting varies throughout the year. These data as presented are only a summary of the voluminous information collected over nearly two years. As summary statistics, however, they seem to bear out the totality of our observations. We see that men are more active in hunting. Women, who hunt only with other women, or with men, do not match the total number of trips made by male hunters. Still, the success rates--the killing of game per trip--are high for women. Men alone have a surprisingly low success rate, 17.2 percent.

Explanation of these data demands several special considerations. First, trapping, as noted in the chart, is excluded. Agta at Nanadukan only trapped game during the latter months of our residence, and these months were not considered in the present analysis. Second, we have included all game killed, both small and major. Women, we found do not kill only the smaller prey, and men the major or larger game. In fact, women seldom bother with civet cat and monitor lizard. It is the men, in fact, during forest stalks, who will often shoot these animals as the opportunity appears. A final complication, not clear in the chart, is that occasionally more than one animal is killed on a single hunt. This skews the success rate slightly.

Without question, women, like men, are hunters. Men hunt more frequently than women, but are less successful per hunt. The success rate of women hunters (30.9%) is nearly double that of the men (17.2%). In terms of productivity, male and

Frequency of hunting[1]			Game killed[2]			Success rate[3]
	No. of Trips	%	No.	Wt. (kg)	%-Wt.	
Women	55	18.6	17	283.75	22.2	30.9%
Men	180	60.8	31	545.6	42.8	17.2%
Mixed[4]	61	20.6	25	446.85	35.0	41.0%
Total	296	100.0	73	1275.60	100.0	

[1] includes techniques of hunting except trapping.
[2] includes all sizes of wild pig, deer, monkey, palm civet and monitor lizard.
[3] $\frac{\text{No. of trips}}{\text{No. of game}}$
[4] a team composed of at least a woman and a man hunting with/without dogs.

male-female teams secured 77.8 per cent of the game by weight. But we must emphasize, that Agta women cannot be considered subsidiary actors on the hunt, used only to drive or process animals, as observed among the Mbuti of Zaire.[9] All women hunting groups among the Agta brought in over one fifth of the game by weight.

As a rule, women do not travel, the long distances to the more remote and usually more provident hunting ranges. Agta women are most likely to hunt in the foothills surround their residence sites. This predilection has little to do with the rigor or danger of long distant travel since travel is not especially dangerous nor remote terrain more difficult to hunt in. The danger and difficulty is in the actual hunting, not in the travel to the hunting ground. Agta often run up and down hills while chasing fleeing pig or deer. These wounded animals often turn upon the hunters, so the danger of gorings or injury by deer's hooves and antlers is ever present. However, neither men nor women fear or often sustain serious injury. Nor is the portage of the kill back to home base a serious hindrance for men or women. If several animals are killed, they are butchered on the spot. The meat is sliced and smoke dried, before it is carried back to camp.

Hunting, for the Agta, is reasonably dangerous and arduous. Agta women are, at least among the people we resided, capable hunters. How, then are they able at the same time to reproduce to maintain the population? How can they integrate hunting, and other subsistence and maintenance tasks, with child bearing and nurturing?

Women and Child Care

Among the Agta, children are very much desired. Having children is not considered a burden or a hindrance to participation in subsistence activities. Artificial means of contraception, if known, are seldom used. Herbal concoctions for inducing abortion are known but no use is recorded. Infanticide is abhorred. During pregnancy Agta women assume their normal workload, in or out of camp.

The workload of women is not identical to that of men, in spite of a fuzzy and, at most, mild division of labor. Women are the main, but not exclusive, caretakers of children, especially those younger than seven or eight years. Women predominate in the performance of several daily domestic tasks. Firewood collection and water carrying is nearly exclusively the domain of women and girls. Only when a woman is busy with sick children, is sick herself, or is out on a trip, will her husband or father collect wood and water. Both men and women cook--Agta cooking is simple--but men are not frequently found boiling the carbohydrate staples or meat. Women and girls expend more than fifty percent of the effort involved in processing foods for cooking. Men do help pound rice frequently. Often teams of two, perhaps husband and wife, pound (husk) rice using a large mortar and pestles. Men were never seen to dig domesticated roots for home consumption, although they dug both domesticated and wild roots while traveling on hunts.

Other differences in the workloads of men and women are found, but are not strictly observed. Women tend to be more heavily involved in house construction, especially in assembling the lean-to shade, common in the dry season. Men may secure the poles, while women almost always gather and install the rattan frond thatching material. In the larger rainy season pole house, both men and women enter the forest to cut and carry out the posts and framing pieces. Men tend to make the floor and women again collect the thatching. Both men and women make the roof and sidings (thatch) of the house. Women do most of the sweeping and tidying up in and around the house. Men and women wash and repair their own garments, as few and as poor as they may be. Children begin household tasks very young, and are mainly responsible for their own maintenance after the age of eight or ten. The workload of girls is considerably greater than that of boys, since much care of younger siblings falls upon older girls. As is true for most activities, however, boys are not excluded from such work. Little boys are often seen carrying infants about, playing with them, and in general functioning as baby sitters.

As in all societies, the main responsibility of infant care is assigned to women, and primarily to mothers. During its first year, an infant is constantly attached to its mother. Breastfeeding is "on demand;" mothers stop their activities to nurse a baby whenever it fusses. A nursing mother goes about her tasks with the baby slung on her back or side in a piece of cloth or blanket. All female informants claim that carrying a baby during hunting is not cumbersome. While infants younger than two or three months would seldom be carried on a hunt, older nursing babies are easily taken. As the Agta say, the babies just sleep; if one fusses, it will be nursed, after which it will again fall asleep in the wrap on the mother's back. Older children (three years and above) can easily be left in the camp; other members of the family or groups who stay behind are assigned babysitting. Furthermore, older children do not need constant attention from an attendant.

To evaluate and characterize the inter-relationships of women's participation in hunting and their success in childbearing and rearing requires a more detailed study of characteristics of female fertility, population parameters, and such specifics as birth spacing and childhood mortality. These data are now under analysis by our research team.

From preliminary observation, we do find that Agta women seem to be highly variable in their ability to produce live births and in keeping the children alive until adulthood. In a small sample of 32 Cagayan women, in or past reproductive age, two had never been able to conceive, (three more lack data) and

27 had produced 111 pregnancies. Of these 111, only 84 resulted in live births. Of these 84 births, 28 died before the time of the census, and thirty six were still pre-pubertal. Of the 28 childhood deaths, 25 occurred before weaning.

A variety of conditions produced the deaths indicated above. None of these deaths is directly attributable to hunting, although many may be influenced by general exposure to environmental conditions. Children are often carried in the forest during any work activity. Since foul weather is common during half the year, babies may be wet, cold, and exposed at all times. Sanitary conditions typical of foraging societies heighten the chances for infection. We are unable to judge at this time if the strenuous activities known to all Agta women, is related to the 27 fetal deaths observed.

In spite of the inroads made by high mortality, the Agta themselves attempt to keep all children alive. Parents try to keep babies dry and well fed, to provide traditional and Western medicines, and to "keep the babies coming." Grief over the loss of a child is, we sense, as great as in our own society, despite the knowledge that many babies die.

To summarize the Agta case: women, men and older children all actively engage in a variety of subsistence and maintenance tasks, working everyday to keep the residential group fed, sheltered, and in reasonable health. Women frequently participate in the acquisition of animal protein. They join in housebuilding, food preparation, and leisure activities. They dominate yet do not claim exclusive control of child care. Women, like their husbands, treasure children, but are not seriously handicapped in their work by children. Women are burdened with firewood collection and by fetching water, but men spend a high proportion of time blacksmithing arrows and sharpening tools.

Hunting is not really a problem for women. Women hunt because the return for their efforts is immediate and significant, and because they are capable of meeting the demands put upon them. Physical exertion, danger, and long distance travel are inherent in hunting, but most other subsistence activities operate in the same conditions. Most tasks in Agta life, whether performed by men or women, involve hard work, risk to self, and many kilometers of travel in the rugged forest slopes of the mountains. Hunting is perhaps the worst of all activities in terms of hardship, but we have no record of an Agta ever dying from hunt.

Implications For Pleistocene Models and Ethnographic Theory

The Agta are not Pleistocene, paleolithic hunters. And, certainly, their culture is organized along very different lines from those of complex stratified cultures found widely today. Agta women and men may, however, be studied as part of our general attempt to understand variation in human societies and cultural systems. Study of the Agta and their organization of gender roles broadens the base of information upon which we construct models of past, present, and future societal adaptations. If we want to understand the foundations of human social organization, we must examine the assumptions and the research upon which present theory is based. By clarifying how and why Agta women hunt, insights may be gleaned that sustain a more inclusive model of the earliest hominid bio-cultural origins.

The evidence suggests that rethinking many current assumptions about human sexual division of labor is in order. We suggest that the model "Man the Hunter--Women the Gatherer," which dominates the anthropology of past and present foraging societies, needs to be more flexible. Given the possibility of women's hunting in a subsistence society, we are required to ask how widespread was women's hunting in the past? What were the underlying motives and conditions?

With few exceptions--Nancy Tanner's book <u>On Becoming Human</u>[10] stands out--scholars of Pliocene and Pleistocene hominids see males as the sole hunters of game animals, and females only as gatherers of plant foods. Archaeologists are beginning to waver in the rigidity of that division, but few are actively investigating the earliest organization of hominid subsistence activities in the light of new ideas concerning sexual division of labor. Isaac and Crader, leading scholars of the African beginnings of hominid bio-cultural evolution, write:

> The acquisition of flesh (meat or fish) is commonly the principal contribution of males, although females may also take part in this aspect of subsistence. The gathering of other foods is often the responsibility of adult females, but all members of the society participate at times in this activity.[11]

> ...<u>division</u> of <u>labor</u> between <u>hunter</u>, <u>scavenger</u>, <u>fishers</u>, who are preferentially <u>male</u>, and <u>gatherers</u>, who are preferentially female, is <u>virtually</u> universal.[12]

In recent years female anthropologists have stressed the importance of gathering and mothering over hunting.[13] If we reject the universal applicability of the Man the Hunter model of the origins of human systems of subsistence and of the early organization of society, we must ask several questions concerning alternatives. What indeed was hunting like in the Pliocene? What actually could have been the capabilities of females? What subsistence behaviors and what forms of cooperation and sharing <u>were</u> adaptive?

The dichotomy of males hunting and females gathering is too divisive and too stark a representation. At first glance, the sexually divided model is elegant, since it posits the protection of females from the dangers of the hunt and from predators. Since females are seen to be nearly always either pregnant or lactating, and these features are seen as critically essential to group viability, we must question the notions that females are less capable, or at least weak in self-defense, and first and foremost involved in reproduction. We must also suggest that the cooperation and sharing of foods and defense may not be predicated upon an exchange of meat, by men, for plant foods and sexual access.[14]

We suggest instead, that males were not just hunters, nor were females simply gatherers. Given the biology and pongid heritage of these hominids, a generalized subsistence strategy was likely. Females were extremely strong individuals, with body and limb musculature enabling bipedal running, grasping of wood and stone artifacts, and inflicting bodily damage on other animals. Bipedalism is not to be underestimated as an early advantage in the pursuit and killing, with or without tools, of game. The exclusion of females from killing is not defensible.

The Agta evidence indicates that pregnancy and infants may diminish participation in very strenuous activity, but not preclude it. As Lancaster pointed out, a carrying device may have been the bipedal hominid females' early invention, with food and baby carried therein.[15] Without a simple sling, early Australopithecines and habilines would have been at a serious disadvantage. Carrying babies in arms would not be conducive to food getting of any sort, either hunting or gathering. Perhaps in the earliest days of transition to bipedalism, a tight group of cooperating males and females, foraging together, eating plant foods and game as chimpanzees do, was viable. Any step beyond the chimpanzee adaptation seems to favor technological introductions. Stone tools dating to the late Pliocene are known in East Africa; without doubt perishable tools existed before that time.

Earlier we asserted that males were not exclusively hunters. The thesis that hunting is the hallmark of humanity cannot be defended. Most male hominids must have spent most of their time foraging for plant foods, alongside the females. The diversity, availability, and efficiency inherent in gathering cannot be discounted as the primary adaptational focus of hominids. If game was sighted, hunted, and killed, all able bodied males and females would likely have joined the pursuit, leaving young to the care of the old or the disinclined.

Ethnographic evidence suggests that females are physically capable of joining the kill. Primatological evidence suggests only that female chimpanzees tend to kill game less than males.[16]

Our Plio-Pleistocene model of hominid origins builds a possibility at odds with the hunter-gatherer division of labor. We suggest the alternative unity of labor. Both females and males hunted and gathered. All, really, were foragers. No early division need have occurred along these lines. In this sense, sexual division of labor is not a foundation of human society. Archaeological evidence neither supports nor rejects the existence of team hunting of big game in the early Pleistocene. Scavenging of dead animals is as plausible as predation of large game. By the time of Homo erectus, organized hunting likely occurred, but Homo habilis was an uncertain hunter.[17] By the time of habilis, the basic adaptational trajectory of hominids must have been set. Thus the generalized nature of early human food procurement seems defensible.

Does our portrayal of women as hunters undercut the importance of females as gatherers and mothers? Not at all. If anything, it strengthens the critical role of females in human evolution. Hominid females surely bore the brunt of the responsibility of keeping the young alive through childhood. Females, carrying young and food, aided by a sling and/or a multipurpose stick, may have dug roots and struck fruits from tree limbs. Faced with a predator, the shaft could be turned into a weapon. In addition, small game, especially young herbivores, may have been dispatched when encountered. The hominid female would have found advantage in elaboration of such technology and subsistence tactics. We suggest female involvement in hunting may have been easily as important as male hunting.

The Agta organization of life support activities would seem to encourage a model of female competence in all spheres of endeavor. Instead of great constraint due to mothering and a restricted subsistence involvement, we see greater capabilities due to the demands of food getting, preservation of the young, and the use of technology. The Agta case provides an example of women's capability in arduous work and child rearing. It illustrates the weakness of those notions of human nature and capability which reflect the particular limitations cast on women today and project a dubious correlation of biology and task fitness.

Agnes A. Estioko-Griffin
University of the Philippines

P. Bion Griffin
University of Hawaii

Notes

1. Helen Fisher, The Sex Contract: the Evolution of Human Behavior (New York: William Marrow and Co., 1982); Ernestine Friedl, Women and Men: An Anthropologist's View (New York: Holt, Rinehart and Winston, 1975), pp. 15-19; Glynn L. Isaac, "The Food Sharing Behavior of Primate Hominid," Scientific American 238, 4 (1978):90-109; Thomas C. Patterson, Archaeology: The Evolution of Ancient Society (Englewood Cliffs, New Jersey: Prentice Hall, 1981), p. 97; Sherwood L. Washburn and C.S. Lancaster, "The Evolution of Hunting," in Man the Hunter, eds. Richard B. Lee and Irven DeVore (Chicago: Aldridge Publishing Co., 1968), pp. 295-296; Ronald L. Wallace, Those who have Vanished (Homewood, Illinois: The Dorsey Press, 1983), p. 54.

2. Richard B. Lee, The !Kung San: Men, Women and Work in a Foraging Society (Cambridge: Cambridge University Press, 1979); Lorna Marshall, The !Kung of Nyae Nyae (Cambridge, Massachusetts: Harvard University Press, 1976); George B. Silberbauer, Hunter and Habitat in the Central Kalahari Desert (Cambridge: Cambridge University Press, 1981); Jiro Tanaka, The San: Hunter-Gatherers of the Kalahari, a Study in Ecological Anthropology, trans., David H. Hughes (Tokyo: University of Tokyo Press, 1980).

3. Naomi Quinn, "Anthropological Studies of Women's Status," Annual Review of Anthropology 6 (1977):181-225.

4. Agnes Estioko-Griffin and P. Bion Griffin, "The Ebuked Agta of Northeast Luzon," Philippine Quarterly of Culture and Society 3, 4 (1975):237-244.

5. Griffin and Griffin, "The Ebuked Agta", pp. 237-244; Agnes Estioko-Griffin and P. Bion Griffin, "Woman the Hunter," in Woman the Gatherer, ed. Frances Dahlberg (New Haven: Yale University Press, 1981), pp. 121-151; Agnes Estioko-Griffin and P. Bion Griffin, "The Beginning of Cultivation among Agta Hunter-Gatherers in Northeast Luzon," in Contributions to the Study of Philippine Shifting Cultivation, ed. Harold Olofson (Laguna, Philippines: Forest Research Institute, 1981).

6. Griffin and Griffin, "Woman the Hunter," pp. 121-151.

7. Madeleine J. Goodman and Lenn Evan Goodman, The Sexes in the Human Population (Los Angeles: Gee Tee Bee, 1981), first distributed in xerox form in 1979.

8. Navin K. Rai, "From Forest to Field: a Study of Philippine Negrito Foragers in Transition" (Ph.D. dissertation, University of Hawaii, 1982).

9. Reizo Harako, "The Mbuti as Hunters - a Study of Ecological Anthropology of the Mbuti Pygmies," Kyoto University African Studies X (1976):37-100; Colin Turnbull, Wayward Servants: the Two Worlds of the African Pygmies (Garden City, New York: The Natural History Press, 1965).

10. Nancy Tanner, On Becoming Human (Cambridge: Cambridge University Press, 1981).

11. Glynn L. Isaac and Diana C. Crader, "To What Extent were Early Hominids Carnivorous?," in Omnivorous Primates: Gathering and Hunting in Human Evolution, eds. R.S.O. Harding and G. Teleki (New York: Columbia University Press, 1981), p. 37.

12. Isaac and Crader, p. 91.

13. Jane B. Lancaster, "Carrying and Sharing in Human Evolution," in Human Nature 1, 2 (1978):82-89; Sally Slocum, "Woman the Gatherer: Male Bias in Anthropology," in Toward an Anthropology of Women, ed. Rayne R. Reiter (New York: Monthly Review Press, 1975), pp. 36-50; Nancy Tanner and Adrienne Zihlman, "Woman in Evolution, Part I: Innovation and Selection in Human Origins," Signs I, 3 (1976):585-608.

14. Fisher, The Sex Contract.

15. Lancaster, "Carrying and Sharing in Human Evolution," pp. 82-89.

16. Geza Teleki, "Primate Subsistence Patterns: Collector-Predators and Gatherer-Hunters," Journal of Human Evolution 4 (1975):125-184.

17. Glynn L. Isaac and Diana C. Crader, "To What Extent were Early Hominids Carnivorous?," in Omnivorous Primates: Gathering and Hunting in Human Evolution.

SEXUAL RACISM IN POPULATION POLICY*

The end point and as it were the purpose of all racism is ethical, or rather anti-ethical, the limitation of the deserts of others, globally, as a group differentiable from the we. The others are not fully, really human, and therefore it is justified to enslave, exploit, or rule them, to manage them "for their own good," having first denied their dignity and undermined the basis of their claims to freedom. The structure of this argument is classic, from the claims of Aristotle that some men are natural slaves or tools, to the claims of the American apologists of the "peculiar institution" in the antebellum south. In the 20th century the argument is stripped of its paternalist pretensions. The recognition of global interdependency calls forth demands for recognition that some peoples are not fit or worthy to survive, that war, famine, and pestilence are the rightful victors in the struggle for the survival of the unfit. And, by a curious twist of 20th century double think, the demand for recognition of this strange imperative of death is stated in the name of ethics, a new ethics suited to the exigencies of spaceship earth.

Sexual racism is of two forms, one of which may be confined to a speculative and theoretical plane, while the other is deadly earnest and practical. Speculative racism of a sexual

---

*At the 1982 conference, Concepts and Strategies: Women's Studies in Different Cultural Contexts an extended version of this paper and a related paper on sexual stereotypes of race were presented. These papers form parts of the authors' forthcoming book, Particularly Amongst the Sunburnt Nations—The Persistence of Sexual Racism in Bioscience.

type confines itself to castigating the races deemed inferior: their men are not true men, but partly child or beast, their contact to be feared or shunned, their development, too soon--precocious sexuality with its inevitable structural correlate, stunted intellectuality. Their women are things of fantasy, childlike or overrefined, complaisant to all comers, toys of imagination, or terrifying traps of insatiable lust.

Practical racism extends such fantasies beyond the realm of imagination. Its concern is with the reproductive side of sexuality, the world engulfing reproductive power of the unknown other, and the terror lest the we become engulfed, displaced and dispossessed by them. Such a vision belongs more properly to the nightmare realm of racist propaganda than to the realm of science or rational deliberations on public policy. Yet the underlying division between the embattled we and the imminent if inferior encroaching hordes of them has penetrated the categories of soi disant scientific discourse, as we shall argue here, and the value laden axioms of population planners. The nisus of this form of racism is directed against the very existence of races deemed inferior--particularly those of the less developed world. Its impact falls most heavily on the women of that world, who are viewed in its perspective not as human individuals faced with complex problems, but as yawning maws of pestilential, perhaps apocalyptic reproductive menace.

Ethics, once the bastion of settled verities has been transformed in the thinking of Garrett Hardin and others into a foundation for the claim that the biological exigencies of spaceship earth may well call upon us to cut off the air supply of the adjacent compartment and would not condemn the drowning of its inhabitants. Race here, for purposes of ecological convenience, becomes a geographic rather than genetic compartmentalizer. Virtue and vice, which were the basis of praise and blame, punishment and reward in classic ethics, are replaced by environmental responsibility and irresponsibility, often reducible to procreation versus non-procreation as entrance tickets to the ecotopian Valhalla or Gotterdammerung.

For Galton the scandal of biology was the failure of "superior types" to outreproduce their inferiors. The "fit" seemed incapable of demonstrating their superior fitness by the only quantitative standard of fitness Darwinian evolutionism can acknowledge. Social policy, Galton reasoned, should mend the failure of (overly social) biology to enforce its own standards: The able should be aided; the poor and helpless should be aided too, to the speedy and painless extinction of their kind.[1]

For Hardin the adoption of a moralistic tone makes possible varieties of elimination Galton never considered. Those who outreproduce our resources are not merely (paradoxically) unfit; they are unworthy, guilty in fact, and deserving of the fate which their choices and our responses shall bring upon them:

> If each human family were dependent only on its own resources; if the children of improvident parents starved to death; if, thus, overbreeding brought its own "punishment" to the germ line--then there would be no public interest in controlling the breeding of families. But our society is deeply committed to the welfare state, and hence is confronted with another aspect of the tragedy of the commons.

> In a welfare state, how shall we deal with the family, the religion, the race, or the class (or indeed any distinguishable and cohesive group) that adopts overbreeding as a policy to secure its own aggrandizement? To couple the concept of freedom to breed with the belief that everyone born has an equal right to the commons is to lock the world into a tragic course of action.[2]

Hardin's answer to his rhetorical question as to how punishment for "overbreeding" shall be brought upon the irresponsible is voiced in terms of coercion--governmental and intergovernmental actions, and quite possibly, "injustices." Hardin writes: "Coercion is a dirty word to most liberals now, but it need not forever be so...The only kind of coercion I recommend is mutual coercion, mutually agreed upon by the majority of the people affected...Injustice is preferable to total ruin." Like Galton, Hardin believes that "legal possession should be perfectly correlated with biological inheritance--that those who are biologically more fit to be the custodians of property and power should legally inherit more."[3]

Joseph Fletcher, the author of Situation Ethics, similarly argues on Malthusian grounds that food aid should be withheld from nations that have "exceeded their biological carrying capacity by spawning more mouths to feed than the ecology allows." He warmly endorses the position of Alan Gregg, a past vice-president of the Rockefeller Foundation, describing "overpopulation as a cancer, adding that he had never heard of a cancer being cured by feeding it."[4] Fletcher, like Hardin, here imputes moral accountability to nations as though they were individuals but reduces the deserts of starving infants to nullity, as though their existence were a cancer. His central premise is that human suffering can be alleviated by allowing or encouraging these infants to die, and he calls upon the authority of ecology (the Malthusian dogma that added food is automatically translated into added reproduction) to give scientific status to his ethical prescription.

Hardin has argued against inter-nation food sharing, against increasing agricultural productivity, against even the attitude of one human being taking responsibility for aiding others across international frontiers, on the grounds that shared resources naturally are squandered (the tragedy of common grazing lands), that growth of resources leads inevitably to population growth which is inherently

destabilizing (literal and naive Malthusianism).[5]   Hardin
pursues the thesis that ethnic selfishness is the only
far-sighted (or "Promethean") ethical policy, and he actively
promotes the idea that war, famine, pestilence and poverty are
humane (because humanistic, putatively future preserving and
promoting) means of population control--especially when thought
of as relegated to the lot of others.

> The wisdom of triage can be fully
> appreciated only if we recognize the
> inevitability of competition; and
> competition between members of the same
> species is inescapable so long as death is
> not a sufficiently effective thinning
> agent--which we prevented from being with
> our fantastic medical advances. Life,
> cooperation, and compassion are all good
> things, but we can have too much of any one
> good thing, considered in isolation and
> elevated to the status of an absolute
> good.[6]

Assignment of equal value to human lives only reduces our
ability to save lives, Hardin argues, or in less extreme
situations reduces "the average quality of people's lives."[7]
On a finite earth we must cease to consider individuals' worth
as absolute, and laugh if need be rather than weep at their
predicament.[8]   Quoting with approval the English physiologist
A.V. Hill, Hardin sums up what he calls the Promethean
problem. Someone must speak for posterity, war, famine,
uncontrolled fertility, and progressive diminution of the
quality of our lives, which are caught up inextricably in a
nexus whose only dissolution is the racist stricture: "if men
will breed like rabbits they must be allowed to die like
rabbits."[9]

'Allowed to die' is a euphemism for euthanasia. And, in
the case of peoples, refers, in Hardin's usage, not merely to
laisser faire but also to the selective withholding of food
grains under principles of triage.[10]   Recognition of a
universal right to food and of the 1948 U.N. General Assembly's

standards for the definition of genocide via compulsary birth prevention, and international recognition of the family as "the natural and fundamental unit of society" with whom irrevocably must rest "any choice and decision with regard to the size of the family" combine to yield a "formula for disaster," an inevitable "Breeding War."[11] The Promethean (hence newly humanistic) view prefers the recognition of the tragic wisdom of ecological succession: "Competition creates environmental fragmentation, and the fragmentation creates a richer world."[12] Such are the dictates of evolution.

Not every advocate of bio-social policies which are racist in effect or intention has the temerity of a Garrett Hardin to represent as new morality the advocacy of mass starvation, the annihilation of entire peoples for the sake of preserving a comfortable life style and preventing any tremor of hardship or discontent from causing static in the Muzak of spaceship earth. Yet many well intentioned advocates of population planning and fertility control, influenced in part by scientifically canonized racial stereotypes and their own keen visions of the terrible conditions which population planning is designed to alleviate and prevent, have worked unstintingly, vocally and silently, in behalf of population programs whose central premises and impacts have been more inhumane on a practical level than even Hardin's visionary images of refusing to throw a life-line to drowning nations. For Hardin's self righteous fantasies bear an obscenity which makes it difficult for humane leaders even to speak them publicly let alone propose them as foundations of public policy. But other, more well intentioned views, are in active use in many nations and internationally which yet rest on invidious perceptions of the world's diverse races and for that reason strike diverse races with an invidious impact.

A widespread premise in the population planning field and in public health in general, arising from the dank and casuistic soil of situation ethics, is the assumption that health practices or fertility control techniques which cannot be countenanced among us may be entirely acceptable when introduced or even imposed among them.

Roger Short has served as head of the British Medical Research Council unit on reproductive biology, located in Edinburgh. It was in that capacity that he wrote: "powdered milk and baby foods are one thing for the emancipated, hygienic, pill-taking Western career girl, but quite another matter for the socially deprived inhabitant of some squalid favella."[13] Short brings to his medical/population work his own assumptions about the relationship of eroticism and fecundity and his own theories of the interspecific and intra-human variability of both eroticism and fecundity. Applying these theories, Carl Djerassi, the developer and exponent of the steroid birth control pill, can make a show of scientific justification for implementing human clinical trials in such nations as Korea, Chile, Thailand, Mexico and India.[14]

The theory that racial variations in fecundity reflect variations in what Djerassi calls "sexiness"[15] is central in the thinking of many population planning advocates, as is the notion that putatively heightened or precocious sexuality is somehow to be associated with retrograde or stunted intellectuality. The complex of these notions is fostered through the idea of a primitive or traditional mentality, which is backward, fatalistic, procreative and conservative, where modern mentality is progressive, optimistic, liberated and constructive. Thus Djerassi achieves an important objective by relying on Short's contrast of the "liberated career girl" with the "socially deprived inhabitant of some squalid favella."

Djerassi's purpose throughout his book, The Politics of Contraception, is to promote steroid contraceptives of existing, new, or experimental types throughout the world. The stereotyping of working mothers as pampered or neurasthenic dilettentes, or of diaphragm users as "a select middle-class group of women, a group I would characterize, only partly facetiously, as one frequenting organic food stores rather than supermarkets,"[16] is only part of the campaign. Djerassi concedes that diaphragms are the safest women's contraceptives,[17] so it becomes necessary to his campaign to argue that environmental circumstances including cultural backwardness and taboos make the Pill a better choice from a population planning standpoint in many less well-heeled groups. Hence, the "squalid favella."

In population planning circles, as often in the field of public health, motivational campaigns are termed educational. Success is called compliance. And resistance is ascribed to ignorance, rigidity and backward attitudes, since values cannot grammatically be described as backward. The values of local populations and the asperity of local conditions combine to form the arguments on which health and population officials from the United States and Third World countries have argued in support of a double standard of benefit-risk analysis as applied to developing and industrial nations. Local ignorance/resistance to fertility control techniques and the inaccessibility of adequate medical care are the chief foundations of these arguments. But the equation of resistance with ignorance is founded on cultural and racial stereotypes rather than on a realistic and other-regarding appraisal of the genuine factors underlying reluctance to use specific birth control techniques. And pessimistic predictions of health care resource accessibility seem often to be founded on prior policy decisions which set population control ahead of other calls upon medical resources.

Djerassi is typical in his remark that the low level of condom use in Arab countries is "largely attributable to cultural factors." He adds that Arab men are "generally speaking, simply not interested in taking responsibility for fertility control. The same can also be said of men in many Latin American countries including Mexico."[18] No data are cited in support of this widesweeping generalization. What supports it in fact is simply the association of traditional valuations of virility with procreative motivations. Similarly, traditional marital values expressed through the outward submissiveness of women in many Third World nations and resulting in poor marital communication have been cited as culprits in the resistance of traditional societies to population control campaigns. However, as J. M. Stycos has shown, the widespread adoption of sterilization in Puerto Rico proceeded without visible disruption of traditional family patterns.[19] While the Puerto Rico sterilization experience has come under significant criticism as a campaign which was ultimately genocidal in impact,[20] the experience clearly demonstrates that traditional roles are not in and of themselves an insuperable barrier to family planning.

Machismo, the stereotypic counterpart of female submissiveness in Latin American societies and other groups originating in warmer climates has similarly been shown not to be a necessary correlate of contraceptive avoidance. Stereotypically, machismo is central in the confounding of virility and manliness with prolific procreation. Thus we read in People magazine: "Machismo is a powerful force in Mexican culture and the proof of virility through fertility is necessary to most men."[21] As Stycos points out, the same myth is promulgated by the Chilean educator-physician, Hernan Romero, the Colombian sociologist-priest Gustavo Jimenez, the Paraguayan population planner Dario Castagnino and many population planning officials, in the 1960s, 70s and 80s, who express discontent with the values and attitudes they attribute to their rural or impoverished compatriots.

The impatience of such leaders, founded in sociological theories, which often merely canonize and crystalize widespread racial stereotypes was epitomized in extremis by James Reston's unusually intemperate column on the "stubborn vanity and stupidity of the ignorant male in Latin America." Plainly the inhabitants of Latin American nations do not share Reston's Scottish roots or Calvinist values. But the felt disparity of values becomes the basis of a racial slur against the "ignorant male," i.e., the non-complying: he is "worse than the baboon and worships the cult of virility long after he has forgotten the cult of Christianity." Interpreting: "The Latin male is not satisfied with love, he must have life--one new life a year, if possible, in order to prove he is good for something."[22]

As for the factual foundation of such claims, upon which much population policy has been based, the empirical work of Evelyn Folch-Lyon, Luis de la Macorra and S. Bruce Schearer has shown, inter alia, that 94% of Mexican men they surveyed in 1978 rejected the statement that having a large family makes a man feel more manly; 81% disagreed with the view that a husband who is willing to limit his family to 3 or 4 children is not a real man; and 92% agreed with the statement that such a decision by a man for family limitation showed concern for the welfare of his family.[23]

The sensitive exploration of situational factors affecting family welfare in a particular rural family in India, as portrayed in the recent Oxfam documentary 39,000,000 + 1 confirms what liberal economists have long contended, that individual and family choices about family size are influenced not by sheer attitudes but by rational decision making in an attempt to cope with limited resources and to provide for family welfare and continuance.[24] Yet the stereotype persists that when "compliance" is reserved, tradition is the enemy to be combatted, and that some peoples are simply not susceptible effectually to efforts at "education."

J.F. Marshall, an anthropologist quoted at length by Djerassi, perpetuates the stereotype of Indian village populations as subsisting at a level of mental deficiency such as to render the inhabitants unlikely to be capable of distinguishing one type of injection from another. Thus Marshall favors injected contraceptives on the grounds that "years of exposure to antibiotics and vaccinations" have rendered hypodermics "entirely acceptable" to rural Indians: "Indeed, a villager who was not given a shot during a visit to a doctor felt himself somehow cheated." Marshall does not speculate that this feeling of being cheated may have arisen from rural Indians' sense of deprivation of medicines, a sense which was poignantly elucidated in the Oxfam film. Rather, he suggests that the problem was simplemindedness compounded with backwardness and suspicion: Injection obviates the need for genital examination or a visit to a "threatening and inconvenient hospital or clinic." But contraceptive injections should be clearly colored (in a hue not associated with danger or disrepute) to limit natives' association of injections in general with contraception, lest resistance to contraception lead to refusal of all injections.[25]

The attitude Marshall expresses here, which is echoed by Djerassi treats the "threatening" and inconvenient character of medical procedures for rural populations in Third World environments as a central argument for reliance on less than fully voluntary modes of contraception and proposes the substitution of such contraceptive modalities for the provision of more comprehensive health care, involving medical examinations and clinical visits. Further the assumption of the backwardness of these rural populations and their inaccessibility to adequate health care is made the basis of an argument in support of their provision with materia medica whose safety is not established, either because they are experimental or because the known risks are at a level which renders their use unacceptable in countries like our own.

By less than fully voluntary contraception we refer to such proposals as those of Leo Szillard and John Platt that contraceptive steroids be placed in staple foods such as rice or salt, in the interests of public policy, with price supports to ensure their "voluntary" use by target populations in the non-temperate world. Djerassi and Platt object to placement of contraceptive steroids in public water supplies on the grounds that animals other than humans would also be affected. But they perceive no moral difficulties' in manipulating human populations through the use of food and threat of famine to achieve what governments have determined as their policy objectives, without regard to the interests of the individuals affected. Djerassi voices only technical objections to Platt's scheme, which he calls "extraordinarily optimistic": "It is the little word 'if' that pushes any possibility of such an approach well into the twenty-first century." Platt, whom Djerassi calls "an extraordinarily innovative thinker," even offers an obscene allusion to Gandhi's "famous march to the sea to break the British salt monopoly" as an illustration of how dependent human populations are on salt, oblivious of the irony of his proposal of a new salt tyranny on the same terrain.[26]

Depo-Provera, a synthetic progesterone, widely used for contraceptive purposes, especially in rural populations of developing countries, is a drug whose administration raises practical problems in the immediate present as distinguished from the speculative, somewhat futuristic problems posed by the provocative fantasies of Aldous Huxley, Leo Szillard, John Platt and William Shockley. Illegal, in the United States and other industrial nations, Depo-Provera is promoted as a contraceptive of choice for less developed nations. Long term injectible contraceptives account for 79% of contraceptive use in Kiribati (the Gilbert Islands), 63% in Niue, 42% in the

Solomon Islands, 30% in Tonga and 46% in Tuwalu. An estimated 5 million women worldwide use Depo-Provera. A Depo-Provera injection blocks fertility for a period of 3 to 6 months. Its side-effects include menstrual disruption (amenorrhea), as well as heavy, irregular bleeding, especially in the first weeks of use. Other side-effects include weight gain or loss, acne, loss of hair, severe depression, loss of libido and/or orgasm, headaches, dizziness, blotchy complexion, elevated blood sugar and fat levels, nausea, discomfort in the extremities and breasts, and vaginal discharge. In laboratory tests, Depo-Provera has been associated with malignant breast tumors in beagles and endometrial cancer in rhesus monkeys. Women who receive Depo-Provera injections during a pregnancy which has not yet been ascertained sustain a possibly increased risk of congenital malformation to their offspring. High concentrations of Depo-Provera are found in the breast milk of women who have received the injection post partum, but the impact of the hormone on nursing infants is unknown.

The FDA's prohibition of Depo-Provera for contraceptive use in the United States took these risks and disadvantages into account. The agency even warns pregnant women against the ingestion of any progestin drug and, in the interests of avoiding a double standard, prohibits the marketing of this drug abroad. However, the use of Depo-Provera abroad is strongly supported by AID, the International Planned Parenthood Federation and by many national authorities abroad.

In her recent book Sex and Destiny: The Politics of Human Fertility, Germaine Greer describes the forced injection of Khmer women with Depo-Provera by public health authorities in Thai refugee camps in the early 1980s. These women, who had only just escaped the overt genocide of the Pol Pot regime, "were anxious to rebuild their families," and by March of 1980, 20-30% of married women of childbearing age in the Thai refugee camps were reported to be pregnant. Thai authorities, "who wanted no Khmer babies born on Thai soil," rounded up Khmer women with sticks for Depo-Provera injections. The injections were given indiscriminantly to pregnant and nursing women, despite their abortifacient and anti-lactational effects. "Even children received the injection and experienced the same symptoms as the women."[27]

The tragic victimization of the Khmer people, by the Pol Pot regime, the Vietnamese conquerors and the Thai population bureaucrats forms the background to an extreme case of the genocidal administration of a contraceptive whose side effects, minimally, have been described as "menstrual chaos." But, even in its normal use, Depo-Provera is administered only semi-voluntarily.

We refer to Depo-Provera administration as only semi-voluntary on the part on the recipients, not because the drug's effects last from day to day, but because its side-effects are rarely subject to full disclosure and still more rarely monitored. Indeed, the absence of adequate clinical care and the difficulty of medical examination are, as we have suggested, among the principal grounds urged in support of Depo-Provera over other contraceptives whose use may be more readily discontinued. Donald Kennedy, Commissioner of the Food and Drug Administration under the Carter administration argued in 1978: "Quite obviously, a drug that may not be suitable for approval here could well have a favorable benefit/risk ratio in a less developed nation." Depo-Provera, continues to be manufactured by the Belgian subsidiary of Upjohn Pharmaceutical Corporation and marketed to any nation that will accept it. In view of this situation, Kennedy left the door open to future legislation which might legalize the export of Depo-Provera "for nations with higher birthrates, lower physician-patient ratios and less readily available contraceptive methods," even when the drug is not regarded as safe enough for domestic use.[28]

A bulletin of the International Planned Parenthood Federation in London disseminates a paper presented in Thailand in November 1981 by Pramilla Senanyake and Renuka Rajkumar, entitled, "Improving Public Confidence in Depo-Provera." The paper highlights negative publicity surrounding Depo-Provera and expresses concern at the withdrawal of Swedish aid funds for Depo-Provera in Sri Lanka and Kenya. It decries the discontinuance of Depo-Provera use by War on Want, a UK charity, following publication of the Minkin Report, which cited the evidence of Depo-Provera's unsafety. The IPPF paper recommends that family planning personnel should combat the "anti-Depo-Provera propaganda" seen to emerge from the international women's movement, by the use of reassuring testimonials from "satisfied users," medical authority, mailings, press lunches, pre-recorded radio tapes, briefings and the appointment of lobbyists. Discussion of Depo-Provera should be introduced as part of a general concern with women's health, in much the way that other sensitive issues, had been dealt with, such as female circumcision in Egypt and the Sudan, and family planning in Nigeria. The "misleading information" of the Minkin report should be combatted but, "If, after investigation, it is found to be correct for example, that women have not been counselled about the side-effects that accompany the use of Depo-Provera, then we should admit that this has occurred while making sure that, at the same time, we can point to action to remedy the complaint." In "combatting adverse publicity on Depo-Provera...contact with key people on the local scene is essential. But other key people on the scene include those working at a high level for international organizations--both governmental and non-governmental. They may be able to help to make sure that there is an effective well-informed channel of communication to counter anti-Depo-Provera publicity at the international level." In a public relations campaign of this kind, "honesty and openness is the best policy." The risks of the drug, of course, are known, but too much is at stake to allow Depo-Provera to fall into disuse. The function of honesty and openness is to reassure: "Do not leave room for criticism."[29]

Justification of the use of Depo-Provera in Third World contexts is sought in the heightened risk of maternal mortality in the less developed countries and the extreme penury and medical deprivation of their inhabitants. Thus Frederick T. Sai, former director of medical services of Ghana and a former officer of the International Planned Parenthood Federation, typically argues that in Third World countries the risk of pregnancy outweighs the risk of Depo-Provera.[30] But such considerations do not justify the withholding of information about risks or the transference of risks from potentially pregnant to contraceptively compliant women. Djerassi's arguments in behalf of the contraceptive pill that considerations of health risks are outweighed by local conditions among the poor or ill educated are likewise fallacious. The diaphragm, he argues, "is totally unsuitable for the impoverished woman living in a hovel, lacking running water, toilet and privacy," although it "may be ideal, for instance, for the motivated American woman willing to use it."[31]

Ethically, impoverished women are as entitled as middle class women to full disclosure of health risks and are fully as concerned with the impact of those risks, as becomes evident when full disclosure is made. Platt's argument that the training of paramedical personnel sufficient to conduct medical examinations of the 100 million Indian women of childbearing age would delay implementation of mass population control measures by "five, seven or even ten years," affords no support for the policy of administering unproven drugs without medical follow up. If a proper work up and close follow up are sound medical practice, then they are so for all populations. Even the formidable argument about the heightened risk of pregnancy in marginal or subsistence environments is nugatory from an ethical point of view. Such risk argues only for the need of improved health care not for the supplanting of health care provision by unmonitored injections, still less for the subjection of unwitting populations to unknown or uncalculated risks.

What founds the policy decisions of population planners who argue for the double standard can only be the presumption that life in a hovel or favella is probably of so diminished a quality and value that risks to health or life are insignificant in this context and the need for birth control paramount. Where ethics argues for equality of positive human entitlements and biology places paramountcy on the value of human life, the resultant in bioethics is a view which regards the individual as the best arbiter of his or her biosocial future. Where considerations of social policy diverge from such a standard, the underlying cause, at least in the present instance, seems to be the presumption that the squalor of life in the favella diminishes the value of that life to those who live it or bear the primary responsibility for its continuation. Such a presumption, founded in stereotypes whose power does not rest in factual data but grows from the projected horror or sense of guilt about the unacceptability of others' lives, is the epitome of what we mean by racism, diminution of the deserts of others, globally, as peoples, on the grounds of their presumed inferiority.

Madeleine J. Goodman
University of Hawaii

Lenn E. Goodman
University of Hawaii

1. See the discussion, references and critique in Goodman and Goodman, The Sexes in the Human Population (Los Angeles: Gee Tee Bee, 3rd ed., 1984).

2. Garrett Hardin, "The Tragedy of the Commons" in P. Reinig and I. Tinker, eds., Population: Dynamics, Ethics and Policy (Washington: AAAS, 1975), pp. 14-15.

3. Hardin, p. 15.

4. Joseph Fletcher, "Give if it helps but not if it hurts," in William Aiken and Hugh La Follette, eds., World Hunger and Moral Obligation (Englewood Cliffs, N.J.: Prentice-Hall, 1977), pp. 104-114.

5. See Goodman and Goodman, The Sexes in the Human Population for a critique or neo-Malthusian Models, pp. 92-118.

6. Garrett Hardin, Promethean Ethics (Seattle: University of Washington Press, 1980), p. 71.

7. Hardin, p. 70.

8. Hardin, pp. 69, 64, 61-63, etc.

9. Hardin, pp. 65, 50.

10. Hardin, pp. 56-61.

11. Hardin, pp. 50-52.

12. Hardin, p. 45.

13. Carl Djerassi, The Politics of Contraception (San Francisco: Freeman, 1981), p. 11.

14. Djerassi, p. 137, citing Short (1978).

15. Djerassi, loc. cit.

16. Djerassi, p. 19.

17. Djerassi, p. 19.

18. Djerassi, p. 16.

19. J. Mayone Stycos, "Husband-Wife Communication and Fertility," in J. M. Stycos, Family and Fertility in Puerto Rico (New York: Columbia University Press, 1955), pp. 166-180.

20. R.R. Jenkins, moderator, "Depo-Provera and Sterilization Abuse Discussion," in H.B. Holmes et al., eds., Birth Control and Controlling Birth (Clifton, N.J.: Humana, 1980), pp. 129-130.

21. Maggie Jones, "The Law versus Machismo," People, 3 (1980), 13.

22. James Reston, "The Cult of Virility in Latin America," New York Times, April 9, 1967.

23. "Focus Group and Survey Research on Family Planning in Mexico," Studies in Family Planning 12:12 (1981), pp. 409-432.

24. "39 Million and 1," London: Oxfam Film, 1975.

25. Djerassi, pp. 155-156

26. Djerassi, pp. 170-179.

27. Germaine Greer, Sex and Destiny: The Politics of Human Fertility (New York: Harper and Row, 1984) pp. 179-181.

28. Rachel B. Gold and Peters D. Willson, "Depo-Provera: New Developments in a Decade Old Controversy," Family Planning Perspectives 13:1 (1981), pp. 35-39; Carol Levine, "Depo-Provera: Some Ethical Questions About a Controversil Contraceptive," in H. B. Holmes, et al., eds., Birth Control and Controlling Birth: Women-Centered Perspectives (Clifton, N.J.: Humana Press, 1980), pp. 101-105.

29. P. Senanyake with Renuka Rajkumar, "Improving Public Confidence in Depo-Provera," Second Asian Regional Workshop on Injectable Contraceptives and Implants, Chiang Mai, Thailand, November 9-13, 1981.

30. Gold and Willson, p. 36.

31. Djerassi, p. 47.

FEMINIST VALUES: ETHNOCENTRIC OR UNIVERSAL?

American feminism over the past decade has had an immeasurable influence on individual attitudes and institutional policies, both nationally and internationally. Yet many foreign women scholars and leaders whose policy goals seem very similar to ours question the applicability of American feminist values to other societies. It is my purpose in this essay to disentangle the several strands of values that have been wound together in the dominant belief system of contemporary American feminism, and to examine each for its universality.

By American feminism, I mean the multi-faceted efforts by American women to redefine their roles and rights in American society. Such a broad definition obviously includes some groups that might be uncomfortable with the term "feminism," precisely because it has taken on, even for many American women, a more specific value association than "equal rights for women." Like any revolutionary movement, the American women's movement tends to be identified with the most extreme positions put forward by radical feminists. It is from such challenging ideas that the movement has drawn its strength and dynamism. However, the broad support for the movement by American women comes from the fact that the dominant values of the movement spring from deeply held American beliefs in individual rights, equality, and justice. I will argue that the values of American feminism define the American women's movement, that the radical stance of some feminists is an issue of degree, not substance; and that it is the underlying American value system that disturbs women in other cultures, particularly in developing countries.

This essay is not meant to present an exhaustive review of American feminist theory. Rather it is a first step in linking American feminist thought to debates over the validity of current theories concerning socio-economic development, particularly as they relate to women. In the process, I will identify and examine the issues supporting, and separating, two aspects of the American women's movement: Women's Studies and Women-in-Development. Both these groups were represented at the conference "Concepts and Strategies of Women's Studies in Different Cultural Contexts," held at the University of Hawaii in November 1982, where the ideas discussed in this essay were first presented. This conference, therefore, provided an ideal opportunity to explore the values that undergird American feminism, particularly as they manifest themselves in Women's Studies, and to reflect on their universality, particularly through the responses of the participants from the Pacific Islands and Asia.

Feminist Values

Essentially what American women have been demanding over the past decade is that women should have the same rights as men: equal opportunities for education and employment, equal pay for work of comparable value, equal access to credit and clubs, equal benefits and pensions. These demands are part of the equity revolution of the sixties which started with the Black civil rights movement but which quickly expanded to include Native Americans, Hispanics, Asians, white ethnics, the handicapped, and senior citizens. The demand for equal treatment by clearly identifiable groups was _de facto_ an admission that the melting pot concept was not only a myth but was no longer a desirable ideal. These various groups argued that people should be allowed to be different and still receive equal opportunities and justice under American law. Their complaints illustrated the unpalatable fact that discrimination was still pervasive.

This recognition of persistent racism in the United States contributed to the condemnation of the Vietnam War, for many saw the war as racist and the military service as particularly onerous to Blacks. Many of the same women and men who had been actively working and demonstrating for civil rights joined the anti-war movement. Yet it seemed that in both these movements it was the men who did the leading while the women did the typing. Nor did these male leaders simply discriminate against women in job assignments; many were individually credited with the statement that the only position for a woman in the movement was prone.

"If everyone is equal, why not women too?" asked the activist women as they began to look at their own exploitation by the men in these movements that laid claim to moral rectitude. After all, they argued, the right of the individual as paramount is a fundamental American value. The search for religious liberty--the right to seek salvation of one's soul in one's own way--was responsible for much of the early European settlement of the states. And of course, each soul is equal. The connection between Calvinist beliefs and the work ethic embodied in the White Anglo-Saxon Protestant (WASP) value system which today pervades our country has been amply documented. Briefly, Calvin preached predestination: some people were born to be saved, others were predestined to Hell. Since none but God could know who was to be saved and who not, society began to assign values to individual behavior. Good people lived simply, went to church, and worked hard. In the resource-rich new land, hard work was quickly rewarded. Imperceptibly, "rich" was added to the attributes defining good.

The ideology of our current administration in Washington is a classic example of this belief: if you are rich you are good. If you are poor, it must be because you are lazy or spendthrift, and, therefore, you are bad. "Rags-to-riches" is the WASP definition of success; Horatio Alger, the hero. Wealthy dynasties such as those of Carnegie, Rockefeller, and Kennedy are celebrated; the way their wealth was accumulated is irrelevant. Indeed, these beliefs seem to work for many Americans; our country is affluent beyond the dreams of most people in the rest of the world. We seem to others to worship materialism.[1]

The WASP concept of the right of an individual to work hard and become rich did not seem to apply to women. The counter-culture of the sixties transferred the value of individual rights from seeking wealth to "doing your own thing." Children of the affluent middle class were put off by the pursuit of money and material goods that characterized their parents, whose own goals were formed during the Great Depression of the thirties. These "flower children" celebrated love and nature; they turned their back on affluence...at least for a time. This strand of individualism was open equally to women and men.

Egalitarianism and Individualism

Thus the two dominant, but overlapping, values of the women's movement, as for all Americans, are egalitarianism and individualism. As women began to organize in the sixties, they not only demanded equal rights under law, but also insisted that women have as much right to "do their own thing" as do men. Women do not need to accept a subordinate role in the suburbs, playing chauffeur to the kids and the dog. Women do not need to throw away their fine university educations on years behind the vacuum cleaner.

Indeed, much of the anger that has welled up within the women's movement comes from the feelings of exploitation voiced by well-educated suburban housewives. It was these women, rather than established professional women, who flocked to

106

meetings in the early seventies of the National Organization for Women (NOW) with its emphasis on the consciousness-raising group. For this reason, NOW has emphasized individual values within the family more than the professional organizations founded about the same time. Groups such as the Women's Equity Action League (WEAL) and the Federation of Organizations for Professional Women (FOPW) have focused on achieving egalitarian national policies toward women, especially with regard to employment and education.

Egalitarianism and individualism are distinct concepts, however merged they may seem in the women's movement. Egalitarianism in the American context means equal rights for citizens under the law: to vote, to a job, to equal pay, to pensions, to an education. Women in Washington spent two decades, from 1960 to 1980, trying to expand federal legislation to include women equally. During that time, as women's issues gained in visibility and legitimacy, such legislation became increasing difficult to pass. A major reason is that the issues being addressed had changed from those concerning women as citizens to issues such as those of battered women or abortion, that concern women as individual women.[2]

Although the women's movement was demanding equal protection under law to ensure the right of every woman to have an abortion, or to leave a husband who beats her, there is a subtle difference: these issues relate directly to the family; earlier issues related simply to women's equal access to rights already accorded men. More recent issues concern private life; while equal rights under law issues generally dealt with public life. It is much easier for most men to grant public equality; treating women in the home as equal individuals is another matter. Furthermore, equality in the workplace is a basic demand of all who work. As a result, there is almost universal support for public equality for women. The current debate over women's rights revolves around issues of individual rights and roles for women within the private sphere of sex and family.

The dominant view within the women's movement is that equality and individual rights can be applied within the family. Radical feminists in the sixties denied this possibility and viewed any male-female relationship as exploitative. The logical outcome of such a view is women living apart from men, whether in lesbian relationships or not. The identification of feminism with lesbianism in the minds of many observers has continued to plague the women's movement, leading many young professional women to eschew the term "feminism," while clearly supporting the goals of the women's movement.[3]

Sex Differences

At the heart of the debate over equality within the family is the issue of whether women and men should be considered absolutely the same. This issue, in turn, requires consideration of the biological differences between the sexes. The easiest way to reconcile women's demands for equality in the private sphere is by emphasizing the right of each individual to make her own choices and minimizing any differences between the sexes. Equality is thus defined as equity or fairness rather than as sameness. Thus, women can bear children but men can feed them as well as women except for breast feeding. Men can cook and women clean up, or vice versa. Early movement women championed marriage contracts that laid out the division of household chores.

An alternative way of dealing with the issue of housework has been to assign economic values to each household activity, and thus prove the wage value of women's household work. Indeed, an organization was formed under the banner of "Wages for Housewives" to promote this. The idea of paying women to stay home and attend the house and children was intended to give greater status to women's work in this sphere. Such a view can too easily be turned into a conservative justification for keeping women at home, "in their place." This reversal was illustrated recently in Italy where a neo-fascist party took up the cry of wages for housewives. Furthermore, if monetary values are given to every activity, what of love, beauty, and creativity?

As the issues of abortion and family violence drew greater attention during the sixties, the feminists had to base their claims for women's rights on their uniqueness, not on their sameness, for it is women who bear children and women who are usually beaten. Assertion of women's rights on both issues infringes on men's traditional assumptions concerning paternity and authority. To demand abortion rights or to seek shelters for battered women requires the acceptance of women's biological differences. Thus the women's movement began increasingly to reconsider women's nature and to wonder if, in insisting on absolute equality, women were not being pushed into imitating men. Women began to realize that equal access to clubs, or jobs, or universities has usually meant women's equal entry into a man's world or a male bureaucracy, and it's the women who adapt.[4] Academic women began to recognize the male bias in curricula and set up Women's Studies courses and women's research centers. Books and articles appeared on women in the arts, in history, in science, in the corporation, or in government. One author even argued that the hope for American business was the feminization of the workplace[5], while another believed that female attributes were more suited to the Age of Communication than were male attributes.[6] In all of these trends there is acceptance of the difference between men and women.

Some feminists, acknowledging women's biological differences, have argued that women are morally superior to men. Indeed, this assertion ran through the arguments presented early in this century by the suffragettes[7] and it tends even today to undergird the women's peace movement. This can be a dangerous stance, allowing, for example, such radical religious leaders as the Ayatullah Khomeni to blame the moral ills of Iran on women for discarding the veil. Nonetheless it continues to be a pervasive belief held by both women and men.

A second set of assertions arising out of the recognition of biological differences revolves around the belief that women are by nature more nurturant than men. This concept has been used as an explanation of why the environmental movement is dominated by women. But this same belief can also reenforce conservative political insistence that women's place is in the home and that mothering is only for women.[8]

Recognizing that any claim to moral superiority or special attributes too easily leads to a questioning of equality and provides a rationale that puts women back into traditional roles, most leaders of the women's movement prefer to emphasize the rights of each individual woman to equality both under the law and within the family. Paternity leave and househusbands are championed. The strains of the double bind are ignored, but with few children and long working lives, the heaviest household tasks don't last too long. A couple can surely deal with equal household tasks more easily when children are no longer at home. It is within the context of children and their upbringing that the equality of husband and wife is most questioned. Solutions to the dilemma of women's work on the one hand and of household and family responsibilities on the other, are neither easy nor obvious. Simplistic solutions based on the mere assignment of "value"--often equated with cash value--to women's contributions within the family do not directly address the question of equality. They tend to presume the legitimate confinement of women's efforts to a rather stereotypic mold within the family sphere and thus propose perpetuation of inequality in both private and public

lives by underscoring women's differences.[9] Growing praise
for the family, both in the United States and in the United
Nations, suggests a reaction to women's demands for equality
that could reverse many of the freedoms recently won by the
women's movement. These are the issues that I expect to
dominate debates within the women's movement during the next
decade. But I do not believe that feminists will retreat from
the underlying values which proclaim each woman's individual
right to equal treatment.

The Individual and Society

Almost nowhere in the literature spawned by the women's
movement is there serious discussion of social responsibilities
of women, or of men. Indeed, the majority of persons who
identify themselves as new feminists express the notion that
historically, women were "conned" into providing the glue of
society while men were out "doing their own thing." Hence,
most American feminists eschew the whole idea of being a
volunteer. To them this means playing "grey lady" in the
hospital, organizing charity balls for the old folks home, or
holding a fair to make money for the school. Yet the same
women provide hours of volunteer help in a multitude of
organizations: feminist, environmental, and political.
Perhaps the pertinent distinction is between time spent trying
to change the present organization of society and time spent
providing free community service.

As with family responsibilities, women today demand that
men spend equal time on social support systems or,
alternatively, that the government develop services to replace
those previously undertaken by volunteers or the family.
Clearly, in contemporary America, individual rights take
precedence over societal responsibilities, whether for family
or community. In the name of egalitarianism, women now claimed
the same privilege long enjoyed by men.

The emphasis on the individual as the primary building block of society can be traced back to many strands of thought that arose in Europe during the Renaissance and Reformation. Social Contract theorists such as Hobbes, Locke, and Rousseau debated the characteristics of <u>man</u> in the natural state and designed societal rules based on their philosophical not analytical, observations. Their projection of women's roles, however, were more "realistic," drawn up not with reference to proposed ideals of political stability, social equality and participation but descriptively, by reference to the lowest common denominator of women's social, sexual and economic functions. Contemporary women anthropologists argue that the portrayal of women's roles in primative societies in textbooks still tends to be based on myth, not reality; women historians and theologians have shown how women lost many privileges during the so-called renaissance or rebirth of Europe; women scientists and philosophers illustrate how sexual stereotypes have conditioned biological thought and influenced experimental conclusions.[10] In other words, much of the thinking upon which the foundations of our contemporary industrialized society are laid is, in its essence, chauvinistic. It provided the philosophical rationale for freeing men from the hierarchy of the church-state; but by emphasizing the predominance of the individual man, it put his woman further under his control, with little channel for appeal to societal standards or rights.[11]

The primacy of the individual over society also asserts the rights of the individual owner over land and resources. In response, the environmental movement works for preservation of our great natural heritage for future generations against immediate short-term individual gain. In other words, environmentalists are demanding a better balance between the unfettered rights of the individual or collection of individuals in a corporation and the right of society to clean water and clean air and to forests, marshes, and beaches. They are also concerned with indiscriminate exploitation of farmland, minerals, and oil. Some women environmentalists talk of the "rape of the earth," further establishing the parallel between feminist thought and environmental concerns.[12]

In conclusion, it is clear that American feminists have utilized as the philosophical basis for their movement the fundamental American values of egalitarianism and individualism. These are verities deeply held by all American women and men. What feminists have done that is revolutionary is to insist that women should be equal to men and should have the same rights to develop their individual skills and psyches. What was once a radical challenge is today the cornerstone of the American women's movement. Indeed, opinion polls show that a majority of women and men support women's rights under law. Even conservative women base their argument favoring the housewife role on individuals having entered into a marriage contract.[13] While early feminists inveighed against the housewife role, activist women today are more likely to demand equal rights to social security and pensions for women who do make such a choice. And they demand better ways to collect child support payments when a man deserts his family. All of these policies continue to be based on equal individual rights.

Yet by pushing these concepts to their logical extremes, feminists have revealed the weakness of a philosophy which gives unfettered rights to an individual over family or society and which interprets equality as sameness. Most feminists have chosen to ignore these weaknesses, fearing that any modification of their demands would be seen as a retreat.

Exporting Feminist Values

Since World War II, the United States has assumed a leadership role in the reconstruction and modernization of societies worldwide. Beginning with the Marshall Plan for war-torn Europe, the US has loaned or given money to other countries to assist in their industrialization. Economic development theory used the U.S. of the post-war era as its model of "modern." This was the period in which women were urged to give up their wartime jobs in factories or government and retreat to the suburbs. Obviously, development theory has been exporting the male values which are anathema to the feminists. By the seventies, empirical data began to show that development too frequently was having an adverse impact on women. As this process became more widely understood, women concerned with socio-economic development agitated to have the fruits of development reach and benefit women as well as men.[14] This group, which began to be known as Women-in-Development (WID), emphasizes cultural variation and differences among people in different countries, and so argues that development should be based on local values and needs.

In their criticism of prevailing development theory, WID adherents have found allies among adherents of two groups of early development specialists, those favoring the basic needs approach and those calling for appropriate technology. All three movements condemned the capital intensive macro-economic approach to development, which has frequently resulted in the rich getting richer and the poor getting poorer. They called, rather, for small-scale technology, village participation in planning, labor intensive enterprises, and programs that reach women. Above all, they called for adapting theories to local situations and designing projects in response to local needs as articulated by the local group.[15]

Interest in the impact of economic development and social change on women of the developing countries has increased exponentially on American campuses in the last 10 years. In the early days most of the Women-in-Development work was done by anthropologists; they were quickly joined by political scientists, rural sociologists, and home economists. Interest also soared among women concerned with the implementation and impact of development programs. Policy-oriented women in Washington conceived an amendment to the Foreign Assistance Act of 1973 calling for the integration of women into development programs, which Senator Charles Percy (R. Ill.) introduced. The U.S. Agency for International Development, the World Bank, and most major donor agencies set up WID offices to ensure that women as well as men were beneficiaries of their programs. Several independent research centers and consulting firms have been established both in the United States and abroad to support these efforts.[16]

Meanwhile, Women's Studies courses expanded throughout the country and, in 1977, the National Women's Studies Association was established. This organization of academics aims to support women faculty primarily on university campuses. Because some early Women's Studies courses contained large amounts of consciousness raising and because men were often barred from the courses, some university administrators questioned the academic validity of the programs, while others thought of them as advocacy rather than substantive courses. Consequently, within the Association, great emphasis is placed on scholarship in order to give legitimacy to the subject matter. Furthermore, because of the possible loss of academic merit for women teaching Women's Studies, only committed feminists tend to do so. This tendency exaggerates the tension between the feminist emphasis on egalitarianism and the hierarchical structure of the university. Feeling embattled, many Women's Studies faculty members, with their students, have formed closely-knit groups that presume to be the only true representatives of feminism on their campuses.

As a result, many Women's Studies professors dismiss Women-in-Development research as too applied, too hasty, and generally deficient in scholarship. They also argue that, because the funding source is often the U.S. Agency for International Development, the results are suspect or tainted. Finally, as self-appointed keepers of American feminism, they have tended to argue for the universality of their views and question the feminist credentials of those WID practitioners who argue for adapting feminist values to varying cultural situations.

In 1981, several leading WID adherents from major land-grant universities began to discuss the need for a professional association of WID specialists who would be drawn from donor agencies and consulting groups as well as from university and research centers. The Association for Women in Development was formed in May 1982 and held its first national conference in Washington in October 1983 to bring together scholars, practitioners, and policymakers.

Development Theory and Women

The subject matter of WID is social change, whatever the cause. As critics of development theory, WID specialists question the use of GNP (gross national product) as the measure of development. Alternative measures have been attempted to get beyond availability of food, clothing, and housing, to meet basic survival needs, into more illusive standards for health, sanitation, and education.[17] These measures are much more accurate in assessing women's status in a country than is per capita income: the Arab countries provide obvious illustrations. In questioning that money is the measure of all things, WID specialists join a growing body of women and men in the U.S. who are critical of American materialism. But it is difficult to incorporate this concept into a feminism that is striving for equality with men in the terms of success as perceived in the United States: equal pay at all levels.

As critics of a development theory that argues for the universality of economic phenomena and trends, WID adherents emphasize local variability and advocate adaptation of programming to the norms of the community. This does not mean an uncritical acceptance of local hierarchies of power, but rather the recognition of alternative value systems which, while changing rapidly as a result of modernization, may still differ from our own. In particular, this means understanding the tension between individual rights and societal or family needs in a different philosophical context. When doctrinaire feminists have visited developing countries and argued for the freeing of women from the bondage of their families, the vision evoked of the parlous state of unattached women is often considered worse than the prevailing patriarchy. Local women leaders have criticized dedicated American feminists for trying to design programs for women which assume greater individual autonomy than exists and have called these efforts counterproductive.

The point here is that development is a dynamic process; change can further exacerbate the daily struggle of women for survival, or it can ameliorate their drudgery, and provide new opportunities for education and income. Even with revolution, nations draw heavily on their cultural traditions. The tenets of American philosophy which granted unfettered rights to the individual over society are not widely held nor easily exportable.

Even more difficult to export is the idea that women and men are the same. Ivan Illich has recently provided a new theory as to why women have less status in modernizing societies. He argues that women held greater advantage in a society which preserved gender assignments of economic activity and where women and men were necessary to each other for survival. In industrial societies, tasks are genderless, with the result that women are assigned the most lowly. This leaves only sex as the difference between men and women. No wonder this was the focus of the first attack by American feminists.[18] As noted above, there is danger in acknowledging biological differences between men and women, lest the response be back to economic assignments by gender, in the home and in the marketplace. Yet this particular strand of feminist thought is already under reconsideration at home, making it all the more improbable that it will be adopted abroad.

We have, then, two national organizations of women concerned with research and policy: the National Women's Studies Association and the Association for Women in Development. As aspects of the women's movement, these organizations share the fundamental beliefs of egalitarianism and individualism. While they have different substantive bases, both groups also support demands for increased employment opportunities for women in their respective fields. Embedded as it is in academia, Women's Studies seeks to legitimize theory and scholarship about women; Women-in-Development, on the other hand, wants to influence policy and programming and so emphasizes pragmatic research and field experience. To this extent, the differences between the two groups is similar to those between many other organizations that divide over the academic versus the applied.

In addition, however, are the value perceptions of the two groups. Women's Studies, as the inheritor of early feminism, continues to espouse the early feminist interpretations of egalitarianism and individualism. As a group they tend to ignore criticism on the grounds that alterations of the basic philosophy will weaken the movement, and to be intolerant of those who suggest modification. Women-in-Development is founded on the premise that any theory based on national experience travels poorly; it seeks to moderate the impact of socio-economic development on women in the name of social justice. As a group, WID adherents accept local definitions of the balance between the individual and society and try to work within local definitions of women's roles.

These different approaches may be seen more clearly by referring briefly to several recent issues which have divided adherents of these two groups.

Infant formula. For some years, feminists in the United States have inveighed against the advertising campaigns of international conglomerates to convince women in developing countries to stop breast-feeding and use infant formula instead. In particular, they attacked Nestle's tactics of sending saleswomen dressed as nurses to visit newly delivered women in the hospital. Incorrect use of the formula has led to many infant deaths; sterilization of feeding bottles is obviously difficult under sanitary conditions prevailing among all but the affluent in most developing countries. Incorrect measuring or purposeful ekeing out of the powder over long periods of time leads to malnutrition. The problem is particularly acute in Africa, where commonly inherited lactase deficiency means that babies cannot digest cow's milk and its use in formula leads to severe diarrhea. Boycotts led by American women were largely responsible for creating the publicity that led to the passage by the World Health Organization in 1981 of a set of guidelines which spelled out acceptable advertising methods.

The intent of the boycott was to stop all export of the formula to developing countries. Women in those countries were increasingly critical of this effort, for they saw no concerted attempt in the United States to prohibit the sale of the formula. They argued that women had to work to survive and they had to be able to bottle-feed their babies. Furthermore, many felt that allegations about incorrect use of the formula were attacks on the intelligence of women in their countries. They felt that instead of receiving support from women in the U.S., their interests were being subordinated to a theoretical international stand.[19]

Depo-provera

This injectable contraceptive has been used in developing countries as part of the USAID-supported family planning program. It has many advantages over available methods: pills must be taken regularly, not easy even in the clock-tied U.S.; IUDs (intra-uterine devices) exacerbate vaginal infections and so are more hazardous in developing countries, where infection is more common and treatment less accessible, than in the U.S.; condom use must rely on the cooperation of husbands; diaphragms require a level of cleanliness not easy to attain. Perhaps the greatest advantage of Depo-provera is that one injection lasts three months and may be obtained on a regular trip to market; furthermore, husbands do not need to know--a not inconsiderable advantage in many male-dominated societies.

But Depo has not been licensed for use as a contraceptive in the U.S., tests reported in 1979 found the drug to be carcinogenic when taken in large quantities. There is strong opposition, particularly among a large sector of women in the health movement, to the sale overseas of this drug that is not acceptable in the U.S. itself. In addition, there is increasing concern in developed countries over the safety of chemical contraceptives in general and a widespread return to barrier methods. There is a growing worldwide demand for greater emphasis on developing male contraceptives. For all these reasons, the women's health movement has campaigned against the continued promotion of Depo in USAID-funded programs.

On the other hand, statistics from Thailand, where Depo has been used for more than five years, do not indicate any undue hazard, according to proponents. They also point out that women in developing countries face greater risks from pregnancy than from the drug and that Depo presents no greater risk than the less effective pill. Advocates of the drug feel that comparisons of risk between the U.S. and such countries are fallacious, that different standards must be recognized, and most particularly, that in countries where population explosion is a reality, Depo works and women like it.

This line of reasoning is winning converts, especially as retesting of the drug has cast doubt on earlier results which indicated high risk. At an international meeting in Geneva in 1980, sponsored by the feminist journal ISIS, (Rome, Italy and Carouge, Switzerland) grassroots women's health groups decided not to pass a resolution against Depo after hearing the presentations of women from developing countries. In 1983, the U.S. Food and Drug Administration took the unusual step of arranging a re-hearing on Depo. The radical feminist Women's Health Network testified against the use of Depo, but the Women and Health Roundtable pleaded instead for careful monitoring. The FDA has not yet issued its ruling.[20]

Multi-National Corporations

An economic phenomenon of the last decade has been the trend by multi-national corporations to move factories from the U.S. and other high labor cost countries to developing countries where labor costs are low and governments often grant tax advantages. Textiles and electronics have been particularly affected, industries that employ large numbers of women. Many feminists in the U.S. have condemned this movement of industries, both for the jobs lost to women here and out of concern for the women exploited in the developing countries. Multi-national corporations are said to seek a docile labor force and regulations in many free trade zones specifically prohibit union organizing of workers. Hours are long, the pay is low, and there is little job security, since management prefers to hire unmarried young women. Nonetheless, these jobs are eagerly sought after, particularly by young rural women who have few job alternatives to living in villages and working 10 to 12 hours a day at subsistence activities merely to survive. Furthermore, in most of these countries, women who marry do not usually wish to continue to work; as did the New England textile workers, they work to earn a dowry and then leave.[21]

Conclusion

These three cases are prime examples of the many policy issues on which many American feminists have taken a view based on theory that does not accord with the reality of women's lives in developing countries as seen from these women's own perspective. In none of the cases is there an easy solution. It would be healthier if all women breast-fed their infants; but surely that must be an individual woman's choice. Depo-provera is by no means a perfect drug, but how can American feminists, with their demand at home of the right to control their own bodies, object to allowing the same choice to women in developing countries? Conditions in most factories are onerous; women employees are undoubtedly exploited in the name of profits. But subsistence life is even harder; money is scarce and much needed. How can feminists who insist on equal employment opportunities object to the opening of more jobs for women in poorer countries?

I have argued that American feminism built its strength and persuasiveness on the basic American values of egalitarianism and individualism. The radical message of American feminists is that these values should apply equally to all women. In the ensuing debate it is clear that most American women and men have embraced the public application of egalitarianism: the Equal Rights Amendment has the support of the majority of citizens of the country. But equality within the private sphere of the family brought greater questioning, particularly as women began to demand legislation which was female-specific. Most Americans also support the concept of individualism. Feminists, by arguing that women have the same rights that men have, put individual women's interests before their families; or alternately, in the name of the family, they have underscored the weakness of a philosophy that does not temper individual rights with responsibilities to family and society. On the whole, American feminism as expressed through Women's Studies has rejected any modifications to their clear stance: movements need ideology. To the extent that they claim for themselves the term "feminism," their views and values remain ethnocentric.

But the movement does not remain stationary. Indeed, the intellectual challenges posed by the feminist critique are producing some of the most exciting thinking of the century. Much of it is pointing in one clear direction: the fundamental tenets of current American beliefs must be reexamined, whether the research and ideas are coming from scientists, or theologians, environmentalists or Women-in-Development specialists. What all of these theorists and technical specialists are asking for is a reconsideration and revaluation of basic American beliefs. This requires scrutiny of the philosophical bases of contemporary industrial society, at home and abroad. In this respect, feminists are in harmony with the growing unease around the world toward the continuing export through development of these unexamined values. Change is inevitable, and necessary. But the goal should be societies where women have equal rights, where men and women can choose occupations and roles without gender limitation, where there is a reasonable balance between individual rights and support for the family, society, and the environment.

Irene Tinker
Equity Policy Center
Washington, D. C.

1. Max Weber, The Protestant Ethic and the Spirit of Capitalism (London: Allen and Urwin, 1904); David M. Potter, People of Plenty (Chicago: University of Chicago Press, 1954); C. Wright Mills, White Collar (Oxford: Oxford University Press, 1956); See also Irene Tinker, "America: Melting Pot or Plural Society," New Frontiers X, no.2 (1965).

2. For a detailed exploration of women organizing for change see Irene Tinker, ed., Women in Washington: Advocates for Public Policy (Beverly Hills: Sage Publications, 1983).

3. See Susan Bolotin, "Voices from the Post-Feminist Generation," The New York Times Magazine, October 17, 1982, for the persistence of this linkage.

4. Noelle Beatty, ed., Women & Power: An Exploratory View, proceedings from a Radcliffe and EPOC Symposium, 1979 (EPOC: 20012 S Street, N.W., Washington, D.C. 20009).

5. Micheal Maccoby, The Gamesman (New York: Simon & Schuster, 1976).

6. Elsa Porter speaking to the Washington Women's Network, Dec. 9, 1982 on "Women in Management."

7. Jean Bethke Elshtain, "Moral Woman and Immoral Man: A Consideration of Public-Private Split and Its Political Ramification," Politics & Society (1974).

8. Jane Roberts Chapman and Margaret Gates, eds., Women into Wives: The Legal and Economic Impact of Marriage (Beverly Hills: Sage Publications, 1977); Ann Dally, Inventing Motherhood: The Consequences of an Ideal (New York: Schochen, 1983).

9. A variety of feminist views are presented in Karen Wolk Feinstein, ed., Working Women and Families (Beverly Hills: Sage Publications, 1979).

10. Susan Carol Rogers, "Women's Place: A Critical Review of Anthropological Theory," Comparative Studies in Society & History 20 (Jan. 1978):123-162; Madeleine J. Goodman and Leon Evan Goodman, "Is there a Feminist Biology?," International Journal of Women's Studies 4.4 (1981):616-636; Elise Boulding, The Underside of History: A View of Women Through Time (Boulder: Westview Press, 1976); Mary Daly, Beyond God the Father: Toward a Philosophy of Women's Liberation (Boston: Beacon Press, 1973).

11. For a very different argument which arrives at similar conclusions see Ivan Illich, Gender (New York: Pantheon, 1983).

12. Elizabeth Dodson Grey, Why the Green Nigger? (Wellesley: Roundtable Press, 1979).

13. Mark E. Kann, "Legitimation, Consent and Antifeminism," Women & Politics 3, no. 1 (Spring 1983) suggests that the contract theory's use by anti-feminists in

contemporary America has added to their respectability and success.

14. Irene Tinker and Michelle Bo Bramsen, Women and World Development (New York: Praeger, 1976) gives a state of the art review as of the International Women's Year Conference in Mexico City in June 1975.

15. ILO classics of this debate include: E.F. Schumacher, Small is Beautiful: Economics As If People Mattered (New York: Harper & Row, 1973).

16. See also Irene Tinker, Gender Equity in Development: A Policy Perspective July 1982 (EPOC: 2000 S Street, NW, Washington, D.C. 20009).

17. For a discussion of PQLI (Physical Quality of Life Index) see Measuring the Condition of the World's Poor (Washington, DC: Overseas Development Council, 1979).

18. Ivan Illich, Segregated societies to offer opportunities for the disadvantaged, whether Blacks in pre-integration U.S. or women in less developed societies. For statistics on women in the professions see Ester Boserup Woman's Role in Economic Development, London: Allen & Irwin, 1970. Chapter 7.

19. Dana Raphael, ed., The Lactation Review (The Human Lactation Center Ltd: 666 Sturges Highway, Westport, Conn. 06880); Jane Cottingham, ed., Bottle Babies, (ISIS: Case Postale 301, 1227 Carouge, Switzerland).

20. Anne S. Kasper, "Women's Health and the FDA: A Case Study in Consumer Lobbying," Women in Washington: Advocates for Public Policy (Beverly Hills: Sage Publications, 1983).

21. Irene Tinker, Women, Energy and Development (EPOC: 2001 S Street, N.W., Washington, D.C. 20009) for time budgets; Irene Tinker, Toward Equity for Women in Korea's Development Plans (EPOC: 2001 S Street, N.W., Washington, D.C. 20009) for discussion of women in factories.

PART II

Practice and Experience

MATRILINEAL HERITAGE:
A LOOK AT THE POWER OF CONTEMPORARY MICRONESIAN WOMEN

From the end of World War II until the 1970s, few
foreigners were permitted to visit Guam or the Pacific Trust
Territory. The high volcanic islands and coral atolls of
Micronesia were accessible only to U.S. military and government
personnel and to a handful of ethnographers and journalists.
The latter offered us a picture of Micronesian women that was
intriguing: many island women governed themselves, owned and
worked land, fished cooperatively, orchestrated their own
sexual lives, and spoke their minds freely. Yet, overall, the
view we have of these women's social status is puzzlingly
contradictory.

From the anthropologist H.G. Barnett, we get the impression
that Palauan women are accorded important rights, but only to
the extent that they're willing to augment or consolidate the
power of men:

> The Palauans live in a man's world for which
> they give women credit....the men are
> disposed to be quite generous in their
> acknowledgment of women's worth if the
> admission does not alter the fundamental
> reality of male dominance....They believe
> what they say about the importance of women,
> so much so that they are almost carried away
> by their gratitude in praising their women
> to an interested outsider. The men enjoy
> their candid admissions of indebtedness...
> and the proofs they adduce have been known
> to trap sympathetic but unwary foreigners
> into believing that the Palauans live under
> a matriarchal system presided over by
> respected, kindly, elderly woman.

A former World War II correspondent revisiting postwar
Micronesia counters: "Women, I gathered, wielded tremendous
power in Palauan society, although it was not easy to get a man

to admit it."[2] Twenty years later, another writer agrees that women "are in many ways the ultimate power brokers."[3]

We might resolve this difference of opinion by deciding that Barnett, as the Palauan-speaking ethnographer, is correct. But no matter who the source is, the literature is full of ambiguities and information gaps. Often, the writer is so thoroughly convinced that women's activities are tangential to society that when evidence to the contrary is mentioned, it is simply left hanging. Thus, we have Roland Force alerting us to the existence of Palauan female chiefs. He writes that these women help formulate village policy, and sometimes sit in on the klobak, or men's council. A few hold male titles and permanent places on the klobak. But we never learn any significant details about their roles and activities. Force reveals only that "their political power is considerably more restricted than that of male chiefs."[4]

The debate over subordinate versus superordinate status could be continued indefinitely, but a more fruitful approach might be to describe the types of power that some contemporary Micronesian women do have, and try to pinpoint the factors that have allowed them to retain that power. I propose to begin making that delineation, using data I collected in 1982, while working as a consultant to several Pacific Island departments of education.

Four Dimensions of Power

I sought out Palauan and Ponapean women as my primary informants and asked them to participate in a three-hour interview, at the end of which they would assess their own political, economic, and social status. Asking the women to describe their own activities was a means of eliciting information that might not fit into conventional Western constructs. Requesting that the women help evaluate their own power was one way to avoid the trap of assessing them according to how closely they emulate male styles of social and political participation. Weiner pointed out that Trobriand Island women, for example, have a subtle, but crucial, role in the ritualistic Trobriand economic exchanges, based on their spiritual importance to their culture. Women's power, Weiner stressed, must be reckoned with, "even if it appears limited and seems outside the political sphere."[5]

At the beginning of each interview, power was defined as the ability to make decisions, and ensure that others would comply with those decisions. Because one part of the interview dealt with personal issues, such as deciding whom and when to marry, and how much education to pursue, "domestic" decisions were taken into account, but the emphasis was on "public" participation and influence.

The four dimensions of power I analyzed are in agreement with the categories suggested by Peggy Sanday's framework for evaluating women's status,[6] but adapted to reflect my lesser focus on female economic interests. Women's marketing activities and control over extradomestic material goods seemed not to be appropriate indicators of power in societies where access to a central marketplace is weather-dependent and therefore sporadic, and the cultural emphasis on generosity, sharing, and other communal values makes it difficult for anyone to amass, or to dispose of material possessions unilaterally.

The interviewees were thus asked to respond to the following four categories of questions:

I. Female political participation. What kinds of public policy decisions did the women make? Could they allocate authority, mold public opinion, influence male policy-makers? Could women be mobilized to act as a group?

II. Female control over strategic resources, specialized knowledge, and skills. Did women own land, have rights to fishing areas, control other means of production? Could they acquire the scientific and technical expertise to lessen the islands' dependence on foreign resources? Was there a value placed on their knowledge and skills?

III. Female solidarity. What were the systems of mutual obligations/mutual help? What were the functions of formal and informal women's organizations? Did the women and the community view them as effective?

IV. Personal power. What pressures did women feel in making key life decisions about education, work, marriage, children? Were their childhood expectations being realized? What doors were closed? Were there comparable restrictions on everyone in the culture?

In a fifth set of questions, women were asked to consider their overall power, and compare it to that of their peers, their mothers, less educated women, women of higher and lower social status, and the women of the more isolated, outlying islands.

Participants in the full three-hour interview included 11 Palauan and Ponapean women and eight Guamanian[*] (Chamorro) women. They ranged in age from 20 to 65. They included women who were never-married, married, divorced, and widowed. Some were never-employed, others held clerical, sales, and professional positions. Since Ponape and Palau are hierarchical, clan-based societies, the women surveyed represented clans of ordinary and chiefly lineage. The Palauan and Ponapean women were the main informants in this study. The Guamanian women, all of whom now live in California, were interviewed because they could discuss and analyze their status from a double perspective, that of Westernized women who are, at the same time, participants in a culture whose values of

---

*All but one of the women born in Guam preferred to be called Guamanian, rather than Chamorro; thus, the term Guamanian is used in this paper.

132

hospitality, friendliness, cooperation, and social
interdependence are similar to those of other Micronesians.[*]

Because the formal interview sample was small, I
supplemented the data by discussing women's influence and
prestige with many of the Palauan and Ponapean men and women I
talked to, and with American women I encountered who were
married to Micronesians. Whenever possible, I also mapped out
the proceedings at department of education meetings, to see who
spoke, whether their comments were neutral or pointed, whether
they could attract allies, and/or whether they could
singlehandedly influence others into making policy or taking
action. I also noted women's mannerisms, facial expressions,
and general physical presence. In fact, I found that one of
the most striking things about Palauan women is their lack of
conformity to Western (or Asian) notions of restrained, docile,
self-effacing "feminine" behavior. But before these
differences are discussed, the women's perceptions of their
roles should be reported. Below, following a brief sketch of
Palau's geography and economy, the Palauan women speak for
themselves. Later sections discuss Ponape and Ponapean women.

Palau

The Republic of Palau (or Belau) is an archipelago of 350
lushly-vegetated islands, coral atolls and mushroom-shaped,
rocky outcroppings, about 500 miles east of the Philippines.
Hot, humid and rainy throughout most of the year, the islands
support a population of some 12,000 people, of whom about 7,000
are adults. There are only 3200 jobs in the wage sector and
almost half of these are in government work (including

---

*The people of Guam do not view themselves politically as
Micronesians, but since geographically, and in many senses,
culturally, they're part of the Micronesian group of islands,
Micronesia is used very generally here to include Guam.

education); the rest are in light industry, tourism and private retail trade.[7] Fishing and subsistence agriculture supplement cash incomes and are the sole livelihood for many people.

Despite a succession of four foreign administrations (Spanish, German, Japanese, and American), the traditional culture in Palau has not been overtaken by the transitional culture (an amalgam of American, Japanese, and European bureaucratic structures, styles of political protest, etc.). The two cultures coexist side by side. At department of education meetings, many of the Palauans chew betel nuts, as they discuss problem-solving models and goal-setting procedures. And the electronic ping of Pac-Man is heard in the distance, as the women inform a male administrator that he should have provided coffee for a long work session.

Palauan Women: "A Man Who Has No Sisters Is Unlucky"

When I began interviewing the Palauan women, several informants stressed that Palauan women traditionally choose the male chief of their own clan--an important social and political responsibility that is mentioned only once in the literature[8] even though much of the material on Palau is specifically about political leadership and factionalism.[9] Because the chief is looked up to as the person who defends his people's rights and customs, his is not an empty role in Palauan society, and the women's right to choose him means that they partake in his power. Whoever aspires to be chief must pay close attention to the thoughts, needs, and feelings of the women who appoint him. The men of the village can veto this appointment, but as one informant explained, their veto is merely an expression of disapproval that the women can override:

> The chiefs in the village can object to the women's choice. If the females of the clan have another alternative, they might reconsider their decision. But if they choose the same one again, that guy is going

to be it. Already, there has been a court
case where the chiefs of one village got
together and signed a petition to get rid of
a chief who is now deceased. They didn't
like him. So they took it to the court and
the chiefs lost because they have no right
whatsoever to decide who will be chief. Now
they each have to pay $500, plus seven
percent interest, and they have a certain
time left to do it. If they do not pay,
they will probably be in jail, those ten
chiefs.

It's the women's prerogative to decide who the chief will
be, she added, because it's the women who will provide the
chief with the money he needs to carry out the many traditional
obligations he has as the clan's leader. The women will also
prepare and contribute any feast food that the chief needs for
the rest of his life, which is likely to mean that the women
are committing themselves to an enormous financial
responsibility.

It is this type of financial obligation, which is far more
binding upon both single and married women than it is upon men,
that is a major source of women's power and prestige. For
many, it's also a burden. Women are expected to provide money
and food for every Palauan "custom." The customs are observed
not only to mark births, deaths, and marriages, but to
celebrate and assist with house-building, boat-buying and other
expensive endeavors. Women have been known to come up with as
much as $5000 to contribute to a brother's new house--a demand
that would strain the budget of all but an upper middle-class
American and is especially difficult on Palauan salaries. It's
no wonder that people in Palau say, "a man who has no sisters
is unlucky" and "a Palauan woman is a Palauan man's money."

The women seemed to agree, however, that accepting these
financial obligations gave them leverage within Palauan
society, and a feeling of security. As one woman described
this feeling: "People here define themselves and find their
identity in relationship to the group. The Palauan concept of

the chain of giving is that maybe you suffer by helping, but you know also that if you don't have a penny, you will not starve. You can complain about it, but you need to feel involved with people, with the community."

The system of mutual obligation was explained in detail by another woman who stressed that Palauan women are in many ways more powerful than the men, not only because of their financial role but because they make all the major decisions about the food that is exchanged at the customary feasts. In Micronesia (and other Pacific Island areas), it should be noted that food and feasting have profound social, emotional, political, and economic significance that has no counterpart in Western culture. The securing of food is a major preoccupation that until recently consumed most of an islander's time and work life. Food thus symbolizes work and is at the same time a reward for working. The amount of food provided at a feast not only indicates the feast-giver's economic, social, and sometimes political importance, but the sharing of food also serves to cement the bonds of kinship and community, reminding everyone that generosity, sharing, and concern for the group are the basis of island culture. Guests not only consume food during the festivities, but take home baskets of food in an amount proportionate to their social and political position, marital status, and willingness to contribute money to that particular custom. The money doesn't pay for the food. It is a more abstract exchange that ties the giver and receiver together in the knowledge that eventually there will be reciprocation, more exchange, and again more reciprocation. Women are at the epicenter of this intricate network, determining the nature and extent of the exchanges and who the givers and receivers will be. One informant traced the lines of supply and exchange that would be set up for a typical wedding:

> If, for example, a woman is getting married,
> the mother of the bride decides on the

amount and types of food. She may say okay, we need ten baskets of uncooked taro, one pig of so many pounds, one big pot of fish, one big pot of pigeons, one pot of bats--a very special food--one big pot of crabs or oysters. It depends on the mother, if she wants to show off, maybe foreign foods, too, like cases of canned milk, sugar, rice.

Then the relatives are called. And the ones who get the most food are the sisters of the groom. There is a reason for this. The sisters give the biggest amount of money because it's their responsibility to give. Then the groom's aunts will get the second largest amount of food. Actually, the female relatives of the groom--not the male relatives--will divide the food.

A date is then set for giving the money, and the women relatives of the groom provide money that will go to the parents of the bride. It used to be $200 and now it is more like $1000. Some people have even spent $7000. They give that money to the parents of the girl and that money opens the door to the rest of the customs. Once this money changes hands, that's it. The bride is obligated. When the women relatives of the groom need food, they won't be reluctant to go to the bride for it.

Although men, too, contribute money to the customs, a single man from a clan that is high in the Palauan hierarchy might be expected to give $5 or $10, whereas a married woman from the same high clan would be expected to give a vastly greater amount. "If my brother has a house party, my brother who is younger may give $5 or $10 just to help," one woman said, "but I might be expected to give up to $10,000. It's the sisters who will buy the house."

Eventually, there will be a return on the investment, but repayment may be spun out over a lifetime:

If my husband's sister comes to me and says, "my niece died, I want a pig--200 pounds-- and four sacks of rice, I say, "sure." Then I turn to my brother and I say, "I need a pig and four sacks of rice." And my brother

turns to his wife's brothers and it goes
around and around until someone decides to
stop the chain. But that evening I will
have a pig and rice. And I will give it to
my husband's sister and she will know where
it came from. And the same will happen six
months later, when I need money.

Most often, the hard-working women will not only collect
the money, but will also be the ones to earn it, "When I think
about words to describe Palauan women, I think of beautiful but
oppressed," one outspoken woman teacher said. This informant,
who has run for political office and lost, feels that "it is
like shoveling a pile of sand with your eyelashes" for a woman
to try to progress to an administrative job within the
educational bureaucracy. Highly conscious of her own and other
women's positions within the traditional and transitional
cultures, she offered this assessment of her own and others'
status:

Within my immediate family, I think I have
more power than my younger brothers,
although maybe not over my older brother.
Because I am the second oldest child,
because I have a better education, and
because I already contribute to the customs,
I have established my position in the
family...

Within my clan, I don't have much power. I
yak, yak, yak, I give my opinion and I get
scolded for it. Sometimes, they agree with
my idea...

As far as being a woman in this society, I
think a woman is more oppressed than a man,
because the responsibility for customs falls
on her. She contributes money, almost to
the point where she doesn't have enough to
provide for the people she lives with. It's
unfortunate because then she cannot begin to
bloom in her own environment or grow....The
women are so giving. They contribute when
it's called for, and when they return to the
family, they still have to perform, to take
care of the children, the household
responsibilities....The men contribute their

138

little share, they give it to the wife, and
then they float. But the females feel the
burden. They keep it in their hearts, day
in and day out. Women cannot grow if
they're overburdened with these kinds of
cultural responsibilities and family
expectations.

In her clan, this woman said, her female relatives had
innovated a type of Christmas club, in which the 14 women who
participated set aside $10 every pay period, and took turns
being the recipients of that sum. They were also beginning to
insist that the men contribute more money to customs:

We're beginning to have more male
participation because everything is costing
more money and the pressure is building up.
Before, someone would announce that
something was needed and a single man would
say, "well, should I (contribute) or not?"
But as a woman, single or not, I have to do
it. It's a duty. So now, in my family, the
men are made to give. We go collect
contributions from them.

Although the women's role in carrying out the customs
pervaded all the interviews, some of the women pointed to
several other social mechanisms that buttress female influence
and prestige. If being able to tap into formal and informal
lines of communication/information is one characteristic of
powerful people within organizations, Palauan women could step
into the top ranks of company management with aplomb. Aside
from the formal women's networks that all but one of the women
belonged to, an informal system ensured that women could be
called together on the strength of the convoker's social
status. The purpose of the meeting was unimportant, my
informant explained, since attendance depended on the social
and political credibility of the other participants. "We women
have our messengers," she said, adding:

If I send the word that there will be a
meeting, the women will say, "Oh, who will
be there?" And if the right women are
there, everyone will make sure to come. But
if you (as a non-Palauan) call a meeting and

you have no introduction, it doesn't matter what you have to offer. The women won't make it.

Finally, as one woman pointed out, there is the sense of power inherent in the matrilineal tradition, in knowing that, no matter what happens, you have the land you inherited from your mother's lineage:

> The women here are so sure of themselves...maybe it's that we know for sure that we have land....Even if I don't get land from my husband, I still have it from my mother and nothing can change that....Also, some women today convince the man to build a house on their family's land, so if anything happens (to the marriage), they have the house...

> The women, I think work harder than the men. But speaking for myself, I would say we have equal power. Right now, my husband cannot stop me from going to work. Sometimes he tries. I cannot picture myself staying home all the time, doing the housework. I'd rather be out working....The women here have equality with the men.

Ponape

The state of Ponape, which includes the large, volcanic island of Ponape itself, as well as 39 other tiny islands and islets, lies 400 miles east of Truk in the central Pacific. The most easterly of the Caroline Islands (Palau is the most westerly of the Caroline group), Ponape is the wettest island in the Pacific, with an average rainfall of 180 inches along the lowlands and coast and far more rain in the interior. Ample fresh water induced the Japanese to introduce large-scale commercial agriculture, when they ruled the island before World War II. But Ponape's isolation from foreign supplies during the war caused over-exploitation of land and marine resources, which has since slowed economic regeneration. In 1979, only 3600 people out of the population of 22,000 worked for cash, primarily in government jobs. Everyone else--a far larger

percentage than in Palau--depends on subsistence farming and
fishing.[10]

Like Palau, Ponape was subject to four foreign
administrations (Spanish, German, Japanese and American) until
1978, when Ponape joined the Federated States of Micronesia.
Unlike Palau, Ponape was also subject to the strong influence
of Christian missionaries, who gradually converted the local
population, established schools, and tamped down interclan
violence. The changes imposed by the Germans were as
far-reaching. The Germans brought with them the concept of
private land ownership and replaced matrilineal inheritance of
land with a patrilineal land system. Only recently were the
laws altered so that parents' land could be passed down to
female as well as male children.

Ponapean Women: "Their Mind is Kind of Open Now"

While the Germans excluded women from land ownership, they
allowed matrilineal descent and title inheritance to continue
as they had for centuries. Thus, membership in the clans that
are the basic social and political unit of traditional Ponapean
society is reckoned through the woman, as are the titles that
are important in Ponapean life. But the mother's title only
goes to her male child. A man is a "naniken" or prince if his
mother is in a princely line; a woman gains a title through
marriage to a man who has or acquires this honor. The titles
delineate status within the traditional Ponapean culture, and
yams, pigs, and sakau--the major exchange goods at feasts--are
the material means for winning and enhancing prestige. Women
may plant and tend the sakau, and raise the pigs; but at
traditional ceremonies, men pound the sakau into the soporific
ritual drink and men present the gigantic prize yams as gifts
to the chiefs. A sufficient number of these gifts elevates a
man's position in the social hierarchy, whereas the avenue to

social status for a woman is less clear-cut, less a question of "do's" than "don't's."

Women are also limited in their access to the wage economy. Ponapean women are only beginning to work as salespeople, hotel personnel, typists, secretaries, and teachers. These jobs are invariably low-paid. Consequently, when one woman was asked where she would find money in a crisis, she responded:

> If I needed money, I would first turn to my husband. If I were single, first my parents, but if they weren't working, then my brother. It's not so much that my brother would have more money than my sisters, but as I said, we kind of consider men to be the head, the number one, and the second would be the female. But if my brother wasn't working, I would go to my sister.

Another woman agreed that she, too, would have to turn to her male relatives for money, but she pointed out that a special bond between women would lead her to expect help from her female relatives--help that would be her due even if her relative's husband refused her request:

> For money, I would, of course, go first to my husband, then my parents and then, perhaps, my husband's parents. After them, I would go to my male relatives because it's they who work and have money. But really, I might go to my aunt instead of my uncle. He could refuse me, but she can't. Because it wouldn't look nice if she refused me.

The avoidance of censure by others and the power of gossip are strong themes in Ponape, and, as a result, few women are willing to actively rebel against the role that the church vouchsafes to women. The missionary influence has established itself in Ponape in a way that it was never able to do in Palau. Women are taught to be modest, quiet, domestic, to say little in public. The church provides for women's organizations that are, quite literally, sewing circles. But the church is by no means a monolith, and individual teachers and administrators at the mission schools may encourage girls to continue their education. Some need very little overt support to look beyond their mothers' lives and envision something different for themselves. For one informant, who is now a secretary, with occasional thoughts of running for political office, school was a ticket to a larger world, and an outlet for an energetic, expansive personality:

> For me, if it wasn't for my own insistence, I wouldn't have the kind of education that I did. My father was for it and I had some teachers who were encouraging me, but I think it was my decision. When I was going to school here in Kolonia, my mother said, "Why should you go to school? You're going to be a housewife." She even came to the mission to take me out of school, but I said, "No, I'm not coming." After that I went to high school in Saipan, and then college in Honolulu.

As Ponapean women become more mobile, and bring back new visions of autonomy to those at home, more and more of the latter are realizing that education, and with it, a place in the cash economy, increases one's alternatives. As one 20-year-old typist recalled:

> I saw some of my friends stop school and during the weekends go to the taro fields with their families. During the week they stay in Kolonia, around the house. If they need money they have to ask for it. I saw that it isn't good to stay at home. You can't do what you want to and can't go where you want to. I wanted to go to the occupational school in Palau and my parents said no. But I went. I told them I would go. Then I told them I would go. Still I told them I would go. And then they accepted it. It is much better to work. Now I would like to go to school more.

One of the very few women educational administrators reaffirmed that it's rapidly becoming apparent to most Ponapean women that education is a key to change:

> As the adult education specialist, I am really working hard for women. Now we have

classes for nutrition, health, sewing, and
home gardening. By my observation, at first
the interest wasn't really strong. But now,
it's really surprising. Most of the
community know that these classes are really
useful. Especially the women know this.
Attendance is increasing, interest is
increasing. I really like the idea of
carpentry. If there were money for it, we
would have those classes and women would
take them...Some of the ladies would like to
go fishing. But men have the canoes. Only
men build the canoes and the ladies collect
shells. If we could have classes in canoe
building, we would have to talk to them and
explain it, but they're really good people.
If you explain something, they will accept
it.

Perhaps because of Ponape's change in political status, and
their consequent hard look at the future, or perhaps for other
reasons (e.g., women's new visibility all over the world),
there are more options available to Ponapean women now than
there were even five or ten years ago:

Before, maybe you wouldn't have such a good
life in this culture if you didn't get
married. If you go to the bar and you're
single, people will talk and just give the
bad side. But if you're married, they think
nothing will happen. Women marry for
protection in a way. But nowadays, maybe
it's changing. Before, they wanted their
daughters to get married, but maybe they're
kind of educated now. Most of the girls,
they're going to school. And when they get
out, they have their jobs. So their mind is
kind of open now.

For the most part, though, the women are still caught in a
cultural quandary, compounded by the overlay of missionary
ideas on traditional Ponapean ways. What is truly Ponapean is
often difficult to separate out from what seems traditional
because it is unmodern, the vestige of a 19th century colonial
attitude that the church hasn't shaken off. One woman
commented that she could go out and drink sakau, the local
euphoriant, with seven men, and no-one would say anything

because drinking sakau is so unmistakeably Ponapean. "But if I went out to drink beer with men, people would talk about it. They would say to my husband: 'How come we saw your wife with these guys?'" The gossip would be negative even though sakau is more potent than beer, and beer is often drunk as a chaser with sakau. But the relative innocence of one or the other is not at issue. Beer drinking in bars is not considered ladylike behavior. That this may be a missionary/colonialist view, with little relevance to traditional Ponapean culture, is, unfortunately, not readily apparent to Ponapeans who are socialized into the mix of these influences. That Ponapean women should be restricted by these Victorian values, seems particularly ironic when one reads of women who were canoe-builders, sailors, carvers, and settlers of new lands in the Book of Luelen--a Ponapean history set down by a 19th-century village chief who wrote the book to remind Ponapeans of the events of their past.[11]

However, there are more important restrictions than those surrounding beer-drinking. One salient example is the difficulty of breaking into politics. "Sometimes I joke to my husband that I want to be a politician," one woman commented, "and he says, no, he couldn't stand to hear me criticized. I told some women in my church group the same thing and they said, 'why get yourself in trouble?' I think we still have low opinions of ourselves. Like politics is a man's job, only for men."

Another woman agreed that:

> Women are not really recognized, as of now.
> We did have two ladies who tried three years
> ago to be on the congress, but they couldn't
> make it. They tried their best to mobilize
> the women, but the belief here is really
> strong that even if a lady is really smart
> or has whatever degree, she just can't make
> it in politics. Maybe after 10 or 15 years,
> if we do have more educated people, then
> ladies could be recognized. The beliefs are

fading, but right now they believe that women shouldn't be politicians.

When the Ponapean women were asked to compare their power and prestige with that of women from other cultures, none felt they could make that comparison. But an American woman in her twenties who lives with a Ponapean man disputed the idea that "the women here are not really recognized":

> I think the women have a lot of say here, more than we women have in the States. I think they're treated more like equals. Maybe I'm treated particularly well as an American, but I've been living here for two years, participating in the customs, asking questions, observing. I see that whenever the family members meet to discuss something, the women have as much to say as the men. If the women decide a house is needed, the men will do the building but the women will do all the planning. The women work very hard here, harder than the men-- they cook, they sew, take care of the kids, plant, harvest, make the copra, collect crabs, sell what they make. Maybe for that reason, they make a lot of decisions.

It is age, this woman thought, that brings with it power and respect:

> In my boyfriend's family, all the women boss the rest of the family around, but it's especially the older sister who does it. She decides what's going to happen and everybody does it. Nobody talks back to her. She calls my boyfriend; he goes. She can beat him up and he has to go along with it, not because she's a woman but because she's older. And it's the women who act as disciplinarians. If a kid gets drunk, it's usually the father who sits back while the mother beats the kid up.

Despite their somewhat anomalous position, then, the Ponapean woman universally said that when they thought about the women they knew (albeit not necessarily themselves), the words that came to mind were "self-confident, hard-working, strong." One woman said:

I would have to say self-confident most of
all...I think the men have more power...but
some of the families, even though they say
men are the head, you will find that the
woman is the leader...Some of them are kind
of tough women. Some people, you know,
believe in medicine and there are women who
have power as medicine women. I don't know
how they do it, but if they say something,
the men will agree. They'll say, "okay,
let's do it. Whatever the lady says." It's
not really that they're afraid of these
women. It's not that they think the women
have the power to damage, as much as to
heal. It's kind of that these women change
your thinking...So what they say, you
follow, and you say, "oh yes, that's good."

Cultural Bias: Some Caveats

Age, tough-mindedness, and the ability to heal seem to be
the prerequisites for true female power in Ponape. Similarly,
in her discussion of women's status within the Native Hawaiian
Movement, Haunani-Kay Trask (in manuscript) points to the
kupuna (an older woman with considerable life experience) and
the kahuna (an older woman possessing spiritual wisdom) as
being the only two politically influential roles allowed to
Hawaiian women.   It begins to be apparent that the attributes
of female power in the context of the Pacific Islands is at
odds with perspectives in the West, where a woman's age and
tough-mindedness are, unhappily, rarely regarded as
credentials, and the ability to heal has been viewed as satanic
or extranatural.[12]

It should be stressed that Western modes of social analysis
are often inappropriate to people who are neither Western nor
Eastern. Superficial similarities, including fluency in
English, may lull one into thinking that Western measures are
applicable, but there are cases of carefully constructed
research attempts that have yielded bizarre findings. Francis
L.K. Hsu, for example, reports on a study made of Carolinian
and Chamorro children in the 1950s. The children were given a

147

series of projective psychological tests, including the Rorschach and Bender-Gestalt tests, which Bender herself interpreted. The researchers concluded that "either large-scale antisocial behavior with unconscious self-destructive aims or death-like apathy might be expected from the younger generation"--results that have in no way been confirmed during the ensuing 30, years as those children have grown into adulthood.[13]

It becomes clear, then, that in the end, the people best qualified to assess their own status are the women themselves.

General Conclusions

By their own account, Palauan women have high status, high social and economic participation, and a healthy degree of personal power albeit limited participation in the politics of the transitional culture (women are, however, represented in the Palauan congress and at least one important community agency head is a woman). As we've seen, the women are the vital links in the Palauan "chain of giving" that ties the community together economically, socially, and psychologically. Although their status rests in large part on their economic productivity, this is perhaps a necessary but not a sufficient explanation of their power: in some cultures, women's work may keep the family alive and yet be regarded as secondary or inferior.[14]

It is likely, then, that not just economic participation, but a cluster of interlocking factors underlies and perpetuates the Palauan woman's power. A feedback system--a loop--can be identified, in which working hard makes it possible to contribute to customs; the contributions bring with them prestige, and the prestige reinforces the obligation to keep working and giving, since prestige, power, and duty to the extended family are inextricably interwoven. Along with recognition and obligation comes a sense of psychological security and identity: the industrious woman has her solid place in the order of things and credit is given where credit is due. Moreover, although the hierarchical nature of clan society places some limits on social mobility (but at the same time contributes to a secure social identity), the Palauan woman can enhance her social standing through hard work and generosity. Her prestige is therefore not dependent upon marriage (which may be temporary) or children (who may turn out badly). She is burdened, but she is also in control of her sources of self-esteem.

The Ponapean woman's status is far more ambiguous. By their own account, the island women "think low of ourselves" and consider "the man the head, the number one and then the second is the female." The women are expected to be modest, unassuming and domestic, and as the literature on the education of nonwhite, non-middle-class children in the U.S. has so frequently documented, low expectations (by others toward the child) dampen that child's aspirations and chances of achievement. With less education and less access to the cash economy, women have less economic clout and fewer sources of influence and prestige. In contrast to "a Palauan woman is a Palauan man's money," one hears Ponapean men say, "what is most important to a man is land, women, and food." Land is first and a woman's birthright does not entitle her to the land, so marriage is an economic and social necessity. Consequently it is dangerous to be too assertive, too educated, too outward-looking. And yet, Ponapean women are breaking out of these strictures.

Precisely how and why is a legitimate subject for further research. Does the matrilineal heritage--even weakened by the loss of the land--serve as a source of identity and self-esteem? Alice Schlegel suggests:

> It is probably that the importance of the woman as the linking factor in the descent group gives to womanhood a dignity that may

be lacking in societies which do not have
this belief. In psychological terms, this
is saying that in matrilineal societies
there is a cognitive set toward the
importance of women that has an effect in
mitigating male dominance. This is an
intriguing theoretical problem and one that
could be investigated further.[15]

Just how important is matriliny and matrilineal land
inheritance, to the ego-strength of Palauan women? How do
these women reach consensus when they choose a chief or
redistribute food and money? How do Ponapean medicine women
change people's thinking? How do Palauan and Ponapean women
view the range of roles available to American women? These are
questions that we can hope the Micronesian women themselves
will address and answer. To have Micronesian women look
critically at contemporary American women's roles would be an
exciting prospect for several reasons. First, such a study
might bring to the surface our most deeply-embedded,
unconscious assumptions about ourselves and other women, as
ideas about female autonomy, individual ambition, and
relationships to men and children are analyzed and challenged.
Then, too, it would be enlightening to see how American women's
efforts to evolve new social structures are perceived by people
from traditions that have long sanctioned women's economic and
social support networks, multi-parenting (in parts of
Polynesia) and involvement of men in child care (in parts of
Melanesia). Finally, it would be edifying indeed to be given a
model of feminine social and psychological development by women
enculturated into values so different from our own. That model
would certainly not be built on the "deficit approach" that
assumes that women's self-realization is contingent upon

successfully competing with men. Just what the model would be
is a tantalizing question.

Jane Margold
Oakland, California

Donna Bellorado
San Francisco, California

Notes

1. H.G. Barnett, Being A Palauan (New York: Holt, Rinehart and Winston, Inc., 1949, 1960), p. 18.

2. Robert Trumbull, Paradise in Trust (New York: William Sloane Associates, 1959), p. 165.

3. Dale Gumb, "Palau," Micronesian Perspective, 1977, Honolulu, Pacific Islands Research Institute.

4. Roland W. Force, Leadership and Cultural Change in Palau (Chicago: Chicago Natural History Museum, 1960), p. 40.

5. Annette B. Weiner, Women of Value, Men of Renown (Austin: University of Texas Press, 1976).

6. Peggy Sanday, "Female Status in the Public Domain," in Michelle Zimbalist Rosaldo and Louise Lamphere, eds., Woman, Culture & Society (Stanford: Stanford University Press, 1974), p. 192.

7. U.S. Department of Energy, Territorial Energy Assessment (Internal DOE working document, 1981), pp. 54, 57.

8. Gumb, loc. cit.

9. Arthur J. Vidich, Political Factionalism in Palau (New Haven: Pacific Science Board, 1949), cf. R. Force, 1960.

10. U.S. Department of Energy, pp. 103, 105-106.

11. Luelen Bernart, The Book of Luelen, trans. and edited by John L. Fischer, Saul H. Riesenberg and Marjorie G. Whiting (Honolulu: University Press of Hawaii, 1977).

12. Haunani-Kay Trask, "Fighting the Battle of Double Colonization: The View of a Hawaiian Feminist," Unpublished manuscript.

13. Francis L.K. Hsu, Psychological Anthropology (Cambridge, MA: Schenkman Publishing Co., 1972).

14. Claude Levi-Strauss, Tristes Tropiques, trans. by John Russell (New York: Atheneum, 1964.)

15. Alice Schlegel, Male Dominance and Female Autonomy (New Haven: HRAF Press, 1972), pp. 141, 142.

THE SOCIOCULTURAL DYNAMICS OF RURAL
WOMEN'S ORGANIZATIONS IN RAJASTHAN, INDIA[*]

Introduction

As part of the Government of India's efforts to involve
rural women in the development process, attempts are being made
to establish and strengthen women's associations. India's most
recent Five Year Plan states:

> For promoting adequate developmental efforts
> for women at different levels and creating
> needed channels for women to participate
> effectively in decisions that affect their
> lives, grassroot level organizations should
> be promoted.[1]

Local level women's organizations include mahila mandals,
literally "ladies circles," which were originally established
as part of the Community Development Program of the early 1950s
with the intention of providing training and information to
rural women in fields such as nutrition, education, health,
mother and child care, home improvement and adult literacy.[2]

In an effort to ascertain the extent to which mahila
mandals are educating women for involvement in rural
development, I spent 15 months in Rajasthan, a northwestern
state of India, investigating these groups in two villages.[3]
As an anthropologist, I was particularly interested in the
extent to which the local socio-cultural context influenced the
structure, operation and effectiveness of mahila mandals which
have been essentially imposed from outside the village.

---

[*]An earlier version of this paper was presented at 82nd
Annual Meeting of the American Anthropological Association,
November 20, 1983 at Chicago, Illinois.

My intention here is to examine some features of the socio-cultural context within which mahila mandals operate and their impact on the functioning of these groups. Specifically, I note the strength of purdah, kinship and social organization, social and economic stratification, the nature of indigenous women's associations, and the lack of local leaders as having distinct effects on the performance of these groups.

Village Settings

I would first like to describe briefly the two villages where I conducted my research in order to convey some idea of the prevailing physical, cultural and economic conditions. Hathawas[4] is a village located in the Jaipur district, approximately 10 miles west of the capital city of Jaipur. It is easily accessible by a narrow, paved road that is frequently traveled by buses and other forms of public transportation. Close proximity to a major urban center has given Hathawas a number of amenities including: two government schools, electricity, three private health clinics, a cooperative seed store and several water handpumps (an important advantage in a semi-arid[5] region).

The settlement pattern of Hathawas is characterized by a main nuclear village around which a number of smaller subsidiary settlements known as dhani or hamlets[6] are dispersed. These hamlets are populated by land owning castes, primarily Jats and Gujars. The main village is made up of 24 different caste groups (jati). The population of Hathawas excluding the hamlets is 1358. Including the hamlets it is approximately 2500.

There is a difference in the degree and kind of work Hathawas women do depending on caste and economic standing. Among families in which men bring home a regular wage, women are not expected, in fact, are not allowed to seek employment outside the home. Jat and Gujar women who live in the hamlets

are actively engaged in most aspects of agricultural production
in their own family's fields. While all of the Rajput families
in Hathawas owned land, the majority of Rajput women were
secluded within the walls of their compound and did not leave
its confines even to labor on family-owned land. In contrast,
some women of the Raigar caste (a leather-working caste) could
be found engaged in diverse remunerative activities:
agricultural labor, basket and fan making, and construction
work such as the transportation of stone.

The mahila mandal in Hathawas had been functioning for
about a year and was started primarily to give training in
tailoring to women under the central government's TRYSEM
(Training of Rural Youth for Self Employment) program. It
consisted of 15 registered members[7] ranging in age from 17 to
34 years old and one very active unregistered Brahman woman in
her 50s. The women were of six different caste groups
including five low caste members. The training course, held in
a Brahman house, was taught by a tailoring teacher who came
from Jaipur for four hours per day, six days a week, for four
months.

Other group activities were supposed to include: soap and
tooth powder making, cooking demonstrations, learning one's
signature and instruction in "basic knowledge" (learning
answers to questions such as "Who is the Prime Minister of
India?"). The tailoring teacher, with occasional help from the
village nursery school teacher, did teach the women to write
their names. The other activities were under the scope of
duties of the female Village Level Worker (Gram Sevika). She
was supposed to visit the village weekly, but in fact came
infrequently and most of the mahila mandal members could not
recall anything she had taught.

The second village, Minapur, is located in the southern
part of Rajasthan in a sub-humid hilly region approximately 65
miles south of the city of Udaipur. It is more remote and

accessible only by a "fair weather" road serviced by two buses a day. Udaipur district has a large tribal population and in Minapur more than half of the 1775 villagers are adivasis (a term meaning "original inhabitants").

Minapur's settlement pattern is characterized by a separation of the tribal and non-tribal populations. There is a main village consisting of 13 different caste groups. Scattered among the hills surrounding the main village are the dwellings of the tribal population. Although the two groups are separated physically, there is a certain amount of interdependence. The adivasis go to the main village for shopping and for various services (e.g. tailoring), while the villagers, particularly the Patels, a farming caste, depend on the adivasis to supply agricultural labor, firewood and fodder for animals.

The main village of Minapur is electrified, but this service does not extend to the tribal population. There are two primary schools, one serving the tribal population, the other in the main village. Sources of drinkable water are limited to a few widely dispersed wells. The nearest medical resource is a male nurse located about one mile away in the next village and a small hospital is available in the nearest town seven miles from Minapur.

Many adivasi men are employed in military or police service and may be stationed as far away as Kashmir or Bihar. Although these men occasionally visit Minapur and send money to their families (albeit irregularly), the women are generally responsible for the daily decision making and household management in their husband's absence. Consequently, we may regard these as female headed households and approximately 15 percent of adivasi households in Minapur fit into this category.

Tribal men not employed outside the village and tribal women earn a livelihood primarily through agricultural labor, selling wood for fuel, and occasionally working for the Public

Works Department on road construction and repair. Most adivasi families do not own any land other than the small plot directly surrounding their house. This homestead land is usually planted with corn and male and female family members contribute labor to its maintenance. Processing and preparing food are considered female tasks as are animal care, collection of fodder and fuel, water gathering, household cleaning and maintenance, and child care.

The mahila mandal in Minapur is in a state of decline. Sometime around 1980 the female teacher of the tribal primary school was approached by a female extension worker known as a Lady Nutrition Extension Officer (LNEO) and asked to begin a mahila mandal. The teacher agreed and began gathering women together in the late afternoons to teach them literacy skills. All of the members are tribal women who are either relatives or close neighbors of the teacher. Most women were not interested in learning to read and write[8] and, hence attendance was irregular. The women requested tailoring instruction instead so the LNEO at first made an effort to come to the village two or three times a month to teach tailoring, knitting or to talk about health and nutrition. Currently, a few women gather informally on some afternoons at the house of a member who has a sewing machine. Meetings are held also when the LNEO visits, which is now infrequently, perhaps once a month.

Cultural Factors Affecting Mahila Mandals

I have analyzed the following factors which have bearing on the success of government sponsored groups in rural Rajasthan.

Strength of Purdah

Purdah, or female seclusions, sharply curtails women's mobility and denies them the important social resource of being able to interact freely with other women in the community.[9] Unable to associate with other women in their village, secluded women fail to develop an awareness of the potential of group action. Rigorous _purdah_ militates against the formation of strong women's associations.

Purdah in the strictest sense refers to the practice of physically separating females "through the use of boundary markers such as curtains, veils, and walls and also non-physical markers such as teknonymy."[10] The custom of strict _purdah_ among the Rajputs of South Asia is well known and is still evident in Rajasthan. When I first arrived in Hathawas I was surprised that I saw no Rajput women and naively assumed that there were no Rajput families. I was amazed, when in the course of collecting census information, I encountered a fort-like compound containing more than a dozen Rajput families.

It would be inaccurate to say that all rural Rajasthani women are equally secluded. Most rural Rajasthani women practice a variant of _purdah_ known as _ghungat_, described by Sharma[11] as the customary veiling of a married woman before her husband's elder male relatives and most elder males of the village. Concomitant with covering one's face is the understanding that one should remain silent as well. As Sharma points out, _ghungat_ insures that women will be publicly passive and essentially restricts their social effectiveness in public situations.[12] This was clearly exhibited during my first visit to Hathawas when I accompanied a male Block Development Officer (BDO) on an inspection tour of the _mahila mandal_. The members, all married but one, were assembled on a rooftop and the BDO sat before them. The BDO attempted to take attendance and elicit answers to some questions. With the exception of a few shy responses from the unmarried girl, his queries were met with veiled silence.

The degree to which females are segregated and the means by which this is accomplished varies by religion, caste, class and region.[13] Studies which illuminate these differences are important to consider, particularly in the context of women's participation in development activities and groups such as mahila mandals. Rajput women in Hathawas could not participate in mahila mandal activities unless they took place within the walls of the compound to which they were confined. The practice of ghungat by other women of the same village reveals that to some degree all rural Rajasthani women are subjected to codes of modesty which restrict their mobility and limit the possible location of mahila mandals. At least three of the tribal women in the Minapur mahila mandal expressed reluctance at meeting in the house of the female village school teacher fearing that her husband might come home while they were present.

It should be clear at this point that purdah can and does operate to isolate women from other women in the community and the outside world. An alternative view, however, is to see it as a unifying mechanism which fosters alliances among women who reside together, usually female kin. Gender segregation places women in close proximity with one another, and hence, they come to rely on each other.[14] As Pastner suggests, female bonds tend to function similarly to links in a segmentary lineage system. Generally, female kinswomen may be at odds with one another, but band together in a common situation against men.[15] Pastner cites behavioral options available to the women of Panjgur, Baluchistan, that may result in a compromise of men's control. Such behaviors include the withdrawal of sexual favors and refusal to perform domestic duties.[16]

The reason that these female tactics work, according to Pastner, is that males are aware of their dependence of females for maintaining the domestic sphere of society.[17] Ultimately however, we must admit that most women are economically dependent on men and this dependency must limit their degree of influence. Women in rural Rajasthan do work together within the context of the extended family, sharing domestic tasks such as child care and food preparation, but this cooperation may be

a structural consequence, more a result of being at the same
place at the same time than a conscious effort to help one
another. Sharma suggests that "cooperation between women...is
very important, but is 'given' by the structure of household
relations rather than developing spontaneously as a result of
their predicaments as women."[18] The extent to which women
are able to organize themselves both within and outside the
domestic sphere demands an examination of other factors such as
kinship and social organization.

Kinship and Social Organization

An examination of features of social organization may tell
us something about the potential for the emergence and success
of women's groups in an area. In her study of two Ijaw
villages of the Niger Delta, Leis discovered that descent and
inheritance systems, residence rules and polygyny were factors
that operated to bring women together into effective
groups.[19] In Patani, a village in the north, several active
women's associations were in existence. Korokorosei, a village
in the central Delta area, however, contained no active women's
organizations.

The descent system exhibited in Patani is patrilineal.
Residence after marriage is virilocal and each year Patani
women are assured an adequate amount of land to farm which
belongs to their husband's patrilineage. Patani women produce
surplus food which they sell in the market and most are
economically independent of their husbands. Inheritance in
Korokorosei is matrilineal so that rights to land are passed
from mother to daughter. However, residence patterns in
Korokorosei are also virilocal and, after marriage, a woman
might move far from her mother's land. She may also be far from
her husband's mother's land so that she is not assured of a
plot to cultivate each year. Korokorosei women produce for

household consumption only and there is no market available for surplus produce or other goods.[20]

Polygyny exists in both villages. Because Patani co-wives hold equal amounts of land, they are all able to fulfill their food-producing responsibilities. Furthermore, their economic independence frees them from competing for financial aid from their husbands. Korokorosei co-wives however, must find their own landholdings which are inevitably unequal and they are also in competition for their husband's economic resources.[21]

Because Patani women farm land belonging to their husband's patrilineage and inheritance rights are passed on to their children through the children's father, they have much more in common with other women in the residence unit. Korokorosei women however, are less integrated with other women in their area of residence because kin ties and distant farms to which they have rights pull them towards other groups. Membership in women's associations is more common for Patani women who share similar loyalties with women living nearby. Korokorosei women continued to maintain a strong identification with their matrikin and attempts to organize women in the village failed.[22] Leis suggests that in West African societies, "the separation of women from their own kinsmen and incorporation as strangers into a kin group whose members have no other loyalties at least sets the stage for the formation of women's associations."[23] Clearly, a study of such structural features as they relate to the formation of women's associations in various cultural settings would yield valuable information for those interested in utilizing women's organizations in development.

Following Leis' example, we may ask how features of social organization such as kinship, residence and marriage rules, and inheritance rights in rural Rajasthan influence women's formation of or participation in associations. Marriage prescriptions in north India require caste endogamy and village

161

exogamy. Residence after marriage is patrilocal. Women leave their natal village and go to live with their husband's family, often in an extended household. Inheritance rights to property (land) are passed through the male line. Although laws now require that daughters be given a part of their father's estate, in practice, few ever actually receive their share.

As we have seen, the segregation and seclusion of rural Rajasthani women keeps them from associating with other village women. However, what goes on within the context of the extended family? Lamphere[24] suggests that in societies where the domestic and political spheres are integrated, as among the Navajo, women are cooperative with other female kin. There is an egalitarian ethic within the domestic group and society as a whole which emphasizes individual autonomy.[25] Women generally have control over their lives and there is consequently no need to attempt to influence some "authority figure" in the hope of altering one's position. As the same options are generally available to both men and women in obtaining help from others, there is no need to "work through men."[26]

This situation changes in stratified societies where stratification extends to the household level. "The authority structure of the patrilocal, patrilineal extended family, where father has authority over son and husband over wife, brings about conflict rather than cooperation between women in these groups."[27] In India tales of antagonistic relationships between mothers-in-law and daughters-in-law are numerous. Even the bonds that might develop between daughters-in-law are only temporary, as child bearing and differential economic success of husbands tend to create differences and dissension among women. As Lamphere notes, "women's strategies revolve around 'working through men,' either their husbands or their sons."[28] I would suggest that this is particularly true in instances where women are confined primarily to the domestic sphere.

The relationships that exist within the extended family are carried over to wider village relations as Sharma points out, "to a large extent, relations between older and younger women within the village community are modeled on those that exist between them in the household."[29] This pattern was illustrated by one of the lower caste Hathawas women's reference to an older Brahman member as gaon ki saas or village mother-in-law. The two were not related, were not even of the same caste, and yet the younger woman thought of the older woman as a mother-in-law. Kinship, then, strongly influences the pattern of interaction among both kin and non-kin.

Kinship obligations also affect participation of rural women in mahila mandals. Sharing daily domestic tasks is informal among daughters-in-law, but mothers-in-law expect their daughters-in-law to help with everyday work in the house and fields. It is therefore often difficult to involve younger, recently married women in groups such as mahila mandals. In Hathawas one mother-in-law frequently came by to collect her daughter-in-law before the tailoring class was over.

Indigenous Informal Women's Associations

As noted earlier, women in an extended household help each other with daily domestic tasks. While it is possible, as Dixon suggests, that "girls who work together on a regular, cooperative basis may well develop strong bonds of solidarity,"[30] the network that forms may be limited in the type of help it can render its members. As Sharma states, "there are limitations to the kinds of positive help that women can give each other" which may prevent them from banding together as an "effective group."[31] However, the importance of the support that women can give each other must be recognized. At this point, it is appropriate to consider the seminal work of March and Taqqu[32] on informal women's associations.

Unlike formal organizations, informal organizations lack a legal recognition and the boundaries, membership and hierarchies are less distinct.[33] Kinship, residence patterns, and women's work patterns "represent the most fundamental bases for association and shared world views among women, and are often widely accepted among the men and women of a society as principles for association."[34] These principles should give us a basic understanding of what constitutes informal women's associations. With these criteria in mind, it becomes clear that informal associations of women do exist in rural Rajasthan. To discern the nature of these associations and place them in a development context, it is important to review March and Taqqu's discussion of active and defensive associations.

These authors distinguish between defensive and active women's groups. Informal associations may be classified as defensive if they are based on alliances formed as a response to daily and/or periodic crises and hardships. Defensive associations of women represent attempts of a disadvantaged group to utilize whatever resources they have, e.g., labor, emotional support, or material resources, to meet the needs of its members.[35] In contrast to defensive associations which respond to emergencies as they arise, active women's associations _pursue_ actions directed towards specific objectives. Through active informal associations women are often able to amass material resources and to develop leadership abilities and organizational skills which allow them to reduce their dependence on men, alleviate some constraints operating against them and hence, effect change.[36]

The distinction between active and defensive informal associations is an important one because it determines the extent to which such groups are "receptive to development interventions."[37] According to March and Taqqu, women's associations that utilize defensive strategies are not appropriate for the intervention of development programs. The strength of defensive tactics rests in their flexibility, and in the resourcefulness that emerges in response to a particular crisis. I would suggest that such strategies are developed and work best outside public scrutiny or, "invisibly." Intervention in these associations risks undermining women's ability to cope successfully with scarcity and hardship while at the same time offering no appropriate alternative. As March and Taqqu point out, "The poorest of the world's poor cannot sustain such well-intentioned but ill-conceived assaults on their meager defenses."[38]

Informal women's organizations which pursue active strategies may or may not be appropriate for the introduction of development schemes. Generally, "the more explicitly the purposes of any particular informal association are focused upon economic or political objectives within the community, the greater its potential role in planned change."[39] Those associations of women that insure an equal distribution of productive resources and decision making among its members are most likely the best suited for development intervention.[40]

Given the nature of activities women perform together and the type of help that they can offer each other, the informal associations of rural Rajasthani women are defensive ones. Unlike areas of Western Africa, Latin America and Southeast Asia where we find active rotating credit associations, market women's cooperatives, mutual aid societies and so forth,[41] such visible and instrumental ("active") associations of women are lacking in rural Rajasthan. Women within a household help each other in daily situations. One woman may watch another's children while the mother takes a bath, for example. Women also depend on female kin at special times such as marriage and birth. When asked who they would call to help them during a marriage, Minapur women said their daughters and husband's brother's wives. In Hathawas, during a marriage in the household where I resided, neighbors lent utensils so that food for guests could be prepared and females of the same caste came to help with the preparation. The aid that women offer each other can be counted on, but is not strictly accounted for, i.e., it is based on informal principles of reciprocity.

Related females are bound more strictly by kinship obligations as noted above. During the final stages of the tailoring program in Hathawas, the sister of one of the members gave birth to a baby in another village. The mahila mandal member was called away to the village to help. The tailoring teacher argued that she should stay, finish the course, and attend the final meeting where she would receive a sewing machine. In this case, there was a conflict between group participation and fulfilling a kinship obligation. In the end, the woman left to help her sister, but returned to be present at the distribution of sewing machines. The meetings she missed were ignored by the sympathetic tailoring teacher.

Lack of Local Leaders

Lack of local female leadership is also prevalent in rural Rajasthan. Village women's organizations cannot be strengthened or vitalized unless there is a woman who is dedicated enough to see that meetings were convened, and who can act as a spokesperson and liaison between the women of the group and the female village level workers. In neither mahila mandal did I find any woman willing to assume a leadership role.

This reluctance to take a leadership position may in part reflect the unwillingness of rural women to risk losing their defensive network for an uncertain new association. In her study of two villages in Himachal Pradesh and Punjab, Ursula Sharma wrote that she found "a real dislike among women of taking any role of leadership or authority over women beyond the roles already written into the kinship structure of the household."[42] Since female neighbors do occasionally elicit help from one another at times of marriage, to borrow utensils, etc., asserting authority over a neighbor risks disturbing the "informal reciprocity" that exists.[43] One woman who normally convened the mahila mandal in a large village I visited said that she encountered difficulties when she asked for small donations from members to help buy equipment or materials as the women suspected she would keep the money for herself. The mahila mandal members believed that she was receiving money from the government when, in fact, her position was voluntary. Consequently, even those women who are potential leaders might be reluctant to assert influence for fear of arousing suspicion, and perhaps alienation from their neighbors.

Low levels of education among rural Rajasthani women may contribute to the dearth of local leadership. Figures from the 1971 Census indicate a literacy rate of 4.03 percent for rural Rajasthani women.[44] This is the lowest female literacy rate of any state in India. Rajasthan also exhibits one of the highest levels of disparity between male and female literacy rates in India.[45] Lack of participation in the formal school system limits the development of a female populace trained and confident to take up leadership positions, but formal education alone should not be taken as the sole criterion for leadership. There may be illiterate village women whose personal attributes make them well suited to be leaders.

Recognizing the importance of tapping local leadership, efforts in India have been made to work with local women who seem to have the ability to gather women together. They have been called gram kakis or village aunties. The gram kakis chosen by government officials to convene women may, however, exhibit leadership qualities by a Western definition. We must ask what it is that is getting the job of leadership done in rural Rajasthan, i.e., what shape leadership takes among women themselves. There is stratification within the household in rural India as we have seen. Some women, notably mothers-in-law, do have a degree of authority over their daughters-in-law. One indigenous "model" of leader/follower appears to be the mother-in-law/daughter-in-law relationship. Would it be possible to find an older, well-liked and respected woman, a gaon ki saas (village mother-in-law) to fill a leadership position? It is curious that relations within the household may be extended beyond it, but the authority role appears not to have been removed from the domestic sphere. Further studies of cultural concepts of leadership as well as attributes of successful local female leaders would be helpful.[46]

Social and Economic Stratification

Even if women are allowed relative freedom to move about the community, interactions are often influenced by other factors such as caste and economic relations. In Hathawas, low caste people were restricted to the use of two water handpumps. The well is often cited as one area where women can congregate, but such was not the case in Hathawas where women of high and low castes did not associate with one another. In addition, households within a given community are linked by economic relations. Male and female members of some households provided labor for wealthier families in both villages I studied.

The social and economic stratification systems influence group participation and interaction among participants. In Hathawas, the mahila mandal met at a Brahman house. This posed no problem for members participating in the tailoring program. However, an occasional activity included cooking demonstrations. Since these demonstrations were held in a Brahman house, low caste women were prohibited from participating due to cultural rules of purity and pollution.

Some studies of mahila mandals have pointed out that they tend to be dominated by middle caste or landowning castes[47] and have not met the needs of lower caste women. The caste system in rural Rajasthan is still strong and studies have revealed that the location of mahila mandal activities will have bearing on the caste composition of its members. Seth[48] notes that when mahila mandal meetings are held in buildings located in low caste areas, the majority of members are of low castes, since high caste women are not supposed to venture into low caste areas.

That most mahila mandals appear dominated by elite castes may be related to economic conditions and work schedules of women. In Hathawas many men worked in jobs outside the village. Their wives remained in the village and did not work outside the household (39.34 percent of Hathawas women did domestic work only. This figure excludes agricultural work). The majority of these women belonged to middle and upper castes. After their morning work was done, some did have leisure time available to sew or gossip with other women. Lower caste Hathawas women however, were involved in extra non-domestic work such as agricultural labor and construction work. The most frequent absentees from the tailoring program in Hathawas were two women of a leather-working caste (considered "untouchable") who worked as agricultural laborers. In Minapur, although all members of the mahila mandal were tribal, there were some economic differences between the women. At least one member was hired by the family of two others for agricultural and other occasional labor. Those who participated most frequently were economically better off. The husband of one, for example, was a Subinspector of Police. They were able to hire agricultural labor to help at peak periods.

Impact on Mahila Mandals

As noted above, village women who have free time. do occasionally gather at times to gossip or sing. Mahila mandals originally were conceived of as a way to "tap this nonformal gathering."[49] Some mahila mandals did start as bhajan mandals, i.e., as associations of women who gathered together to sing bhajans (religious songs). The activities of these groups were later diversified to include programs consonant with the goals of the Community Development Program. Such instances of utilizing indigenous groups are rare, however. Instead, most mahila mandals have been imported from outside, and set up specifically as vehicles through which development programs can be implemented. This approach may have some positive aspects. For instance, setting up new organizations may leave the existing "defensive" informal women's associations intact and able to perform their functions. However, groups that have been organized based on some model developed outside the village, and which strive to meet externally imposed goals through programs planned at the central level will be influenced by the prevailing socio-cultural and economic conditions of the area. I have outlined some of the factors above and here will summarize the impact that they have had on the structure, operation and ultimate success of mahila mandals in the two villages I observed.

In examining the structure of mahila mandals I focused on the interactions and relationships between the participants. I was concerned with whether or not these reflected the pattern of relations (social structure) of rural Rajasthan. Could the principles of kinship organization, caste system and economic relations that obtained between women in the village be seen in the interactions among the participants of the mahila mandals? With some qualification, the answer is basically yes.

As we have seen, kinship greatly influenced the manner in which women interacted with one another. In addition to the instance already cited in which a lower caste woman referred to an older Brahman woman as a "village mother-in-law," there were other Hathawas cases where women applied kinship terms to other members to whom they were not consanguineally or affinally related. Thus, one woman spoke of another of the same caste as being like a devrani (husband's younger brother's wife). When asked if she knew any of the women before joining the mahila mandal, one Kumhar (potter) woman replied, "I did not know anyone before, because I am a newlywed. Sushila is like a jethani [husband's elder brother s wife]. Manfuli is like a jethani also. Sita is like a nanand [husband's sister]."[50] Only one woman was of the same caste as the speaker. Thus, fictive, if not actual, kinship ties defined how women interacted with one another.

Economic relations linked some members of both mahila mandals. In discussing her relationship to the other women in the group, one Hathawas woman of a lower caste said the following: "I knew them all before [joining the mahila mandal] because they are all in the same village....We take pots from the Kumhar's house. My husband does labor work at the Brahman's house so I know them. Others I know from coming and going with them." She saw her relationship to others primarily in economic terms. There were those who provided goods and services (in this case water pots) and those for whom she and her family provided labor.

In Minapur women did not refer to each other as kin, but one member did suggest that they were all jati bhai (caste brothers). In all cases Minapur mahila mandal members said that they knew all the others because they lived near, or were of the same village. I was interested in determining whether or not women felt they were making any friends (saheli) with other women of the group, whether any different types of links

might be evolving that would bind the women together. I
thought that perhaps women meeting in an informal setting might
lead to friendships which would form the basis for solidarity.
One young married Brahman woman did say that she had made
friends with another newly married woman who had just moved to
the village. All others said that they had not made any
friends.

The women in both mahila mandals recognize that they are
sister villagers, but the social, economic and kinship
relations that exist among them have not been overridden by any
sense of group solidarity. To the extent that no group
consciousness has emerged, that women do not feel equal to
others as members of a group, these mahila mandals continue to
mirror the traditional social structure rather than act in any
way to alter it. An awareness of group and the efficacy of
group action is critical if rural women's organizations are to
be effective.

To be fair, I must qualify this in one respect. In
Hathawas the mahila mandal did consist of women of different
castes, both high and those considered "untouchable." There
was no segregation of castes. Women of high and low castes did
sit next to one another and talk to one another. There was no
discrimination on the part of the tailoring teacher who
answered questions of all women and helped each in her turn.
This is not to say that caste distinctions were abolished--none
of the low caste women entered the kitchen of the Brahman
house, for example. However, the mahila mandal did provide a
sort of "time out," a place where women of different castes did
sit, and for a time at least, interact relatively freely with
each other.

Impact on Operation

In this section I would briefly like to note how some of
the socio-cultural factors that have been mentioned have

bearing on the operation of mahila mandals in terms of time, location and relevance of activities.

Cultural codes of modesty for women, manifested in such practices as ghungat and strict seclusion of females, limit the mobility of women and impinge upon the possible location and time of mahila mandal activities. Women who are confined to a compound cannot participate in activities that take place outside its walls. Recognition of the hectic daytime schedules of women has led to the suggestion that literacy classes and other development activities be held at night. In Minapur, particularly, where women must come from isolated homesteads, travel at night is forbidden.

In addition, restricted mobility also affects the extent to which activities are relevant or not. Much has been written about the need to teach women income generating skills as a means to achieve economic independence. Given the fact that most rural Rajasthani women are rarely allowed to venture out of the village, the most useful programs initially will be those that will allow women to earn an income at home or within the village itself.

Cultural values associated with purity and pollution altered participation in cooking demonstrations held in Hathawas by excluding low caste women. Cultural concepts of purity and pollution and values associated with Hinduism (or other religions) would certainly affect participation in particular programs: midwifery (the birth process is considered polluting), and poultry rearing (orthodox Hindus eat neither poultry or eggs) are examples.

Successful operation of mahila mandals demands that the time of various activities be compatible with the daily and seasonal work schedules of women. In Hathawas, the tailoring program was held between 12:00 P.M. and 4:00 P.M. Most women found this time suitable as it allowed them to finish their morning domestic work and return home in time to begin the evening's work. One of the complaints that surfaced while talking to members of the Minapur group was that there was no set time when they were supposed to meet. When the LNEO arrived in the village it was expected that the women drop what they were doing and attend the meeting. Some expressed a desire for a fixed time or advance notice so other arrangements could be made for the completion of the tasks.

Mahila Mandals and Women in Development

The primary goal of India's most recent Five Year Plan is the alleviation of poverty.[51] It is the task of local level organizations, including mahila mandals, to offer villagers remunerative skill training that will allow them to earn independent incomes. The Sixth Five Year Plan notes that, "Mahila Mandals and other voluntary agencies would be encouraged to take up socio-economic programmes for providing wages and self-employment in rural areas."[52] Mahila mandals are regarded as institutions for combatting rural poverty and hence, form an integral part of India's current development schemes. There has also been a move toward decentralization so that, ultimately, villagers will assume responsibility for their own development. Participation in local level organizations[53] is the key to involving the rural population in the development process. In this section I will briefly discuss the extent to which mahila mandals are meeting the objectives set forth for them by the Indian government.

Some studies have suggested one reason for the low levels of participation and lack of success of mahila mandals is that the programs are not especially relevant.[54] As we have seen, socio-cultural factors influence the degree to which programs are perceived as beneficial to rural women. Many of the programs implemented through mahila mandals have been aimed at women as housewives and mothers. Unfortunately, this approach ignores the other roles rural women may have as animal caretakers, and agricultural workers for instance. As Kelkar states "most of these housewife improvement programmes have proved a failure because they are irrelevant to the needs of women in subsistence agriculture and are unable to augment women's income in any way."[55]

One of the most popular training programs offered by mahila mandals is tailoring. Tailoring is an attractive program to both village women and government officials, but for different reasons. Village women value the skill because they believe it makes unmarried girls better marriage prospects, and married women better wives and mothers if they can sew clothes for their husbands and children. Government officials identify tailoring as an income generating activity. Tailoring and other remunerative skill training schemes however, have frequently failed due to a lack of follow-up services such as the provision of raw materials, credit and market opportunities.[56] Six months after the TRYSEM program in Hathawas ended, one woman had sold her sewing machine and another had begun to pay to have her clothes made. The village itself could not generate enough tailoring work to keep all the women earning from sewing and the women were not put in contact with external markets.

The Block Development Officer and Gram Sevika of Hathawas suggested other income generating projects including the production of soap, tooth powder and hair oil. These items can be produced at home or within the village, therefore, they are appropriate as items to be manufactured under income generating programs for rural Rajasthani women. However, without research on availability of market opportunities, and without establishing links to these markets and sources of raw material and credit, any income generating scheme for women in rural north India will fail. In addition, skill training programs must be combined with educational programs that illustrate the possible applications of such skills. In the instance of tailoring programs, in both mahila mandals I studied, there was a gap between the goals of the government and the perceptions of the village women. Most women saw tailoring as a way to save money by stitching clothes for their children and themselves, while the government regarded tailoring as an income earning skill. This difference in perception is an important one and has contributed, in part, to the failure of mahila mandals to effect economic change.

There was a great deal of difference in the degree of awareness about the existence and activities of the mahila mandals between Hathawas and Minapur. The nuclear settlement pattern of Hathawas was more conducive to a rapid spread of information. In Minapur, on the other hand, awareness of the mahila mandal was confined to its few participants. Even the sarpanch (elected head of the local level council) was not aware of its existence. There was widespread agreement in Hathawas that the mahila mandal was beneficial. The participants noted that they had the benefit of learning tailoring and getting a sewing machine. Some did sense the inherent value of learning something new, but there was no systematic effort to teach others their newly acquired skills. After the tailoring courses ended, mahila mandal attendance ceased almost entirely. When the next meeting was called in Hathawas, only three women were present. Both participants and non-participants acknowledge that a mahila mandal is helpful for women, but these new associations have not come to be valued to the extent that they are being perpetuated by the village women themselves after the conclusion of a particular government program.

Although it is a stated objective of the government to have villagers take responsibility for their own development through participation in local level organizations, mahila mandals have not met this goal. In Minapur and Hathawas, there has been no change in the level of consciousness among members about social, economic and political conditions or about what they can do to alter their situation. A frequent reply of Minapur women to almost any question was a resigned "What can we do?" Part of the problem is that the village level workers who are involved with local associations are inadequately trained and are not capable of inspiring in rural women a "critical consciousness."[57] The participatory strategies of rural development applied in the context of adult education,[58] for example, have not been incorporated into the establishment and strengthening of government-initiated mahila mandals.

These associations are not active ones as defined by March and Taqqu. To date, they have been politically impotent. The sarpanch of Hathawas said that there was no connection between the panchayat (village level council) and the mahila mandal, suggesting that horizontal links between mahila mandals and local level political institutions are absent. In the two cases I studied, mahila mandal members did not offer, nor were they solicited for, input into village political decisions. The potential of group action for effecting social change and influencing the local political process is clear. There have been instances where members of village women's groups have successfully censured male distillers of alcohol and habitual drinkers.[59] I have heard from the participants of a case in a southern Rajasthani village where women successfully blocked construction of a water handpump in an area of the village that they did not feel was convenient. Such examples illustrate the efficacy of group action and lend support to the government's efforts to organize women at the village level. The key component absent in most mahila mandals is an awareness of the potential power of group action by the members themselves. Mehra[60] suggests that mahila mandals have been the targets of a welfare oriented approach with women as passive beneficiaries rather than as active participants in the development process.

Mahila _mandals_ have too often become the end itself rather than a means to the end, that is, development.[61]

Janice S. Hyde
Syracuse University

1. Government of India, Sixth Five Year Plan (1980-1985) (New Delhi: Government of India, 1981), p. 425.

2. Committee on the Status of Women, Towards Equality (New Delhi: Government of India, 1974), p. 333.

3. Research was conducted from September 1981-December 1982. Funding was made possible by a Fulbright-Hays Doctoral Dissertation Research Abroad grant (1981-1982) and a Shell International Research Studies Fellowship (1982-1983).

4. The two names used in this paper, Hathawas and Minapur, are pseudonyms.

5. The typology of ecological regions was taken from B.L.C. Johnson, India: Resources and Development (London: Heinemann Educational Books, 1979), pp. 50 52.

6. For a fuller discussion of dhani composition, see Pauline Kolenda, "Sibling-Set Marriage, Collateral-Set Marriage, and Deflected Alliance Among Annana Jats of Jaipur District, Rajasthan," in American Studies in the Anthropology of India, ed. Sylvia Vatuk (New Delhi: Manohar, 1978), pp. 242-277. I have borrowed the translation of dhani, namely hamlet," from Kolenda.

7. A woman could be a registered member if her family was eligible for a loan from the District Rural Development Agency (supposedly only the neediest families) and if her name had been written down when a female village level worker asked if she wanted to join. These women received stipends from the government and sewing machines at the end of the course. The number of registered members was limited to 15. Other women could join the mahila mandal as non-registered members to learn tailoring, but would not receive a sewing machine or stipend arranged by the government.

8. The literacy rate for females in Minapur over 5 years of age is 10.29 percent. The literacy rate for adivasi females is 9 percent.

9. Ruth Dixon, "The Roles of Rural Women: Female Seclusion, Economic Production and Reproductive Choice," in Population and Development: The Search for Selective Alternatives, ed. Ronald Ridker (Baltimore: John Hopkins University Press, 1976); Patricia Jeffrey, Frogs in a Well: Indian Women in Purdah (London: Zed Press, 1979); Hanna Papanek and Gail Minault, eds., Separate Worlds: Studies in Purdah in South Asia (Columbia, Missouri: South Asia Books, 1982).

10. Barbara Miller, "Female Labor Participation and Female Seclusion in Rural India: A Regional View," Economic Development and Cultural Change 30 (July 1982):777-794.

11. Ursula Sharma, "Women and Their Affines: The Veil as a Symbol of Separation," Man 13 (June 1978):218-233.

12. Ibid., p. 227.

13. Papanek and Minault.

14. Carol McC. Pastner, "Accommodations to Purdah: The Female Perspective," Journal of Marriage and the Family 36 (May 1974):408-414.

15. Ibid., p. 412.

16. Ibid, p. 411.

17. Ibid.

18. Ursula Sharma, "Segregation and its Consequences in India: Rural Women in Himachal Pradesh," in Women United, Women Divided: Cross-Cultural Perspectives on Female Solidarity, ed. Patricia Caplan and Janet Buira (London: Tavistock Publications, 1978), pp. 259-282.

19. Nancy Leis, "Women in Groups: Ijaw Women's Associations," in Woman, Culture and Society, ed. Michelle Rosaldo and Louise Lamphere (Stanford, California: Stanford University Press, 1974), pp. 223-242.

20. Ibid.

21. Ibid., p. 233.

22. Ibid.

23. Ibid., p. 240.

24. Louise Lamphere, "Strategies, Cooperation, and Conflict Among Women in Domestic Groups," in Woman, Culture and Society, ed. Michelle Rosaldo and Louise Lamphere (Stanford, California: Stanford University Press, 1974), pp. 97-112.

25. Ibid. For another discussion of women's place in both egalitarian and non-egalitarian societies see Eleanor Leacock, "Women's Status in Egalitarian Society: Implications for Social Evolution," Current Anthropology 19 (June 1978):247 255.

26. Lamphere, p. 103.

27. Ibid., p. 105.

28. Ibid.

29. Sharma, "Segregation and Consequences," p. 277.

30. Dixon, p. 307.

31. Sharma, "Segregation and Consequences," p. 278.

32. Kathryn March and Rachelle Taqqu, Women's Informal Associations and the Organizational Capacity for Development, Rural Development Committee Monograph Series, no. 5 (Ithaca, New York: Center for International Studies, 1982).

33. Ibid., p. 30.

34. Ibid.

35. Ibid., pp. 39-40.

36. Ibid., pp. 48-49.

37. Ibid., p. 39.

38. Ibid., p. 40.

39. Ibid., p. 49.

40. Ibid., p. 52, see their Figure 1.

41. Shirley Ardener, "The Comparative Study of Rotating Credit Associations," Journal of the Royal Anthropological Institute of Great Britain and Ireland 94 (July to December 1964):201-229; Kenneth Little, African Women in Towns: An

Aspect of Africa's Social Revolution (London: Cambridge University Press, 1973), see especially Chapter 4; Nancy Hafkin and Edna Bay, eds., Women in Africa: Studies in Social and Economic Change (Stanford, California: Stanford University Press, 1976); Marion Misch and Joseph Margolin, Rural Women's Groups as Potential Change Agents: A Study of Columbia, Korea and the Philippines, Report submitted to USAID (Washington, D.C., 1975).

42. Ursula Sharma, Women, Work and Property in North-West India (London: Tavistock Publications, 1980).

43. Ibid.

44. Government of India, Census of India 1971, Part I, General Report (New Delhi: Government of India, 1972).

45. David Sopher, "Sex Disparity in Indian Literacy," in An Exploration of India: Geographical Perspectives on Society and Culture, ed. David Sopher (Ithaca, New York: Cornell University Press, 1980), pp. 130-188.

46. For a discussion of types of female leaders in an urban resettlement colony see Diane Ashley Per-Lee, "Employment, Ingenuity and Family Life: Rajasthani Women in Delhi, India" (Ph.D. dissertation, American University, 1981), Chapter 7. See also Virginia Shrivastava, "Nonformal Education Programmes for Women in Indian Villages: A Study of Social Change and Leadership Patterns" (Ph.D. dissertation, University of Toronto, 1980) for a discussion of rural nonformal education "teacher-leaders."

47. T.K. Oommen, "Mahila Mandals in Rural Delhi," Social Welfare 16 (August 1969):11-12, Govind Kelkar, "The Impact of the Green Revolution on Women's Work Participation and Sex Roles," paper prepared for International Labour Office Tripartite Asian Regional Seminar, Rural Development and Women, Mahabaleshwar, India, 6-11 April 1981.

48. Mridula Seth, "Working With Rural Women," Social Welfare 23 (March 1977):29-30+.

49 D. Paul Choudhry, personal communication, National Institute of Public Cooperation and Child Development, New Delhi, May 10, 1982.

50. All personal names used are pseudonyms.

51. Government of India, Sixth Plan, p. 32.

52. Ibid., p. 425.

53. Local level institutions include women's circles (mahila mandals), youth clubs (yuwak mandals), and development clubs (vikas mandals). There were no youth clubs or development clubs in Hathawas or Minapur. I did encounter one youth club in a village in Udaipur district made up of 22 males who were supposed to be involved in local development work. The activities, however, consisted of running a small lending library and volleyball.

54. Mumtaz Ali Khan and Noor Aysha, Status of Rural Women in India: A Study of Karnataka (New Delhi: Uppal Publishing, 1982); S.P. Jain and V. Krishnamurthy Reddy, Role of Women in

Rural Development: A Study of Mahila Mandals (Hyderabad: National Institute of Rural Development, 1979), p. 72; Seth, p. 30.

55. Kelkar, p. 40.

56. Rekha Mehra, "Rural Development Programmes: Neglect of Women," in Women and Rural Transformation, Two Studies, ed. Rekha Mehra and K. Saradamoni (New Delhi: Concept Publishing, 1983).

57. This term is taken from Paulo Friere, Pedagogy of the Oppressed, trans. Myra Bergman Ramos (New York: Seabury Press, 1970).

58. For discussions of participatory research strategies, see Max Powdermilk and W. Robert Laitos, "Towards a Participatory Strategy for Integrated Rural Development," Rural Sociology 46 (Winter 1981):688-702; Marja Lisa Swantz, "Research as an Educational Tool for Development," Convergence 8 (Number 2, 1975):44-53; and Budd Hall, "Participatory Research: An Approach for Change," Convergence 8 (Number 2, 1975):24-32.

59. Kunwar Prasun and Bharat Dogra, "Village Women Unite to Discipline Men," Roshini (January-March 1981):29-30.

60 Mehra, op. cit.

61. Shanti Chakravorty, personal communication, Ministry of Agriculture and Rural Reconstruction, New Delhi, August 18, 1982.

FEMALE STATUS AND ACTION
IN TWO DAYAK COMMUNITIES

The Kenyah Dayaks live in the Interior of East Kalimantan in Indonesian Borneo. They live primarily by shifting cultivation, supplemented by male wage labour and by hunting and gathering in the surrounding rainforest. Their technological repertoire is exceedingly simple. In contrast to their "underdeveloped" technology, the comparatively egalitarian relations between the sexes in this group are such as to elicit admiration and envy from many Western feminists.

The purpose of this analysis is to make explicit some of the critical components of what so often has been called, vaguely, "status." Kahn, in discussing his work among the matrilineal Minangkabau of West Sumatra, concludes that:

> It would be almost impossible, therefore, to make any definite statement about the relative "status" of Minangkabau women because of the impossibly subjective nature of the concept.[1]

I would argue that the difficulty in assessing such relative status lies, not in any inherent subjectivity, but rather in the complexity of the issue. The many components of Kenyah Dayak life that have a bearing on women's status are considered here for two main purposes:

First, a better understanding of a comparatively egalitarian system may help the rest of us to structure aspects of our own lives in a more egalitarian fashion. Second (and more important, in my view), effective Third World development must include the active involvement of women; the creativity, imagination and commitment of women must be tapped just as surely as must that of men. A clarification of the high status and effective action of Kenyah women may serve to dispel some inaccurate assumptions and stereotypes about the inherent passivity and subordination of "traditional" women.

From September 1979 to September 1980, I lived and worked in the hinterlands of East Kalimantan, Indonesia among the Kenyah Dayaks. My research--part of a Man and Biosphere project entitled "Interactions Between People and Forests in East Kalimantan"--was conducted principally in two communities: Long Ampung and Long Segar. Rather than focusing on one community or the other as a unit of analysis, however, the research was planned and conducted around specific problematic human actions.[2, 3] Participant observation was the fundamental method. More specific, focused, quantitative studies were undertaken as deemed relevant and practical, given local circumstances. The active role women took in agricultural activity--one of the main interactions between people and forests in the area--prompted me to look closely at the actions of women. This led naturally into investigation of female status, sex roles, power, and other such thorny arenas.

In this regard I supplemented my understanding based on participant observation with a survey of all adult women in the two Dayak communities: Long Ampung and Long Segar. Long Ampung is a community of approximately 500 people, living a quite traditional, riverine lifestyle in an extremely remote part of Borneo. They practice an apparently benign form of shifting cultivation, dominated slightly by women. The men make periodic, difficult journeys out of the community to procure salt, cloth, iron pots, and other things not available locally. All the people have been Christian since the mid-1960s, coming from an animist tradition. Headhunting, penis-piercing, tatooing, and elongated earlobes represent the most exotic components of their tradition. They still live in longhouses.

Long Segar is a daughter village of Long Ampung. Located only two days and two nights by longboat from the provincial capital (Samarinda), where trade goods, medicine, education, chainsaws, ricehullers, and assorted amenities of modern life are much more readily available. The Long Segar community was a part of a formal (ex post facto) Government Resettlement project, and had access to a variety of governmental resources (teachers, implements, seeds, training, and so on) between 1972 and 1980. The approximately 1000 inhabitants of Long Segar are Christian; practice shifting cultivation; and engage in periodic male circular migration. These Dayaks first came to Long Segar in 1963, and continued migrating from Long Ampung until 1972 when the influx was halted by the Government. They have made numerous changes in their lifestyle since they came to Long Segar.

I lived in Long Segar for ten months, and in Long Ampung for one month. The survey mentioned earlier was conducted by my field assistant and myself, in the Kenyah language, by means of interviews. The interview schedule was tested and revised twice during my seventh month of residence in Long Segar, and the final wording and content of the questions were unambiguous and appropriate to Long Segar conditions. Because of Long Ampung's remoteness pretesting was impossible; but only small revisions, discussed in the text, were necessary for the Long Ampung context.

The definition of "adult women" for purposes of this study was any woman who was married, who had a child, or was generally perceived to be old enough to have married or had children. Women in the latter category were identified as appropriate interviewees by their being addressed as "Tinen So-and-So" (Mother of So-and-So).[*] Adults who are not yet

---

[*]Kenyah naming customs are very complex. But one's birth name is dropped once one has a child. Women become Tinen So-and-So (name of firstborn) and men become Tamen So-and-So. They retain these names until one of their children (and to some extent, other relatives) dies, at which point they are

married, and do not have children may call themselves and be addressed as the mother and father of some child they particularly like. I took this to mean general acceptance of their adult status, and interviewed such women accordingly. The reliability of actual age data are questionnable since the Kenyah have little interest in the topic. Approximate ages ranged from 15 to 65.

The fact that I surveyed only women, in this case, represents a methodological decision that I consider, in retrospect, to have been unfortunate. Although time constraints had some bearing on this decision, the crux of it was a noble concern to "right the imbalance" in data available on women as opposed to men. With the benefit of hindsight, I am impressed with the degree to which this analysis could have been improved had I collected comparable data from the men. Male responses would have allowed a useful and probably illuminating comparison between the views of women and men on the topics addressed here. In future, I intend to respond to this bias with balance rather than a reverse imbalance.

The Conceptual Framework

Because of the complexity and general lack of agreement about such terms as women's status, power, prestige, authority, and sex roles, I took a rather eclectic approach to this analysis. The "suggestive" and "tentative" analytical framework put forth in 1978 by Susan Rogers can serve to place Kenyah society in the broader realm of sexual differentiation. Rogers identified two kinds of sex differentiation: ideological and behavioral,[4] and she specifies four possible

---

called by a name determined by the birth order of the child who died, usually followed by their own original name. Another name change occurs when a person attains the status of grandparent.

permutations: 1) societies which are sexually differentiated ideologically and behaviorally, 2) those which are differentiated behaviorally but not ideologically, 3) those which are not differentiated in either way, and 4) those which are differentiated ideologically but not behaviorally. She considers the first two possibilities to be "most worthy of ethnographic investigation" but considers the third and fourth to:

> entail the breakdown of sex roles, and so...[to be]...out of the scope of the study of sexual differentiation. Furthermore, it is unclear if either of them actually does or can exist. They are, however, present in several utopian schemes, and are therefore possible at least within the realm of imagination.[5]

I would like to explore the degree to which Kenyah sexual differentiation approaches the third category. Elsewhere, I have discussed the minimal amount of sexual differentiation-- both behavioral and ideological--among the Kenyah.[6] In agreement with Rogers' point above, I consider traditional Kenyah society to be neither utopian, nor a manifestation of a "breakdown in sex roles." In fact, the situation in Long Segar, a community in transition, seems more one of rigidifying what were very fluid sex roles in response to wider socioeconomic trends (like the greater use of money) and contact with less egalitarian ethnic groups. The following description and analysis are loosely divided into public and private domains.

Women In The Public Domain

In a pilot study of twelve societies, Sanday[7] was able to order, using Guttman scaling procedures, the following four dimensions into a continuously scaled measure of female status in the public domain: 1) Female material control, 2) demand for female produce, 3) female political participation, and 4) female solidarity groups devoted to female political or economic interests. For purposes of comparison, I have organized the following material in a manner that loosely conforms to her schema.

If we look at the data on Long Segar and Long Ampung, we find ample indication that women control material things, and that there is demand for what women produce. Women regularly collect and/or produce and dispose of agricultural goods. They regularly make baskets, beadwork, sunhats, and other useful items, and dispose of them as they see fit--giving, trading, or selling their products, depending on the context. In any attempt to secure a possession of this kind the would-be buyer is inevitably directed to the producer, regardless of sex.

Long Ampung and Long Segar contexts differ in one very significant way. In Long Ampung, there is very little use of money; whereas in Long Segar almost anything can be converted to that medium of exchange. I did not observe a significant difference in people's attitudes and behavior with regard to women's control over the products they grew or created in the two communities, but a probably insidious difference had emerged in the comparative value placed on female as opposed to male products by the outside world. The introduction, on a major scale, of money meant that in Long Segar men suddenly had much better access to a "good" than did women. It also happened, as is often the case, that men's labor was valued more highly by the larger society than was women's--bringing higher wages for a manday than for a womanday of work. Although sufficient time for the implications of this change to emerge fully has not elapsed, there are a number of indications that this change is not in women's best interests, relative to men.

Women's involvement in commerce can be seen as an indicator of at least partial control over produce, and it may be reflective of demand as well, since among the Kenyah, people normally sell what they have produced or gathered themselves.

Tables 1 and 2 provide the responses in the two communities to some questions about sales behavior. These data give some indication of the degree to which the money economy has become important in Long Segar relative to Long Ampung, as well as the kinds of moneymaking possibilities that exist other than selling rice.

Table 1
Women's Involvement in Sales Activities
Long Segar, East Kalimantan, 1980

Do you sell...	Never	Rarely	Sometimes	Often	Regularly	Missing	Total
Handicrafts (man inu)	45.9%	22.7%	25.8%	---	5.2%	0.4%	100.0%
Plants (mula)	33.2%	15.3%	37.1%	1.3%	12.7%	0.4%	100.0%
Forest products (inu inu cen dalau ba'i)	50.2%	17.9%	24.5%	.4%	6.6%	0.4%	100.0%
Trade goods (inu inu cen toko atau kapen)	90.0%	---	2.2%	1.3%	5.7%	0.9%	100.0%

Table 2
Women's Involvement in Sales Activities
Long Ampung, East Kalimantan, 1980

Do you sell	Never	Rarely	Sometimes	Often	Regularly	Total
Handicrafts	78.6%	8.0%	11.6%	---	1.8%	100.0%
Plants	83.9%	8.0%	8.0%	---	---	100.0%
Forest products	92.2%	3.6%	3.6%	---	---	100.0%
Trade goods	91.1%	4.5%	4.5%	---	---	100.0%

In the category handicrafts, are included baskets, beadwork, sunhats, clothes, mats, usually made by women; and knives, musical instruments, and carvings, usually made by men. Although I did not focus on commerce per se, women and men seemed about equally involved in sales, though in different contexts. Women's sales were more likely to occur as spontaneous responses to unforeseen opportunities; men would enter into contracts or do consignments more frequently (perhaps simply because men were more likely to be approached with such requests than were women).

Using a multi-dimensional scaling technique developed by Galileo, designed for "cognitive mapping," I found that among all groups of Kenyah surveyed, the concept "trade" (dageng) is perceived to be substantially closer to men than to women. This may be because of an emphasis in the term dageng on activities normally engaged in by other ethnic groups with whom men, far more than women, interact. Indeed, dageng is perceived to be a rather alien activity, with regard to Kenyah perceptions of ethnic identity; Kenyah consider themselves by contrast to be rice farmers. And Kenyah women are even more basically considered to be rice farmers than are men.

On a daily basis, the production of rice is women's most consistent (and in Long Segar, most consistently profitable) economic activity. Rice can be stored for long periods of time, and since virtually every family in Indonesia prefers rice three times a day, there is always a demand. The availability of a market for rice in Long Segar--because of improved transportation access--is a departure from traditional conditions; and together with the introduction of technology that is disproportionately available to men, appears to have altered the relative contributions of men and women to rice production.[8] In Long Ampung where rice is used for subsistence (and sometimes for what could be termed either charity or insurance) I was able to demonstrate a clear correlation between the amount of rice a family produced and the proportion of their workers who were female. In Long Segar, where rice is regularly sold in addition to providing a subsistence base, a less dramatic, but inverse correlation was found between the proportion of women in a family and the family's rice production. Because of the important role of production as a necessary (though not sufficient) precondition to high female status, one might expect such a shift to have some negative implications for women's lives.

Two related phenomena similarly suggest a potential decline in women's status in the area. First, the opportunity to sell surplus rice, produced by both men and women, to non-Kenyah requires interaction with other ethnic groups. The small stores in the community accept rice in exchange for the kerosene, candy, sugar, tea, salt, needles and such that they sell; and the longboats that ply the Telen River regularly purchase larger amounts from individuals and from store owners for sale in Samarinda, the provincial capital. Though women do sell rice from time to time and regularly trade it in the small stores in the village, there is a tendency for Kenyah men to feel more comfortable and be more competent in dealings with outsiders. Reasons for this include higher male literacy and numeracy, and greater skill in the Indonesian language;[*] and the fact that most other Indonesian ethnic groups have a stereotype of Dayak women as promiscuous. This stereotype makes female Dayak interaction with such men unpleasant, and encourages Dayak men to accept the responsibility to interact with outsiders. One can see that in the long run this could easily function to reduce Dayak women's control over what they produce.

------

[*]Because of better male access to education historically and because of greater male experience in using these skills as wage or contract laborers on expeditions away from the village.

A second important element in this complex of interacting phenomena is a reduction in women's cultivation and gathering of non-rice foodstuffs (ferns, bamboo shoots, vegetables, fruits, etc.). This reduction appears to have occurred in response to the availability of a market for surplus rice and the greater profitability for the family of allocating time to rice production over and above purely subsistence activities. This means of course that women have less vegetable produce available to allocate than they might wish (though they still retain the right to distribute what they do produce or gather). The sale of vegetables and gathered foods is a comparatively risky endeavor, due to the perishability of most such products and the lack of established and dependable marketing outlets.

Political Participation

In comparison to Kenyah women's traditional equality or even preeminence in economic matters, their political actions are rather insubstantial. There are, however, no formal barriers at this point in time to their participation. Long Ampung's public meetings normally take place on the veranda of a longhouse. In Long Segar, the Resettlement Program (which provided various kinds of development assistance to the community between 1972 and 1980) specified that the people were not to live in longhouses. The veranda of the headman's modified three-door longhouse serves as a meeting place there.

Decisions that affect the whole community are taken at these meetings attended by a representative from each household. Households with no men are expected to send a woman; and old women frequently attend, sitting off to one side. Particularly knotty community problems are dealt with by smaller meetings of the male elders. Problems which are still not considered "community problems" are dealt with by respected members of the families involved. Such small family confabs may fail to resolve the difficulty, in which case the problem is brought before the larger group. Women are as involved in these smaller group discussions as are men. Examples of successful small family group problem resolution which I observed in 1979-80, included two threatened and averted divorces for suspected infidelity (one male and one female); one incident in which a man beat his wife and her child by a former marriage with a large plank; one unmarried girl who was suspected of causing herself to abort; and one man who impregnated a divorced woman. His wife was subsequently dissuaded from divorcing him.

Public meetings are called to plan major community activities like the post-harvest or New Year's celebrations; gotong royong (communal self-help) projects, like cleaning up the village, or clearing the airstrip of grass; to welcome or respond to visiting researchers, dignitaries, or public servants; to plan, with would-be developers, how such development should proceed (e.g., an as-yet-unfulfilled promise to start a poultry project by the Resettlement Project); and so on.

Interestingly, though these meetings are the only identifiable formal setting for political activity, there is remarkably little disagreement or debate at these meetings. Kenyah, like many ethnic groups in Indonesia, avoid public disagreement and conflict within their own group. Even in cases where feelings were very strong--such as the selection of a new headman or a suspected act of thievery--the public meeting was conducted with decorum and the appearance of general agreement.

In these formal meetings, women virtually never say anything. Indeed, the only people who normally say anything are the elderly men mentioned earlier. And they talk at great length. One of the abilities that Kenyah men value is to be able to "talk"--in reference to public speaking. And those who have that ability take every opportunity to demonstrate it. Although the Kenyah commented that I had the ability to "talk" they generally agreed that this ability was rare among women.

In order to get a quantified sense of how frequently women attended meetings, I asked them, "Do you go to community meetings?" (Bek dulu tai tira', iko' tai?--literally, if people go talk, do you go?) The phrasing indicates that the meetings in question are the ones on the headman's veranda. These data are presented in Table 3 and do not suggest that there is much difference in the pattern in the two communities. The table also shows that women do have access to this political arena in some sense. The responsibility to take care of small children was one frequently mentioned reason for not going to more of these meetings.

Table 3
Women's Attendance at Village Meetings
Long Ampung and Long Segar, 1980

Do you go to the village meetings?

	Long Ampung		Long Segar	
	number	percent	number	percent
never	39	34.8%	77	33.6%
rarely	10	8.9%	22	9.6%
sometimes	45	40.2%	99	43.2%
often	2	1.8%	4	1.7%
always	16	14.3%	26	11.4%
no answer	--	--	1	0.4%
	112	100.0%	229	99.9%

The existence of strong opposing feelings on particular issues combined with the minimal amount of public debate at meetings suggests that the actual decisionmaking process for community politics does not occur in these formal meetings anyway. It is however my observation that men are far more likely to be interested in and found discussing community issues than are women. Certainly, however, Kenyah women do have the kind of political participation that Sanday identifies, since she explicitly states "even if only through a few token representatives." Kenyah women's participation is more than "token," but not equal to that of men's in these all-household meetings. Their participation in the smaller problem-resolving groups composed of two or more families is equal with that of men.

Women in Groups

Kenyah women group together in two main contexts, the mother's organization and the reciprocal work group. The kaum ibu (mother's organization) is affiliated with the Protestant church in Long Segar. I understand there are women's groups of this kind in all Kenyah villages, though I have not personally observed them in operation in Long Ampung. The purposes of these organizations are religious study, religious singing, psychological and economic support for those who are ill or have had misfortune, and the joint care of a group ricefield. Any activity that is perceived to be relevant for women tends to be funneled through this organization as well. The kaum ibu assisted me, for instance, in choosing two women to take over the function I had been performing of providing birth control pills to women who requested them.

The second context in which women group is called senguyun, and is not necessarily limited to women. Senguyun actually refers to a reciprocal work group and can be all women, all men, or mixed. My observation has been that women seem to dominate in senguyun groups though, and many such groups are all women. All members go to work on one member's ricefield one day, then all members go to another member's ricefield the second day, and so on until each member has had a day of the whole group's work. Senguyun groups are transitory in nature, organized for some particular, bounded activity, though the same people are free to regroup at any time.

Whether or not this kind of women's group falls into Sanday's category "female solidarity groups devoted to female political or economic interests" remains open for discussion. Although work groups of this kind are devoted to women's economic interests, it is important to recognize that these interests are in no way perceived to be incongruent with the interests of men.

Kenyah life is remarkable in the absence of antagonism between the sexes. There is cross-sex teasing, which is almost entirely sexual in nature. Groups of men and women, working together, engage in a kind of stylized repartee in which women maintain that men are the initiators in sexual encounters, and then the men counter with some indication of how the women are really the initiators, and so on. However, this kind of interchange is marked by great hilarity and no identifiable hostility. Improprieties with rather overt sexual overtones on the part of both men and women are quite permissible in group settings where follow-through is perceived to be impossible.

In sum, then, it appears that Kenyah women do have considerable power and authority in the public domain, if we accept Sanday's four criteria. The more general kind of understanding of women's status that I am seeking here, however, requires that we examine the private domain as well.

Women At Home

I was influenced in the organization of this section by the work of Dubisch[9] who proposed four criteria for measuring male/female power distribution within the family: 1) respect accorded one spouse by the other, publicly and privately; 2) interference of one spouse in the sphere of the other; 3) decisionmaking in regard to allocation of family resources; and 4) arranging plans for children. Again, some adaptation of her approach has been necessary, but the issues she raises are important ones, and have been incorporated into the discussion that follows.

Quality of Interaction Between Women and Men

Although Kenyah marriages are occasionally arranged by parents, the more usual pattern is for the young people to choose their own mates. Young people work together in mixed-sex groups, and as they approach marriageable age (between about 15 and 25 for females; and 18 to 28 for males) they begin to consider potential marital partners. Health and hard work are very important considerations, as well as attractiveness and personality. The opinions of parents are very important in marriage choices, since young couples initially live with the parents of one or the other partner.

Courtship begins with the young man spending time at the girl's house. As they become more serious, he will menyat jago', or ask her permission to sleep with her. Although sleeping with a person one is serious about is accepted, having intercourse is not. The young people are expected to refrain from intercourse until they marry, though this rule is sometimes broken. Parents express their opinions throughout the courtship process, and have considerable influence.

The marriage relationship is most overtly one of cooperation in work. Couples who remain fond of each other arrange to spend a lot of time together. Praising one's spouse or expressing loneliness in his/her absence are considered inappropriate, though people do both in private. Spouses are expected to respect each other's wishes and consult each other

197

about important decisions. The absence of privacy in the home facilitates all family members' getting involved in each other's decisionmaking.

The normal variation in personality characteristics among spouses naturally leads to situations in the family in which one spouse or the other is dominant. Men hold a slightly "stacked deck" in Kenyah marriages, since they usually marry younger women (and age carries respect with it). But the reality of both female and male dominance in different relationships suggests that this is not the determining factor.

Certainly there are none of the elaborate, purposeful respectful behaviors so common in the Middle East, in relations between Kenyah husbands and wives. Neither is there the kind of mixed-sex interaction one observes in some contexts in the United States where the reasoned input of women, including wives is sometimes simply ignored.*

Although the input of some persons in Long Segar is disregarded, this response does not seem to be in any way reserved for women. Certainly interrupting generally is far less common among these Dayaks than among many Westerners. But neither was I able to identify any mechanisms for nullifying or disregarding the input of women there. Indeed, the input of experienced, intelligent, articulate women and men was actively sought.

As I observed marital and other kinds of male-female interaction in Kalimantan, I was struck by the rarity with which anyone of either sex interfered with anyone else's autonomy. Orders were sometimes given by both men and women in

---

*e.g., A man speaks, a woman responds, and then another man responds to the first man without recognition of the woman's output. Or a woman begins speaking in response to a man's comment, and is cut off by a second man who wishes to respond to the first man.

the orderly and efficient performance of some joint endeavor; but people did not boss each other around, as men were wont to do in Bushler Bay, Washington, for instance:

> Husbands readily order their wives around, sending them for a pack of cigarettes, ordering them to make a pot of coffee, insisting they keep the children quiet, and so on.[10]

In an attempt to quantify this observation that Kenyah grant each other considerable autonomy, I first posed a survey question in Long Ampung and Long Segar, asking specifically whether anyone had told the respondent what to do that day (A'un dulu dia' ca cuk iko' uyan inu tau ini?). Of the 15% in Long Ampung and the 20% in Long Segar who responded affirmatively, almost none mentioned their husband or any other man as the person who had assigned the task.

Interestingly, of those who had been told what to do, almost all were either very young or very old. This fits with my observation that people rarely tell productive Dayak adults what to do. Local wisdom asserts that the young are told what to do because they lack the experience to know, and the old because they are no longer contributing to the family's subsistence. Family life among the Kenyah is firmly organized around the necessity to work to secure food. People, including the old, recognize the preeminence of this concern and economic decisionmaking is in the hands of those who do the work. Many of the older women in both communities were weaving baskets and mats or taking care of their grandchildren at the direction of the younger productive members of their families. A number of the Long Segar respondents who maintained they had been told what to do were referring to a call for gotong royong (communal self-help) by the leader of the Protestant women's group. Both men and women appear to make their own decisions, by and large, about what, when, and how much they will do--within an overall context that values hard work.

More general, longer term decisions about the allocation of family labor are usually made in a slow, consensual manner with input from all family members. Even then, when the family's wishes are perceived by an individual to be too far at odds with his or her own wishes, that individual may not comply. People who are "forced"--in the sense of strong community or familial pressure--to do something they genuinely do not want to do, occasionally commit suicide; and people are generally afraid of that outcome should they press too hard.

Within particular families, the relative weight given to the opinion of one person over another is definitely more related to age than to sex. And, as noted earlier, a capable woman with a strong personality may make most decisions in a family, even though she may be younger than her husband. Personality and capability are strong factors in determining who will be the most effective and consistent decisionmaker within any given family.

Table 4 provides the responses to the question, "How has it been when your husband has gone on an expedition? Did you help decide? Did he insist [force]?" (Kompin dalau laki ko' tai selai re? Iko' peteneng? Ia ase' tai?) Women in both communities report considerable involvement in this kind of decision, though the women in Long Segar appear to report less influence than the women in Long Ampung. The second question was "Do you help decide how to use the money that your husband gets from his own work?" (Iko' mepoh pekimet kompin pakai uang ya' laki ko' ala' cen gayeng tengen?). In Long Ampung, this

---

*These translations are offered with the recognition that they are only approximate. "Decide" for instance had to be translated into Kenyah in three ways: "nguba,'" "peteneng," and "pekimet." The first derives from uba' meaning want/like/love/desire; the third is from kimet, to think; and I do not know the stem of the second, though that word seemed to be used in a manner closest to our understanding of "deciding."

question had to be amended to substitute "things" (inu) for
"money" since no one normally received money for work in that
community, and money that was earned elsewhere was converted to
goods before returning home. In Long Ampung 90% of those
interviewed gave clear indications that they were or were not
involved. 94% of these reported involvement and 6% reported
not being involved in deciding how to use their husband's
income. In Long Segar, where 95% of the women's responses
could be similarly categorized, 93% reported involvement and 7%
denied involvement in such decisions. This suggests
considerable female involvement in decisions that relate
directly to the allocation of family resources.

Table 4
Women's Reported Involvement in Spouses'
Circular Migration Decisionmaking
Long Ampung and Long Segar, 1980

	Long Ampung		Long Segar	
	number	percent	number	percent
I help decide	84	75.0%	154	67.2%
Sometimes he insists,				
sometimes I agree	3	2.7%	25	10.9%
It's up to him	--	--	17	7.4%
He goes against my will	5	4.5%	14	6.1%
Not applicable/missing	20	17.9%	19	8.3%
	112	100.1%	229	99.9%

The very considerable trust that exists between husbands and wives is another striking characteristic of Kenyah marriages. Although marital infidelity is considered an offense, it is not uncommon, and the general community expectation is that couples will trust each other until proven guilty. Women and men regularly go on excursions, in groups, with people of both sexes other than their spouses. People who exhibit excessive or unfounded jealousy are considered somewhat humorous and both they and their spouses are pitied. The most obvious behavioral manifestation of this trust was the pattern of women staying at the fieldhuts in their ricefields--usually at considerable distance from the village--for extended periods without their husbands or anyone besides children who could be considered a chaperone.

The question, "do you stay away overnight, if your husband is not around?" (A'un to' tudo, bek laki ko' mpi a'un?"), was devised to quantify women's adherence to this pattern, and as an indirect measure of trust between husbands and wives. The responses show that around 84% of the women in both communities stay away overnight (usually at their ricefields) without their husbands.

Most of those who gave a reason for not remaining alone--mentioned fear of killers and spirits. Others mentioned having too many and/or too young children to work regularly in the ricefield. Still others were too old. In addition to the implications of this pattern for marital trust, it seems a rather powerful statement of Kenyah women's autonomy and general community acceptance of their competence to cope.

Some have postulated a relationship between high female status and ease of divorce. The traditional pattern among the Kenyah was very easy divorce, initiated by either party. Each community had one woman who had been married six times. In Long Segar 68% of the women however had been married only once, and the corresponding figure in Long Ampung was 73%. However,

Christianity has been adopted by all Kenyah now, and the Protestants particularly are antagonistic to divorce. Any Protestant who gets divorced now, ironically, must join the Catholic church.

The only divorce that occurred during my fieldwork was prompted by repeated physical abuse--in this case, husband-beating. Because the man was initiating the divorce, however, all their possessions, custody of their baby, and part of the fine levied against the man, were awarded to the woman.

Any kind of violence within the group is generally not condoned. For example, a major upheaval occurred when a man, angered by his stepson, hit the child and the mother with a beam. The community at large urged the woman not to allow him to return to their home and not to feed him; but she forgave him. Several cases of marital infidelity on the part of husbands did not end in divorce largely because the wives were reminded of the shortage of available men.

The male practice of circular migration, or expedition-making, is a longstanding tradition among the Kenyah;[11] and it is a valued activity. It contributes to an imbalance in sex ratio in the community at any given time. The preponderance of women is exacerbated by the longer lifespan of women and the occasional intended temporary male migrant who fails to return. This male option serves to temper women's power and encourages women to treat their husbands kindly. A man can openly consider going away, "in the interest of the family," to earn money or bring back consumer goods when things get unpleasant at home.

The absence of a strict division of labor between the sexes, mentioned earlier, deserves some elaboration here. Certainly there are tasks that women more normally perform, like cooking; but men frequently cook as well. Similarly though men usually pilot canoes, women can from time to time be seen at the helm. Kenyah seem to be singularly nonjudgmental about either sex performing tasks that are most commonly undertaken by the other. The harsh kind of ribbing that accrues in some places to people who deign to engage in activities reserved by that group for the opposite sex is entirely absent. The Kenyah are aware of sex role rigidity among some other ethnic groups they have encountered. Kayah men, for instance, were described to me as responding to floor sweeping in the same way that American men have learned to respond to dishwashing and diaper changing. But the Kenyah merely chuckle about such cultural foibles.

Elaborate ideologies of female inferiority are very potent forces undermining women's status in some places. Among the Kenyah there is no such ideology except that recently introduced by the Christian missionaries. Substantiating my conclusion that Kenyah women are not constrained by an ideology of inferiority were the results of the application of Galileo's multidimensional scaling technique which showed women to be perceived by Kenyah adults as closer to the concept good than were men. They were also perceived to be closer to ricefields, work, and children--all highly valued concepts--than were men.

Sex preference in children is another indirect indicator of an ideology of female inferiority. When asked "Which is better, boys or girls?" (Ya' mpi tiga, laki atau leto?), the vast majority (in Long Ampung, 92%; and in Long Segar, 85%) considered boys and girls to be equally desirable. Of those who specified one sex or the other, a majority preferred girls.

Women's Decisionmaking in Agricultural Production

That Kenyah women are actively involved in production has been shown using a variety of methods: a time allocation study,[12] a Galileo study,[13] an agricultural survey,[14] and participant observation.[15] Sanday has provided good evidence that female involvement in production is a necessary but not sufficient precondition for the development of high status and

204

that highest female status is in societies where men and women share the productive sphere, as they do among the Kenyah.[16]

The particular symbolic nexus, in Kenyah life, between women and rice cultivation, combined with consistent female action in the agricultural sphere prompted me to ask some questions about women's involvement in agricultural decisionmaking, despite my skepticism about the reliability of such responses. A subsidiary impetus to this survey was my recognition that, although many development personnel now recognized that women were involved in production, they were continuing to address men on the theory that men were the real decisionmakers.

The first step in the agricultural cycle is the choice of land for the year's ricefield. Table 5 shows the responses of women in Long Ampung and Long Segar to the open-ended question "How did you choose land [for your ricefield] last year?" (Kompin ngko' mile' tana' uman ca re?).

Table 5
Women's Reponses to the Question,
"How did you choose your land last year?"
Long Ampung and Long Segar, 1980

	Long Ampung		Long Segar	
	number	percent	number	percent
I did not choose	63	56.3%	147	64.2%
I chose	24	21.4%	50	21.8%
My husband and I chose	10	8.9%	19	8.3%
I chose with someone else [not husband]	12	10.7%	---	---
No ricefield	3	2.7%	13	5.7%
	112	100.0%	229	100.0%

From a symbolic point of view, the choice of land for a new ricefield, in families where the husband is present, would be among the most likely agricultural decisions to be taken by men. A new ricefield is most typically cut from forest, and the forest is generally perceived to be more a domain of men than of women. The forest is full of dangers, it is the area where men hunt (something women rarely do), it is an area that traditionally had to be traversed by men on their expeditions to secure salt, cloth, and other important consumer goods. On the other hand, the first activity in clearing the forest for cultivation is performed by women--the hand clearing of brush and small trees using a baing (machete).*

One factor contributing to the lesser involvement of Long Segar women in land choice (64.2% of Long Segar women were not involved, as opposed to 56.3% of Long Ampung women) may be the fact that the land around Long Segar is typically still in primary forest. This kind of forest has larger trees than does the secondary forest that surrounds Long Ampung; and men are more necessary in the land clearing process in primary forest. One could of course also argue that the decreased involvement of Long Segar women is another indication of their declining status.

Returning to Table 5, a number of women explained their noninvolvement in agricultural decisionmaking by referring to their temporary responsibilities at home, brought on by the recent birth of a baby. Although babies are universally loved and adored, women recognize the degree to which small children decrease their involvement in productive activity, and they view this as a disadvantage of motherhood. The major category of women who reported not being involved in choosing land for

---

*As noted earlier, most activities are done by both men and women. But in land clearing, women tend to clear brush and small trees, and men cut down the large trees.

their ricefields were those who could no longer work, due to age or infirmity. There were one or two mature women and a number of very young women who maintained that they could not "think" or "plan," and left such decisions to others in the household. Since all women in both communities were interviewed, this should not be seen as a reflection of the number of households in which women did not participate in decisionmaking, since only about half of the households had only one adult woman in them; a few had as many as five.

A second question, on agricultural decisionmaking was, "Do you help determine the boundaries of your ricefield?" This question was originally worded to ask about the size of ricefields; (Iko' nguba' koda' biu' uma kem?) however, it soon became apparent that the important decision, once the area has been selected and the other families with contiguous ricefields had been ascertained, was boundarymaking within the overall area. The instrument was correspondingly altered to reflect the local condition (Iko' mepoh uyan saang uma kem?; "do you help make the boundaries of your ricefield?"). Long Ampung women are considerably more involved in determining the boundaries than are Long Segar women (61.6% vs. 50.2%, respectively). This, like the choice of land, may relate to the fact that these determinations are occurring in primary rather than secondary forest, and/or it may be another indication of a reduction in women's status. The rationales offered for not being involved in this kind of decisionmaking were very similar to those given for not choosing the land for a ricefield, discussed above.

In Long Segar, I was able to ask the women "Did you help consider how to use the money from selling rice last year?" (Iko mepoh pekimet kompin pakai uang dalau pebeli padai uman ca re?). However, in Long Ampung, since rice is never actually sold, it was necessary to rephrase the question to say "Did you help consider how to use the rice last year?" (Iko mepoh

pekimet kompin pakai padai uman ca re?). Affirmative responses
to these questions accounted for 64% of the women in both
communities, showing no appreciable difference between women's
perceived influence on the disposition of these family
resources, in Long Ampung and Long Segar.

Women, Men and Economics

Because women's economic activity seems, in the Kenyah
context, to be more a private than a public activity, I have
dealt with it in this section. However, it is important to
discuss the value placed on female labor in the wider
society--a question with pertinence to women's status in the
public domain as well. Certainly female labor is recognized as
critical within Dayak society. Women are generally valued for
their industry and responsibility, relative to men. Men's
greater physical strength is likewise recognized and valued.
From the point of view of productivity, within the Long Segar
or Long Ampung contexts, I was unable to identify any inferior
valuation of women's labor.

Similarly, with regard to agricultural wage labor in Long
Segar there is no local sex difference. The daily wage for
agricultural labor is between Rp. 1000 and Rp 1500 (US $1 = Rp.
623, 1980 rate). The discrepancy in financial opportunities
for men and women only becomes apparent when we look at nearby
contract labor possibilities and employment opportunities in
other, distant areas. Kenyah men can make a good bit of money
doing contract logging for the timber companies (up to Rp.
100,000/month), milling logs with a chainsaw for sale to
passing longboats, or by going away to do logging, factory
work, brickmaking, and the myriad other kinds of jobs available
to men in the wider world.

As noted earlier, Dayak men have traditionally gone on
expedition to Malaysia and other areas to work, buy consumer
goods, and bring them home to the village for home use. They

still do this in Long Ampung. There one can intepret the male contribution of consumer goods to be in some way equivalent to the female preeminence in food production, yielding a rough equivalency of contribution.

In Long Segar, however, men bring home money more than consumer goods. Local accessibility of a market there means that money can--again in Long Segar--buy medicine, education, a variety of capital investments like chainsaws, outboard motors, rice hulling machines, and so on. Money can secure for men something they were, from time to time, dependent on women to provide in the past--food. And although women can get money by selling the rice they produce, agricultural labor of this kind is far less profitable than are the wage labor opportunities available to men.

Kenyah interest in money is not a manifestation of excessive greed, but rather an indication of their recognition of the very real benefits that money can provide--benefits that relate to life and death (medicine); and to chances for a less rigorous and physically exhausting lifestyle (education, technology, food). Kenyah women and men are quick to see the advantages available to those who have money. From the point of view of women's status, just as now decisionmaking goes with those who provide the family's needs, one can anticipate that if 1) money remains more available to men than to women and 2) it continues to gain in importance in overall subsistence, economic decisionmaking rights may gradually shift to the men.

In exploring those aspects of Kenyah Dayak life that contribute to the high status of women in these communities, the emphasis on certain aspects of life that undoubtedly appeal to many Western feminists is not intended to glorify or romanticize Kenyah existence. Life in East Kalimantan is difficult for both women and men. Daily work is physically exhausting, requiring often backbreaking labor under equatorial sun. Life itself is regularly threatened by disease and accident. The control of fertility is not yet a practical option for most Kenyah women. Children under five, as in many Third World situations, die regularly. The surrounding forests are full of dangers.

Yet the human dignity that characterizes these women is difficult to ignore, if one lives with them on a daily basis. They have self-respect and confidence in their abilities to cope, as a general rule. As noted, there are various trends in the wider society that may serve to erode these desirable traits. Indeed, outsiders who do not remain in the village for long, go their way unaware of Kenyah women's attributes. Without some special effort to preserve and enhance the traits these women exhibit, the changes referred to in this paper may 1) reduce these women's status, and 2) remove an opportunity that now exists to collaborate with these women in building an effective and humane development strategy which addresses the many needs that exist in these communities. Female action in Long Ampung and Long Segar is built on their high status, and remains desired and effective; it behooves would-be change agents to build on such potentialities rather than, as so often happens, to tear them down.

Carol J. Pierce Colfer
University of Hawaii

Notes

1. Joel S. Kahn, Minangkabau Social Formations: Indonesian Peasants and the World Economy (Cambridge: Cambridge University Press, 1980).

2. Andrew P. Vayda, Colfer, J.P., and Brotokusumo M., "Interactions between People and Forests," Impact of Science on Society 30.3 (1980):179-190. Reprinted by East-West Center, (Environment and Policy Institute, No. 13, 1981).

3. Andrew P. Vayda, "Progressive Contextualization: Method for Integrated Social and Biological Research in the MAB Program," 1982, Unpublished paper.

4. Susan Carol Rogers, "Woman's Place: A Critical Review of Anthropological Theory," Comparative Studies in Society and History 20.1 (1978):123-162.

5. Rogers, p. 159.

6. Carol J.P. Colfer, "Women of the Forest: An Indonesian Example," in Stock, Force, and Ehrenreich, eds., Women in Natural Resources: An International Perspective (Moscow, Idaho: University of Idaho, 1982), pp. 153-182.

7. Peggy Sanday, "Female Status in the Public Domain," in Rosaldo and Lamphere, eds., Woman, Culture and Society (Stanford: Stanford University Press, 1974), pp. 189-206.

8. For an elaboration of this, see Carol J.P. Colfer, "Work and Production Among Shifting Cultivators of Borneo," Paper presented to the Women in Development Group, Utah State University, Logan, Utah, 1982.

9. Jill Dubisch, "Dowry and the Domestic Power of Women in a Greek Island Village," paper presented at the 70th Annual Meeting, American Anthropological Association, New York, 1971.

10. Carol J.P. Colfer, "Women's Communication and Family Planning in Rural America: The Case of Bushler Bay" (Honolulu: EWCI, Case Study 4, 1977), reprinted 1978.

11. Carol J.P. Colfer, "On Circular Migration from the Distaff Side," in G. Standing, ed., Labour Circulation (Geneva: ILO, [in preparation]).

12. Carol J.P. Colfer, "Women, Men and Time in the Forests of East Kalimantan," Borneo Research Bulletin 13 (2):75-85 (Environment and Policy Institute Reprint No. 25, 1982).

13. Carol J.P. Colfer, in Stock, Force, and Ehrenreich, eds., pp. 153-182.

14. Carol J.P. Colfer, paper for Women in Development Group, Logan, Utah, 1982.

15. Carol J.P. Colfer, "Women as Farmers in Agricultural Development," Benchmark Soils News 5.1 (1981):7-8; "The Potential of Women in Agroforestry in Borneo," Pacific Health 14 (1981):10-14; "Home Gardening...Not So Easy," Agenda 4.8 (1981):8-11.

16. Peggy Sanday, pp. 189-206.

This chapter reports the experiences of laborers' wives in a village of the southern Punjab with one type of tubectomy-- mini-laparotomy. The work was conducted on one village in Ferozepur district during 1980-81. Women did not favor tubectomy. They reported pain in the pelvic area and lower back region after the operation.[1] This affected their work capacity and thereby, their relationship within the family to their children and to their husbands.

The women's experiences of pain cannot be declared invalid although that is the status generally ascribed to their reports of post-operative pain by local doctors who cursorily branded it as psychological. They claimed that women were saying they were in pain only to attract attention to themselves. Assuming the pain is real, nevertheless, one is faced with the problem of women complaining of post-operative pain for which there appears to be no immediate clinical explanation as would be indicated, let us say, by the presence of fever and sepsis.[2] The Additional Director of Family Planning for Punjab suggested in an interview (September, 1982) that the low back pain which women associated with their operation was likely to have been caused by spinal anaesthesia.[3]

This chapter begins with a case study describing the unintended repercussions of one woman's operation on her family. The related second section gives an account of women's role in productive process and the nature of her labor load. Since bending and stretching are crucial elements in that work,[4] the mini-laparotomy method of tubectomy in use in field hospitals, may have to be judged unacceptable in the rural areas. In view of the possibility that the causes of post-operative pain might be purely clinical and only subsequently aggravated by work conditions, the third section of the chapter describes the clinical milieu in which the tubectomy operation itself takes place and the attendant hospital conditions. My hypothesis that an operation interacted unfavorably with a woman's role in the productive process and the nature of her labor load would have to be tested under controlled conditions before it could have the standing of "fact." Since my own observations concerning tubectomy operations were confined to one village over a short period of time I would be reluctant to make generalizations for the subcontinent of India on the basis of my data.

In the village where I worked, the demand from daughters-in-law was for adequate contraception, not for sterilization. This was understandable. Women were dependent on their children for labor and on male children for support during old age. Yet at the same time they were not in control of their illnesses by virtue of their low nutritional status and poor hygiene with which the fourth section briefly deals. Nor were they aided in achieving such control by doctors who did so little home visiting.

Traditionally, the young married woman's position within the household has been low. It is still so! By regarding a woman as a target for a sterilization operation as soon as she has two children, doctors merely acknowledge and extend her low status into yet another arena. As one writer noted, "While women may have rights to education and work, the facts of male domination in all institutions conferring high status except that of reproduction and socialization, complicates the position of women with respect to birth control and population planning."[5] Particularly in northern India, a woman's dignity and continued position in her husband's kin group is dependent on her capacity to bear male children. Marshall correctly asserts that women cannot accept family planning until "status recognition and feelings of competence are achievable in ways other than getting pregnant."[6] Until they reach the status of mother-in-law, women in the Punjab today are beings for whom little independence is permitted. To expect young married women alone to bear the brunt of governmental family planning policies in the shape of a tubectomy operation is an additional demand.

During my nine months' field work in the village, I took the view that it was not my place to present a case for family planning to women, assuming there is one. I operated under the assumption that one's right to advocate family planning came only in response to queries by the women themselves, when they expressed it as a definite need. I visited each of the 144 homes in the village and was inside 50 houses many times in the course of observing weaning practices and describing illness among children at the weaning period. Not all of my visits were purely professional; I visited certain homes because I liked the people in them and often I would be called into other homes for tea or roti (food) depending on the hour. Women started asking me about family planning after I'd been about 7 months in the village. "Now we know you properly," one woman declared.

Since research for this paper was undertaken, the Punjab Government, following the examples of the State Governments of Gujarat and Rajasthan is actively promoting primarily laparoscopy, despite the statement of Dr. D.N. Kakar of the Post Graduate Institute for Medicine in Chandigarh that "many deaths due to bacterial infection through the vagina" are associated with laparoscopic tubectomy. It may by added, further, that women are drawn to these camps by deception. For example, an advertisement issued by the Director of Health and Family Welfare in Punjab and published on the front page of the Tribune on Dec. 17th 1983, stated that laparoscopic tubectomy would be available by the "non-exposure method." There was no reality in this.

A Happening of Baisakhi Day[7]

Among the wheat fields on _Baisakhi_ day a mother from an agricultural laborer's family punched and kicked her thirteen year old daughter to death, complaining that the child was "only playing, not working." The child died one afternoon four days later. The case went undiagnosed for what it truly was. Only when the child died did her father's relatives say they had seen her being beaten. The wives of the other laborers were otherwise rigid in their concealment, blaming the child's death on an evil spirit that must have come upon her, they said, since she became ill in the fields.

The mother had been unable to rest after her tubectomy operation due to the pressures of her daily domestic chores of collecting firewood and fodder. By the time of the wheat harvest she was too tired to take on her full share of the work and her husband began to grumble. In a situation like this, where a mother was forced to work in the fields even though she felt unfit and should have been resting, it was not unreasonable for her to expect that her eldest child would take up her mother's share of the work. As Mydral writes, "Comparatively speaking, the setting of south Asian life is such that children are expected to fulfill obligations to parents more than parents to children."[8] Certainly it was quite common in the village to find children, usually the oldest child, withdrawn from school and doing the work of adults. For example, there was the case of two local farm families where the fathers were opium addicts and one was also asthmatic. Both men suffered temporary periods of incapacitation and their children were drafted to look after the buffalos. In another family, the landlord's wife used her male children to superintend the laborers and see that they were working properly. In yet another case an elder brother used to bring his little sister of eighteen months to the fields for his mother to breast feed. In the case of the thirteen year old who died, the child concerned normally worked with the animals in a Darkman (artisan) household. They paid her sixteen rupees per month (the equivalent of one pound) the rate being two rupees for each buffalo. At harvest time she began to help her own family in addition to working with the animals. Her contribution was important at this juncture, given that her mother was not working to full capacity. Perhaps she did not realize that and this enraged her mother since it is only at the wheat harvest that laborers' families can accumulate enough wheat to last them through 8-10 months of the year.[9]

Only eight people accompanied the child to her resting place, for the Jats (farmers) would not spare their laborers from the wheat harvest nor would they loan a trolley to carry her beyond the perimeter of the village to where she was to be buried. The family had no wood with which to burn her and those who had would not spare any. Somewhere she is buried; in a ditch with a layer of mud and bricks as cover (children above the age of eight are supposed to be burnt). Poverty had allowed the family no freedom to keep their traditions, forcing them to abandon a very sacred custom.

I am making no direct connection (though I am certainly making a contextual one) between the mother's tubectomy operation and the accidental killing of her child. In her case the pain ensuing after this operation was an additional oppression to twelve hours work per day on a sub-standard diet. The pain persisted two months after the operation and she commented "after this operation we suffer so much. And then when we cannot work the husbands say 'go and die.'"[10]

Mothers undergoing a tubectomy operation may endanger their children not in the same way as described in this particular

217

case which, let us hope, is exceptional,[11] but always in the sense that children will have to take on their mother's share of the work. In this case, as it happened, the mother lost a child who, as one old laborer put it, "was the equal of us all (men) in work." There is no replacement for her, ever. The mother, sullen and unbelieving of what had happened said simply "Now I can have no more children because of my operation," at this point giving way to the many angles of her grief. She was not with her daughter when she died and she was left with only one male child in the family--a situation of high risk. In fact no sooner had the mother returned from the hospital after her sterilization than her only son contracted pneumonia from which he nearly died. Her other girls were too small to work and already she was taking cognizance of her new situation by depriving the youngest among them, who had third degree malnutrition, of milk, giving it to her only son.

This case study possibly highlights how unrealistic the government norm of two children per family is and, further, the dangers for rural laboring women in accepting that norm. In an economic structure where children are considered labor units and responsible for the support of aged parents, three boys per family may be more realistic. The finality of sterilization is unsuited to laboring women and women from poor households because the kinds of care they can provide to their existing children often cannot prevent deaths given present sanitary conditions within the village and hygienic habits within the household. Many women from among the category of the poor frequently had experienced some form of past tragedy which rendered them fatalistic. One woman remarked "After so many deaths (referring to the deaths of two of her children and several children who were born dead), I have forgotten about little things such as how to be clean."

The Environmental Milieu

Indira Gandhi correctly assessed in her 1981 speech to W.H.O. "that rural women want family planning." I discuss this issue as seen in microcosm in a Sikh village of almost 1,200 people, 8 km from Ferozepur. I found that one particular mode of family planning was in demand--that by injection. While my research is not to be taken as an argument in favor of Depo-Provera, Potts and Selman have pointed out "the valid questions that can be asked about the use of D.P. will not be answered in advance of wider human use."

The mode of family planning favored by the district authorities--tubectomy--was rejected and feared by most village women. They were being offered sterilization. What they wanted was contraception! In the ten known cases of tubectomy in the village, all except one had been associated with some form of post-operative pain. As a social anthropologist, I don't know the source of this post-operative pain but I did notice that 4 cases out of 5 that took place during my stay were in women who were about 30 and who had 4 or more children. The women concerned took little or no rest after the operation from agricultural and household duties involving bending and stretching. Their statements to me reflected that they very much wanted this rest. They complained that the after-effects of this operation were such that they could not cope with household work and field labor. It therefore seems reasonable to describe the work conditions of these women while admitting that their post-operative pain could be situated in a number of contexts. No follow-up case studies were performed to examine the social and economic effects of this operation on working women and on their families. Hence, it was premature to conclude that sterilization suited young women with heavy work loads engaging in particular work activities on a continuous basis. It was unfortunate, therefore, that a former M.P. and member of the small family norms committee should have asked

219

publicly (in a letter to the <u>Times of India</u>, 13th May, 1981) for the resurrection of the report of his committee pleading for greater reliance on tubectomy.

In the village where I worked women did not feel positively about tubectomy because of the extreme pain involved afterwards. Tubectomy was resorted to usually under conditions of pressure and desperation. One woman for example had given birth to nine children, only five of whom had survived, and of the five surviving two had polio. In another family a twin daughter had developed polio and this prompted the mother to have a tubectomy operation. Only in such situations did women favor the operation and thus when the civil hospital in Ferozepur made an offer of 135 rs (less than $10) and a can of ghee to women who undertook this operation it could attract very few persons. I never came across a voluntary tubectomy. Usually behind a woman's tubectomy there were all sorts of pressures from her husband and his kin group as well as the state medical apparatus.

A description of the work conditions of daughters-in-law follows. Throughout, for purposes of work activities, these women are treated as a single category whether they belong to artisan, laborer or farm families. Even a farmer's family was not wealthy enough to employ outside help consistently for all household activities. Well-to-do farmers could afford the facilities of the better hospitals. And in a case described below, one farmer's wife had adequate family help to enable her to take care of herself after the operation.

Laborers' wives have 3-4 months of very heavy fieldwork at the time of the two major harvests of wheat and rice and at the time of the rice planting. This aside, a woman's two most difficult tasks are the daily gathering of fodder for buffalos and the collection of firewood for household fuel. Fodder has to be collected from the landlord's fields from between the wheat. Landlords frequently forbid this since the women also pull out the wheat for their buffalos at the same time. Because of such difficulties in collecting fodder, it might take a woman as much as three hours. The place of gathering may be far off, and the weight on the return journey might slow her down. Fodder collection was usually done in the afternoon, though the land was still wet in the afternoon in the winter months. A great deal of bending was involved in the daily cutting and collection of fodder.[12] Presumably this was how back pain was aggravated, or accumulated. Fodder collection was always a woman's task, even when pregnant. One woman while pregnant was walking a total of four miles daily to find fodder. The fact that sometimes she could not find very much or had no energy to search was reflected in the fact that her father-in-law's buffalo yielded only 1 1/2 kg of milk. A separate journey was required to collect firewood which was in such short supply that often, as one woman put it "one had to go on the trees." Very frequently dried grass and cane sticks were used in the <u>chulas</u> (hearths) to cut down on journeys. The making of dung cakes, used as a principal cooking fuel, also daily took at least an hour of a woman's time. Laborers' families were in so much financial need that they had to do this not only in their own homes but also in the houses of the richer Darkmans and Jats, though some farmers were so indebted that they were getting their own wives to perform this task. The customary payment for this was ten rupees per month. One laborer's wife also got some tea, flour and milk from the landlord. "Mostly all my children are eating over there now," she commented "and they give firewood." Another laborer's wife took help for the same work in the form of a year's supply of grain. It was also a woman's work to mud plaster the house twice yearly. This could take a long time, in that a woman belonging to a laborer family could not gather mud from just anywhere. The wives of those who did not have their own land had to walk outside the village to the ditches.

Considering the nature of these tasks very few laborers' wives were able to do more leisurely tasks such as embroidering pillow cases and bedsheets and one never saw them knitting. The time spent on fodder collection and on performing various odd jobs in exchange for food also explained why they did not put much time into food preparation though economy in any case forced their cooking to be as simple as possible. For example, the prepared dals found in laborers' houses did not always contain all the ingredients of richer masalas (spice-mixtures)--ginger, chillis, garlic, onions--unless these had been stolen from or given by the farmers.

Jat women had just as much work to do because of their greater family resources. In the early morning they had to milk a larger number of buffalos and churn the milk into butter. They had to cook food twice daily for large numbers of people. One Jat daughter-in-law cooked for 24 people twice daily, washing all the utensils with ashes afterwards. The food had to be delivered to the men in the fields. If only one woman was cooking, and two items were being cooked along with chappatis on only one hearth, the food took a long time to prepare. The same Jat woman complained that if her husband's relatives saw her sitting idle they would invent work for her, such as asking her to start making a bedspread or embroidery for the dowry of her sister-in-law. Sometimes also in these families there were large vegetable plots to look after. These were a woman's responsibility.

Although the Jat women still had to cut fodder, fodder collection for them and for the wives of the richer Darkmans was easier and not such a lengthy process. Some of their own land was usually set aside for the growing of barsim (an especially rich type of fodder) so they did not have to walk long distances in the search and in the carrying of fodder.

Most women, landlord and laborer alike, had to do certain unpleasant tasks every day, such as emptying the chabacha or

222

the _toa_. The _chabacha_ is a collecting place for dirty water, situated outside the walls of the house. It is cemented and square in shape. The _toa_, which is situated close to the pump, is a round hole, an arm's length in depth, dug into the courtyard for the purpose of collecting the household's dirty water. It is inside the walls of the house. Emptying the _toa_ often had to be done twice daily and sweeping the courtyard had to be done still more often. In the course of the yearly agricultural cycle, other incidental duties arose such as drying and pounding chillis, cleaning _dal_, rice and other grain. This outline of a woman's work activities excludes all the work connected with caring for children and household washing.

The above household and field activities performed by all daughters-in-law in the rural Punjab meant that few could take ample rest after a tubectomy operation. There were also family complications if they did take such rest. One woman's husband (an artisan) objected to her having sent her son for fodder and compared her with another woman in the village saying "she also had an operation and she is doing much more work than you." He had to employ a woman at ten rupees per month to make the dung cakes because his wife had no strength, and this was no doubt annoying him.

It is instructive to look at the case of one laborer's wife married at seventeen, and now in her middle twenties. She had one son aged three, another of one-and-a-half, and a new-born baby. She had also lost twins. Her father-in-law controlled the family's only buffalo and would not give either her or her husband any milk. It seems to me quite inhumane to ask such women, who have given birth to so many children so quickly, to undergo any more pain! But at the same time many women hate child-bearing and would take a way out if they could. This woman commented on her latest labor. "For three days I was suffering and no-one even asked if I wanted a cup of tea." In the context of this general situation, one cannot ask these women to suffer more. In their terms, which is what we have to consider, having a tubectomy operation is asking them to do precisely that.

The male role in the productive process also gave them very little leisure. If men worked as artisans, they frequently worked a sixteen-hour day in one of the many privately owned small machine tool shops in Ferozepur, which serviced and manufactured agricultural machinery. If they were laborers, men worked a twelve-hour day on the land. Only the Jat men had leisure time, especially in the period of January through March, between the rice and wheat harvests. Assistance from the husband after tubectomy was more a function of the particular husband-wife relationship than of the husband's available free time. In one case where a husband and wife had a co-operative relationship of which the mother-in-law was not jealous or which for some reason, she could not disrupt, the husband arranged for his younger sister to do household chores, and his younger brothers to collect fodder and firewood after his wife's tubectomy. This allowed his wife some rest. Significantly, this was the only case where the woman did not complain of pain. It was an individual case though objectively possible among those farmers who had the money to pay for proper hospital facilities. Among laborers, however, very few were employed on a yearly basis. Most were given a daily wage of ten rupees. The family survival in such instances was too dependent on money coming into the house each day for men to take time off to help women recuperate from surgery in their difficulties even were that culturally acceptable. For a family of eight eating twice daily, four kilo of wheat were required and the wheat price was then one rupee, ninety paise. Dal was between four rupees and six rupees per kilo. A kilo might do a family of that size only two or three days.

The Clinical Milieu

Until very recently tubectomies were done using spinal anaesthesia. They are still performed using this method in some parts of the Punjab and if a woman is fat. In an interview in September 1982, the Additional Director of Family Planning explained that spinal anaesthesia was rather dangerous, meningitis being a possible side effect. He also mentioned that spinal anaesthesia could produce the low back pain of which the women complained through repeated punctures of the spinal canal by a blunt needle. A prominent doctor in a leading hospital also commented that "I myself would not like to have this injection."

It is now considered safer to administer a local anaesthetic in the abdominal region. This is preceded by an injection of morphine and in ideal circumstances the skin is cleansed by gentian violet and by savlon. The woman is then given an injection of xylocaine. An incision is made through four layers: skin, subcutaneous fat, muscle and peritoneum, the incision being normally 3" - 4" in width. The Fallopian tubes are then identified, ligated and the four layers sutured. Normally there are 4 stitches binding together the top layer of skin. In cases of local anaesthesia the woman stays in the hospital overnight, though the wound takes one week to heal. The operation is preceded by a pelvic examination only if the woman is having the surgery in a hospital. Aftercare is confined to those who remain in the hospital.

Tubectomies are often carried out at a camp if there happens to be a government drive for a greater number of sterilizations. On any one day 80 women might be sterilized. The operation itself takes only 20-30 minutes. A doctor did not always perform the operation though he was supposed to be present. As to the sanitary conditions in a camp, these may be deduced from a statement made by the present Director of Public

Relations for the Government of Punjab explaining the stoppage of a sterilization camp by district health authorities at Rupar on Monday 9th August, 1982: "You see on that day it was raining and things are already unhygienic enough!"

However, conditions in hospitals were not always clean either. For example, the day I visited a major hospital in one Punjab city two wards had been closed down because a hysterectomy patient contracted tetanus. There were two subsequent deaths from tetanus in that ward. In one year this hospital had conducted 1,327 tubectomies, 951 of which were from the villages. The majority of these women had 4 or more children and were mainly in the 30-34 age group. The Punjab figures also show the majority of female sterilizations were from the rural areas (21,969 out of a total of 28,011).

As more and more operations came to be conducted by local anaesthesia in the abdominal area and as more and more doctors were available to perform them, tubectomies began to be carried out away from hospitals, in primary health centers, subsidiary health centers and sub centers. These sorts of premises appeared to be unhygienic. Innumerable centers had rooms with dirty sheets over which flitted a liberal number of flies.

For a woman, the possible dangers of this operation would increase in a camp situation where large numbers of women were being sterilized in a short period of time and where adequate individual care and attention could not be given. Lack of proper sterilization of the needle, the syringe, surgical instruments and of the area around the wound has been reported as has the frequent shortage of bandages and of cotton wool necessary to protect the wound while it heals. A number of doctors at one hospital mentioned that sometimes the operations were conducted by a midwife or by a woman health visitor alone, though State health authorities denied this. However, these findings of unhygienic conditions were corroborated by a junior official in the Department of Health. He stated that in one

year there had been 50 deaths: "Whether these were due to
sepsis, tetanus or to the doctor's negligence is not known.
The deaths were reported to the Department of Health but after
that they went unreported."

Female Hygiene and Nutrition

Lack of adequate female hygiene was an important factor in
post-operative recovery because it could delay the healing
process and thereby increase the risk of infection. Women did
not wash the whole of their bodies daily. In many cases there
was no place for washing and a woman had to wash behind a
charpoy. It was quite customary for women even when they had a
washing place, to bathe only once every 7 or 8 days. Each
morning during the winter a woman had to heat water for her
husband and grown up children who then washed and left the
house for their various activities. In the village the water
had to be heated on the chula, fed by dung cakes or by wood.
Heating water took quite some time. Usually a woman rose at
5:00 A.M. when the fire was first lit to make the morning tea.
During the morning she milked the buffalos, made the morning
meal, washed the utensils, did the washing, swept the courtyard
and made the dung cakes. From her point of view, washing
herself was just one more energy expending and time consuming
chore. It was twelve o' clock in some houses before a woman
had time to wash herself and to eat. In the afternoon she
became dirty again after collecting fodder and cleaning the
animal patch. If she were being properly hygienic perhaps she
should have washed then for a second time. Washing patterns
were observed to be related to the intensity of the work load
and to available leisure, not just to the presence of a washing
place. Hence, if particular standards of cleanliness were
necessary after this operation, I doubt if most women had the
energy for it or saw the necessity.

Women do wash themselves after defecating or urinating, though more carefully after the first. They do not take a bath during their menses and it is very doubtful if all socio-economic classes of rural women washed after intercourse. At the time of menstruation old salwar (women's baggy trousers) were used as sanitary towels and these were not changed often enough. Leuchorrhea was frequently encountered in the female population. Female underclothing was not always worn and salwar kameez in certain sections of the female population were worn for a week at a time. The fact that the majority of women did not change their clothes at night meant that dirt could settle into the wound. Many of these hygienic patterns were, of course, class related in that the wives of middle class farmers and the richer artisans washed daily and changed their clothes daily.

I noticed cases of encrustation around the wound area which seemed to delay healing especially since women continued with work activities that would stretch the wound under such circumstances. Healing was also hampered by a woman's poor initial health, particularly iron deficiency anaemia. Women lose iron by not eating eggs and meat (the subjects of a religious taboo) and beans, which are too expensive. Sarson ka (mustard plant), the main source of iron, was widely eaten, but only available in winter months. Fruit is hardly ever eaten by the laboring classes or by poor artisans. The main source of protein is dal but as already mentioned its cost meant that intake of dal was reduced. The shortage of milk meant that usually it was reserved for males, either those who are working or for male children. It is difficult for a woman's body to repair itself given this initial undernourishment.

Other Forms of Birth Control

The nature of work activities in and out of the house, the fact that women rose early, did not cook throughout the day for

themselves and worked the whole day, did make them interested
in preventing births. But their experience with family
planning was limited to tubectomy and to the IUD. The IUD was
disliked for various reasons. Many women thought their
husbands would feel it during intercourse. They also
complained it produced excessive bleeding. New varieties such
as the Copper T, were not available in 1980-81 to these
villagers unless they traveled to Ludhiana, which might arouse
their husband's and in-laws' suspicions. For in most cases
these women would have to go secretly without the agreement of
their families. A woman's right to practice family planning
was limited by the presence of a husband and mother-in-law who
were generally interested not in her welfare but in that of the
wider family unit. The consciousness of the mother-in-law and
members of the male property group toward family planning had
not changed despite a situation in which most children now
survived. Still, quite a number of families had lost
children. So far as I am aware, the figures for the village
were the following: 15 families in which one child had been
lost; 19 other families in which two or three children had been
lost; two other families each having lost four children.
Clearly this social situation had more of an impact on
attitudes toward family planning than the official Infant
Mortality Rate (IMR) of 78/1,000 (the government figure for the
rural areas of the Punjab, released in 1982),[13] which in any
case would not have been known in the village.

There were difficulties with other forms of birth control,
such as the pill. The pill, for example, could be detected
around the house. Also, since the majority of rural women were
illiterate, it was difficult for them to follow instructions
for pills even though birth control pills were available in
Ferozepur. Problems with other forms of birth control related
to overcrowding and to the lack of the husband's co-operation.
Once in the village I and my assistant explained to one woman

about condoms. She very sweetly replied that it was not possible to use them because it took so much time to put them on and during that time the children would wake up: "We have to do it quickly." We also explained to her about natural birth control but she asked us "What should I do with him on those days when I can't have sex?" In the face of these kinds of problems, the greatest demand from the women themselves was for an injectable contraceptive. Often in the course of talking to a woman about her child's diet and asking her questions about her child's diarrhea she would appear not to be listening and would interrupt "Bhainji (sister) we want an injection to end babies. Can't you give injections to stop babies? Aren't there any injections?" This was the woman's preference to which there was no medical response.

Most Punjabis prefer to receive any medicine by injection. This was especially the case with vitamins which they believed would give them more "takar" (strength) if injected. The controversial Depo-Provera injections[14] are marketed in single dose units with a needle attached thereby preventing infection from the needle. Injections have to be given every 6 months, whereas a tubectomy operation is once and for all. This latter mode of family planning accommodated doctors' attitudes if not women's needs.

The Institutional Milieu

It is government policy that the deputy commissioner (D.C.) of a district and all his block development officers are given quotas that have to be fulfilled with respect to family planning. If doctors do not co-operate with officials to reach the assigned targets, it is written into their record that they are "poor in family planning." Doctors in the rural health services are put under pressure by higher officials. Women are also pressured. They are eligible for family planning, so far as the government is concerned, after producing two children.

Considering the present infant mortality rate and, as the government sees it, their own active immunization program (though the people in this village never saw polio vaccine and had been vaccinated only against smallpox) the government considers it safe to push their family planning program. However, the shortage of food among laboring families, particularly of milk, together with the low consumption of dal, and the under-consumption of wheat makes the children of these families very vulnerable to disease. Government policy vis a vis this class is suspect since there are so many children who are at risk.

Women were recruited for the operation at immunization camps or when they went to the doctor or to the hospital on some other matter. The emphasis on tubectomy was not accompanied by an equal amount of effort to get males to have vasectomies. As one doctor remarked, "the burden falls on women of the poorer classes because of the quota system whereby each doctor has targets fixed for him." Naturally he could not and did not put pressure on the well-to-do. There would be adverse consequences to himself if he did.

India's rural health scheme[15] is modeled on that of China's. But it does not function in the spirit which activated the health service in China, namely Mao Zedong's precept that "all work done for the people must start from their needs." The enormous reliance which the state government health services department placed on tubectomy in fact arose because doctors were out of touch with rural women. They were not out among them in the fields nor were they with them in their homes seeing the nature of their work and how this could interact with the medical remedies they prescribed. Rural women were interested in birth control. However, they were not at all interested in tubectomy or the IUD. The major problem therefore was not the unacceptability of birth control as such but rather the doctors' unawareness of the kind of contraception sought by rural women. Doctors regarded village women as ignorant. Freire's remark "How can I enter into dialogue if I always project ignorance onto others and never perceive my own,"[16] was not an orientation the medical establishment would subscribe to. Doctors did very little home visiting[17] and contacted people only when they had to. Unable to learn from the people what their problems were, lack of closeness to the people which they appeared to think was intrinsic to their status, doctors could not identify or respond to rural women's needs.[18] This being so it was arrogant of doctors and health administrators to propagate and implement a policy of tubectomies for women.

It would be foolish to neglect the value system of those who performed operations on the poorer women. It is just possible that these values might contribute to negligence during an operation and in the post-operative period. An official of the health department mentioned privately that "if a woman is ill the main thought on the part of hospital personnel will be to first get something out of her husband and only then to look after her." The attitudes of medical personnel clearly affected the quality of care. Another factor was the generally negligent attitude of society towards women in the Punjab. This was manifested strikingly in the poor ante-natal and post-natal care in the region.[19] For example, during pregnancy it was common knowledge that for female rural laborers work does not decrease, even at the end of a pregnancy. Many women continued their normal work routines of fetching and carrying fodder and wood or many worked in the fields right up until the moment of delivery. This explained why there were so many cases of prematurity resulting in infant death.[20] Instead of evoking a responsive concern from the state health ministry, women were praised. "Our ladies are very strong," commented one high official of the health department, "they will go on working right until the last day and may resume work the next day after birth."

Family planning which claims to make a woman's life easier cannot do so simply by reducing the number of births. The State Health Ministry, being interested only in the abstract problem of controlling population size, collected little empirical data on why women came to the hospital for sterilization and on the results of that operation, intended or otherwise. After effects of sterilization were not considered because the government's overall aim was a restricted one—to control the birth rate at all costs. Post-operative care was confined to dispensing a few antibiotics. Follow up case studies were carried out only in a few selected urban areas. Sterilization was performed with a certain amount of care and attention for those few women from the propertied classes who chose to undergo the operation and who were prepared to pay. For the many who were paid to have this operation, the conditions under which the surgery was undertaken, and the work to which the women returned, were such as to interlock with the physical effects of the operation itself in an undesirable way.

Conclusion

I have sought to outline the social and economic conditions under which sterilization for women becomes problematical. Too soon after their tubectomy village women had to resume the kind of work that was damaging to the healing process. There was no means to avoid that work for long stretches each day, in most cases out of economic necessity and otherwise because of social expectations associated with their daughter-in-law status. Had doctors and health officers been present for a long period of time in a laborer's house, or in a Jat home where there were only one or two daughters-in-law and hence much work, they would have realized the difficulties surrounding a tubectomy operation, given this social and economic milieu. As I see it, any genuine interest in birth control comes from the women themselves, not from the medical profession who are only interested in performing a certain number of operations on a given number of women.

Doctors should be particularly discouraged from sterilizing women of the laboring class in circumstances where no post-operative care is provided. It is in this class that propagation of tubectomies can be a dangerous intervention, productive of family conflict and tragedy. If it decreases a woman's work output, then her children are made to do her work. If she is forced to keep her economic activity at the same level, her children then have no protection against either the hopelessness or savagery of her feeling. Any medical measure which, interacting with given social and economic conditions, renders a woman less caring for her children has to be considered inappropriate and unacceptable.

In addition, family planning programs for women operate under the assumption that women have the right to care for their own welfare. In fact such a consciousness could not exist without the supporting material context. I think that it is important not to propagate any mode of family planning among village women until they request it. There should be no campaign of persuasion. Bondestam's views are relevant here, namely that "to control the reproduction of poor people is a piece of cynicism unless they themselves have asked for it."[21] Women will not request any family planning help until they trust those with whom they are in contact. Access to some of the information provided in certain parts of this article was not obtained in the course of advocating any form of birth control and it is significant that a family planning motive in many women could have been discovered without any incentive being given for its expression.

Women's requests were for a mode of family planning that could be practised without the knowledge of their husband and his kin group. Their wishes in this respect have not been respected or safeguarded and the need for secrecy must be assured. As has been indicated, whatever mode of family planning is adopted as policy, it has to be responsive to the type of work a woman does. Taylor also notes that it has to be sensitive to area.[22] Above all, as illustrated in the case study, it has to be sensitive to the role children play in the household economy, a point developed by Mamdani.[23] It is extremely important that doctors do follow-up case studies on rural women laborers concerning the possible adverse inter-relation of tubectomy with certain types of work conditions. Back ache and pelvic pain which the women ascribe to this operation are admitted by the Additional Director of Family Planning as having a clinical source. From evidence I gathered in the village it would appear that these physical side effects are accentuated by the particular type of work that is part of women's daily routine. A woman's work hours and work practices are unalterable for the time being. The only components of the situation that are alterable exist in the clinical and institutional environments. I am aware of the controversies surrounding Depo-Provera and which make medical personnel reluctant to use it while women themselves show no such reluctance. As Rakusen has noted "Significantly among those women reported to be happy on DP are those whose husbands refuse to allow them to use contraceptives."[24] Young mothers did not wish innumerable children, as did members of their husband's kin group. Neither did they want the only alternative offered to them by the state medical apparatus--tubectomy. These women were caught between the family structure and the state medical structure. Perhaps for this reason there were many illegal abortions. Young women were happy if they had a number of sons and only one girl. Once they had achieved this they said they would be happy if they thought their menstruation would never return. This is indeed Roger Short's point (as quoted in Djerassi),[25] "there is growing evidence that women would welcome a form of contraception that produces amenorrhoea."

This study has intended to bring together information concerning one method of family planning as it affects one particular class of women. In a wider context, evidence is emerging from countries that have developed rapidly (Cuba, Nicaragua) that achievement of literacy levels and economic security must precede any success in the sphere of family planning. Indian writers have also commented on this.[26,27] In the Indian context, sterilization is a political issue. Many times I would hear from landlords during my stay in the Punjab: "This is becoming a state for landless laborers." The actual proportions of landless laborers in the Punjab is 24.7%, which is the largest concentration of any state in the Indian Union. Democratic societies in which the underprivileged have constitutional rights face problems when entrenched elites seek to control the political, cultural and social effects of the granting of these rights. As Meillasoux has suggested, control over the domestic community's reproduction in society as a whole "is not a natural process it is a political enterprise."[28]

Joyce Pettigrew
The Queen's University of Belfast

236

Acknowledgement

I warmly acknowledge the help given to me in discussions of this topic during my one year stay in the Punjab by Dr. D.N. Kakar of the Department of Community Medicine and Professor B.N.S. Walia, Head of the Department of Paediatrics, both of the Post Graduate Institute of Medical Education, Chandigarh. It was indeed Professor Walia's concern over the incident described that prompted me to take a more comprehensive interest in tubectomy. I thank many families in Ferozepur for their hospitality and also the families of Dr. R.P. Kapil of village Saidanwalla and Kanwar Jagjiwan Singh of Village Lohgarh. In the village I thank Sant Kaur, Daleep Kaur and Harbans Kaur for their warmth, kindness and co-operation. I also am indebted to my assistant Louisa Francis for being with me most of the time.

This paper was read at the Eighth European Conference on Modern South Asian Studies at Tallberg, Sweden, 1983 and I thank Dr. Beatrix Pleiderer-Lutze for her comments. I also thank Dr. Eileen Robinson M.D., Dr. Elizabeth Ann Roche M.D. and Dr. H. Peaston, M.D. D.T.M. for reading through earlier drafts.

Part of the research was sponsored by the Nuffield Foundation and I am grateful for their support.

The paper is dedicated to Sant Kaur, midwife, popularly known as Santi, who gave me so much love and whom I miss very much.

1. Dr. Neelambar Hatti of the Department of Economic History, Lund University, Sweden, working from June 1979-June, 1982 in Sirsi, North Kanara District, Karnataka, found that women reported experiences of pelvic pain as well as pain in the lower abdomen after undergoing tubectomy operations. He says (written communication) that he interviewed 105 women between 28-45 years who had undergone tubectomy in the 1970-1980 period. All except 10 were lower caste women from poor households. In the Punjab data there were also many references to headaches. The Additional Director of Family Planning blamed this on loss of cerebral fluid in the course of spinal anaesthesia.

2. Though in certain women who had the operation, the pelvic and abdominal regions were tender to the touch, perhaps suggesting slow, imperfect healing.

3. It should be noted, too, that sulphadimidine was the most widely and frequently prescribed antibiotic in the village. Sulphadimidine happens to cause low back pain.

4. There is not a complete ban on work as such after a tubectomy operation. Doctors said that the wound heals much faster if a woman walks about. They told me that rest for upwards of a week is harmful as it might cause clotting. However, activities that involve persistent bending and stretching will create tenderness in the pelvic area. The number of activities in the village where repeated bending is essential are innumerable.

5. Lorna Marsden, "Human Rights and Population Growth. A Feminist Perspective," International Journal of Health Services 3.4 (1973):568.

6. J.F. Marshall, "Some Meanings of Family Planning to an Indian Villager," in Anthropology and the Development Process, ed. Mathur, H.M., Vikas, New Delhi, 1977, p. 458.

7. The most important day in the Sikh calendar, a day venerated especially by ruralite Sikhs as being the day when the 10th religious prophet of the Sikhs founded the visible Sikh community. The harvesting of wheat is usually begun on that day.

8. Mydral, G., Asian Drama, Penguin 1968, p. 1515.

9. At the wheat and rice harvest and at the rice planting a family would work as a group. At the wheat harvest a family would work from seven in the morning until seven in the evening. If the whole family was working more wheat could be cut and the family could hence earn more both in terms of wheat for food throughout the year and in terms of earnings. Since a husband and wife alone (without the hindrance of small children) could cut only 1 1/2 acre per day all, the older

children had to work so that a food supply could be ensured for the whole year.

10. Indeed as another case illustrates, no warm supportive atmosphere awaits a woman from this social group when she comes out of hospital. This one woman on her return commented on her husband's attitudes. "It was his suggestion in the first place that I went for the operation and now he is grumbling because I cannot work. When I send my son for fodder he complains that I should go and collect it myself." "Now it's two months since you worked!" he told me. I in turn complained to him "If you and not I had done the operation then you would have had me to look after you."

11. Though how exceptional we do not know. A leading pediatrician remarked that he feared the incidence of such events was greater than was realized but that there was no way of monitoring the number of cases.

12. But as M.F. Myles notes: "Backache is a common complaint among poorly nourished, overworked and multiparous women whose muscles are lax and easily fatigued," Textbook for Midwives, Edinburgh: E.L.S. Livingstone, 1975, p. 413.

13. It is said that "Family Planning Services depend on the reduction of the Infant Mortality Rate" ("Health for All: An Alternative Strategy," Report of a Study Group set up jointly by the Indian Council of Social Science Research and the Indian Council of Medical Research, New Delhi, August 1980, p. 90); C.E. Taylor notes that "Although an association between infant and child mortality and fertility levels has been widely accepted little direct evidence has been available either to support the assumptions or define possible mechanisms of interaction," in "The Child Survival Hypothesis," Population Studies 30.2 (1976):263-277. Wider structural changes are involved in the creation of smaller families and until they occur as Caldwell's work suggests "the reproductive pattern is needed to support the economic one." As he points out "As long as children consume relatively little and boys start earning early then high fertility is no disadvantage," see J. Caldwell, Theory of Fertility Decline, New York: Academic Press, 1982, pp. 171, 175.

14. In India, Depo-Provera has not usually been available in clinics but an article in Studies in Family Planning (Vol. II, No. 9/10, September/October 1980 "User Preferences for Contraceptive Methods in India, Korea, the Phillipines and Turkey") reports that where it was, both in India and in Turkey a higher proportion of rural rather than urban women selected Depo-Provera as a mode of contraception. Dr. Harry Peaston and his wife working among the Pathans in Risalpur (a town in the North West Frontier Province forty miles east of the Khyber Pass) in an area of eighty five percent illiteracy (the literacy rate for females in Ferozepur was 24.74%) remark that "After long thought and experience we concluded that a single dose method given by injection was the most suitable mode of

birth control." Report, Clinical Research Unit, Risalpur, N.W.F.P., Pakistan, p. 30.

15. At District level there was a civil surgeon and at block level, an area covering 100,000 population, there would be a Primary Health Centre with a Chief Medical Officer in charge. Each Primary Health Centre had two subsidiary health centres covering a population of 10,000. The subsidiary health centre had a doctor in attendance and each had two sub centres to each of which were attached two multi-purpose health workers.

16. P. Freire, Pedagogy of the Oppressed, London: Penguin Edition, 1972.

17. The Joint Report of the Indian Council of Social Research and the Indian Council of Medical Research, Health for All: An Alternative Strategy, New Delhi, 1980, referred to above, likewise makes the point on p. 94 that home visiting is essential in the context of labour conditions: "Until such time as poorer women have more leisure, services must be made available to them in their homes at times when they are available."

18. David Werner notes in an article "The Village Health Care Programme: Community Suppportive or Community Oppressive" (Contact, Christian Medical Commission, Geneva, 57, August 1980) that when they asked "the pioneers of rural health programmes we visited in Latin America what they saw as the major obstacles to bringing effective health care to the people the most common replies were 'doctors and politics.'"

19. It appears indeed that the poor development of these services is related to explicit official policy to favour family planning as against maternal and child health services. Banerji for example (D. Banerji in Family Planning in India, People's Publishing House, New Delhi, (1976):41, 48) notes that one of the recommendations of the first U.N. Advisory Mission that was acted upon was that "The Directorate of family planning should be relieved from other responsibilities such as maternal and child health and nutrition...This recommendation is reinforced by the fear that the programme may otherwise be used in some states to expand the much needed and neglected maternal and child welfare services...Later on when the necessity of integrating family planning work with the maternal and child health services was finally realized, this was done at the cost of depriving the directorate general of health services of its maternal and child health unit and transferring it to the family planning department rather than integrating family planning with the maternal and child health services... The maternal and child health workers, health visitors, auxiliary nurse midwives, dais who had earlier been concerned only with maternal and child health, now themselves became targets of the family planning 'targets'...there were no targets for maternal and child health work."

20. M. Cameron and Y. Hofvander, Manual on Feeding Infants and Young Children. Food and Agricultural Organization of the United Nations, Rome, 1976.

21. L. Bondestam, and S. Bergstrom, Poverty and Population Control, New York: Academic Press, 1980.

22. C.E. Taylor, Policy Relevant Findings from Narangwal, The Narangwal Population Study World Bank Monograph, forthcoming (pp. 178-204). He notes (p. 203) that the remarkable variation between villages in types of methods shows that flexibility is needed "in the family planning process." This is borne out by an article on rural Kerala entitled "Marked Preference for Female Sterilization in a Semirural Squatter Settlement," Studies in Family Planning, 1979 vol. 10 no. 11/12:332-336 by Leela Gulati. But significantly in this region there is a higher literacy rate, a higher proportion of attended births and a lower infant mortality rate.

23. M. Mamdani, The Myth of Population Control, Monthly Review Press, 1972.

24. J. Rakusen, "Depo-Provera: the extent of the problem - a case-study in the politics of birth control" in Women, Health and Reproduction, H. Roberts, ed., London: Routledge, Kegan, Paul, 1981, pp. 75-108.

25. Carl Djerassi, The Politics of Contraception, New York: Norton and Co., 1979, p. 13.

26. J.A. de Vries in D.G. Jongmans and H.J.M. Claessen The Neglected Factor reports that "only educational factors disclose a consistent association with family planning involvement," Van Gorcum, 1974. Ashok Mitra also remarks "To my mind primary education and literacy cannot brook any more neglect even in the matter of achieving the small family norm," "The Small Family Norm and Literacy," Family Planning News, 10.2 (1969):6.

27. D. Baneriji notes regarding Indian government planners that they did not realize that a family planning programme in attempting to control population growth forms merely one component of a wider spectrum of programmes to deal with social and economic problems, in "Population Planning in India, National and Foreign Priorities," International Journal of Health Services 3.4 (1973):773-777.

28. C. Meillasoux, Maidens, Meal and Money, Cambridge University Press, 1981, p. 35.

GENDER ROLES IN ELEMENTARY SCHOOL TEXTS IN INDONESIA

Third-world countries offer an interesting context in which
to observe the development of gender role socialization of
children as it is influenced by textbooks. In many third-world
countries large numbers of children have only recently begun to
attend formal schools or to receive even six years of basic
education. Gender role socialization of children has until
recently been carried out almost exclusively through the family
and other non-school contacts. The introduction of a
broad-based educational system drastically alters the content
of childhood learning and increases the opportunity for
governmental decisions to influence children's understanding of
various social roles, including occupational roles, and gender
roles. Governmental decisions on the content of public
education may emphasize the preservation, the exaggeration, or
the alteration of traditional patterns. We see efforts to
introduce national pride at the expense of more parochial
identities such as those of ethnicity, religion, and locale in
many third-world countries.[1] Gender role socialization can
also be consciously undertaken, either to maintain or to change
the "traditional" understanding of gender differentiation in
the society.

In this study we will look at Indonesia, a third-world
country with a rapid upswing in primary school enrollments
beginning in 1974. In the early 1970s the Indonesian
government undertook a broad-based assessment of the
educational system which resulted in a proposed new curriculum
and plans to provide textbooks at government expense in
required subjects. The assessment had shown that most children
did not have texts for their courses because they could not

afford to buy them. The decision to create new texts and to provide them free to students raised numerous problems. C.E. Beeby, who participated in the assessment, pointed to problems associated with changing texts:

> ...there is a preliminary question of policy that lies behind any 'crash' textbook scheme in a country whose schools have been long starved of books: how different shall the new books be from the old? It is a question almost every developing country has to answer at some stage...The typical situation arises when it becomes essential to have, as soon as possible, a set of textbooks in the hands of every student, and when there is at the same time an equally strong demand, from politicians and educational theorists alike, for textbooks very different from the present ones, which are often derived from old colonial models that have little relevance to the country's current needs and policies.[2]

Production of Indonesian language texts and mathematics texts went relatively smoothly, but social studies materials were delayed when a governmental decision was made to introduce "Pancasila Moral Education" as a subject separate from social studies. Basically, this subject was to provide political socialization in ways supportive of the current regime, and presumably the content was to be carefully thought out. Since not all bookwriting projects could be tackled at once, private companies were allowed to publish books for use in "Pancasila Moral Education" by following an outline of approved content, presented in the 1975 Curriculum. The content in the 1975 Curriculum proved highly controversial, especially with Moslem religious parties, because it presented other religions (Christianity, Hinduism, Confucianism and Buddhism) as good religions.

This study deals with a series of books printed by a private company for use in the interim, before 1981, when the official books were finally completed. These temporary books followed the 1975 Curriculum outline for "Pancasila Moral

Education" and were approved by the Education Department for use in schools. The books, called <u>Pendidikan Moral Pancasila Sekolah Dasar</u> (hereafter PMP), were published by C.V. Toha Putra of Semarang and all were written by Drs. Abu Ahmadi.

Moral education is a required course for all elementary students in Indonesia, so these texts have some potential for significant impact on students' understanding of appropriate roles. But there are some assumptions that the reader should <u>not</u> make. First, every child does not have a text and indeed there are probably whole schools where very few children have the text. Urban children are more likely to have the books than rural children. Teachers are more likely to have them than students, and teachers tend to rely heavily on texts when they are available. In elementary grades this may mean that the entire text is copied out on the blackboard. Second, the texts considered in this study were bought in Jakarta, Surabaya, Malang, and Jogjakarta, suggesting a fairly wide usage in Java, but not necessarily outside of Java. Third, one cannot assume that the youngest elementary students will even know Bahasa Indonesia, the language in which the texts are written. However, students do begin to study the national language in the first grade, and the vocabulary of these books is very easy.

With all of these reservations, such a study is still useful. These books reflect governmental decisions about what <u>ought</u> to be taught to children. Each book was approved for instruction by the national-level Ministry of Education and carries a formal statement to that effect on the title page:

> In accord with the Master Teaching Design (GBPP) of the 1975 Elementary School Curriculum.

On the back of the title page the following is printed:

> Important!
> The use of the book Pancasila Moral Education by Drs. Abu <u>Ahmadi</u> (volumes 1,2,3,4,5, and 6) is legally approved as an

elementary school students' book by
Declaration No. 123/I.03/E.78 of 4 February,
1978.

At the time I acquired these books no other PMP books were
being sold in the stores throughout Java.

I am not aware of any explicit Indonesian educational
document on the subject of how gender roles should be
presented. But these books and the later series published in
1982 by the Department of Education are based on the same 1975
Curriculum Outline and are remarkably similar in their
treatment of gender roles. There may be no written curricular
policy stating that girls and boys be taught different social
roles, yet in these Indonesian texts, we shall see that there
is a distinct and consistent pattern of gender role
representations which is repetitive. We are looking at public
policy, whether or not we call it a "hidden curriculum," and
that policy is being formulated, either consciously or
unconsciously, in the national offices of the Ministry of
Education by those persons responsible for the preparation and
approval of texts. We shall see that the approved texts
portray new "ideal gender roles," which are quite different
from actual gender roles as they are or have been, at least in
Java. The policy seems to be an effort to change existing
gender roles.

Gender Roles in Elementary Texts: Usage Questions

Before considering specifically the presentation of gender
roles in elementary texts, several "language" questions
concerning usage in Bahasa Indonesia need to be addressed. In
English, one "sexist" element of language is the rule for the
use of he as the generic third-person pronoun when the sex of
members of a category are unspecified or mixed (i.e., a
Governor works hard; he is diligent). Many studies have
examined how this practice influences our understanding and
gender role stereotyping.[3] The Indonesian language does not

present this problem. <u>Dia</u> (<u>ia</u>, <u>-nya</u>) is either he, she, or it. The word has no gender identification. There are words such as <u>pemuda</u> (youth) for which a feminine variant exists (<u>pemudi</u>) so that the general term for youth may be taken to mean males only even when used as a generic. These words correspond roughly to the kinds of distinctions made between hero and heroine, poet and poetess. There are not many of these in Bahasa Indonesia, but there are some.

In written language, a second usage problem presents itself. Rules of capitalization do not seem to be entirely standardized, but generally proper names and official titles are capitalized within sentences and, of course, initial words in sentences are capitalized. Occasionally, other words are capitalized. One anomaly arises in this set of PMP books. In the first grade texts, the word for mother (<u>ibu</u>) is never capitalized but the word for father (<u>bapak</u>) is, even when the two are side by side in a parallel construction. Since these terms are used as respect terms for older people, the terms appear often. For example:

> Pramuka selalu menurut ibu dan Bapak.
> (Scouts always obey mother and Father.)[4]

> Di sekolah, Heri dan Eni membantu Bapak dan
> ibu guru.[5]
> (At school, Heri and Eni help male (Father)
> and female (mother) teachers.)

In the first grade book these terms appear eight times in parallel situations, where neither is the initial word of the sentence. In every case <u>ibu</u> is not capitalized and <u>bapak</u> is. In the second grade book and all succeeding books, <u>bapak</u> is not capitalized, except in one third grade book. Children just learning to read learn the words for mother and father very early, and (if they have books) could be influenced to see father as more important than mother. Numerous discussions with Indonesian language teachers and other Indonesian speakers did not result in any clarification. Most said that neither should be capitalized unless used as a title for a specific person.

Gender Role Content

Most studies of gender role content in American school books look at the types of activities boys and girls and men and women engage in. The texts considered here are moral education texts and as such most of the roles presented are directly normative. The people described in these books are idealized and have very little personality. For the most part, these are not stories with a lot of action.

Mothers, Fathers and Other Adults

Mothers and fathers are prominent in the books for classes one through three and are nearly absent in later books where the lessons are oriented to knowledge of governmental institutions and structure. Table 1 presents all the activities and characteristics ascribed to mothers and fathers in these texts. Clearly the second grade text spends more space on family relations than do the texts for the other grades. In the second grade, mother is described three times as "staying at home," while five times father "goes to the office." Mothers indeed do nothing other than household chores, child care, shopping, and prayer. Mothers eat and bathe after father. Fathers have occupations, lead children, support the family, protect the family, and in general head the family. Fathers eat and bathe first.

These are very unidimensional characterizations of mother/father roles; almost all portrayals of parents are in the context of a family of five (mother, father, two daughters, and a son). The strong normative character of the described parental behaviors are shown in the following:

> After eating, Eni (girl) and Heri (boy) leave for school. Father goes to the office. And mother stays at home. That is

orderliness in a family. It must be cultivated in the family forever.

And again:

> Heri's father works in an office. He makes his living every day. He fills the needs of his children. He pays the children's school fees. He guards the security of his whole family. These are the responsibilities of the head of the family. Heri's mother cooks in the kitchen. She cooks the children's food. She washes the children's clothes. She brings up and takes care of her children. She prays for the children. These are the responsibilities of the mother in a family.[6]

There certainly are gender role norms in Indonesia which give women primary responsibility for the kitchen and the children. But, for most Javanese children, the distinctions drawn between father and mother are not realistic. Mothers are not just housekeepers. Women frequently play an important economic role in the family. And it is doubtful, in fact, given teacher's salaries in Indonesia, that a father who is a teacher, like the one described in the text, could afford the house pictured, the school fees, and basic necessities, if he were the sole support of his family.

Hildred Geertz described the economic role of women in rural Java:

> ...actually there is little of the man's world that they cannot participate in and still less that they do not know about. In the rice-growing cycle, there are certain tasks traditionally performed by women. After the harvest, in which men rarely engage, the rice is brought home by the women; and frequently its disposal, including complex financial transactions, is also in their hands. The market is dominated by women, and even the rich successful wholesalers are as often women as men. Women own and dispose of property as freely and competently as men.[7]

Table 1
Statements about Mothers and Fathers by Grade

	Mother	Father
1st grade	Bringing up children Tells children to be careful	Is head of family Leads his children
2nd grade	Brings up and teaches children Shops at the market Stays at home (3)* Bathes second Takes rice second at meal Cooks food in kitchen Washes clothes Brings up and guards children Prays for children Works in kitchen	Gives food Is a teacher Has responsibilities and rights Goes to office (5)* Tells children to be industrious & obedient Bathes First Takes rice first at meals Seeks a living, fulfills needs of family Pays school fees Protects family
3rd grade	With difficulty, gives birth to and cares for children Breast feeds, feeds, bathes, clothes children Shops in the market	Guards safety and fills needs of children Pays for his family's living Looks out for health of children Tells children to help mother
4th grade	Prepares food and flowers for Temple (Hindu)	None
5th grade	None	None
6th grade	None	None

*Numbers in parenthesis indicate that a statement appears in that grade-level book more than once.

Women do not plow or carry loads as heavy as those of men, and they do not do road repairs or carpentry, but it is women in Java who are thought to know how to handle money. As Douglas points out, most families in Indonesia (and especially the Javanese) are matrifocal, meaning the mother is dominant in ordinary family affairs, but formally patriarchal meaning that higher status and respect go to the father.[8] Geertz puts it succinctly in the case of Javanese women:

> The dimension of responsibility for major decisions of household management ranges from dominance by the wife to a point of almost complete equality between husband and wife, with discussion over every major decision. Rarely is a Javanese wife completely under the shadow of her husband, but there are many husbands who have passively surrendered to their wives.[9]

The role of mother in texts does not show this female-dominant aspect of the family at all and, instead, the father is given the role of economic provider alone. This is in fact a rare pattern in Indonesia and occurs primarily among high government officials and others with secure incomes. In these cases, a wife may not take on remunerative work (though she still contributes a lot to the family by overseeing child care) and will have servants to do the household chores. In short, the role described in the text is more characteristic of the very small Javanese urban upper class than of the typical family. Emphasis is put on the normative element of respect, (father eats and bathes first) with no recognition of the real division of labor in the family. Outside of school, girls and boys do see mothers frequently fulfilling an economic function in the family, so it is doubtful they will not learn this behavior. But it is possible that they could construe this shifting of economic function entirely to the father as indicative of how things ought to be, or even misperceive the value of mother's contribution to the economic welfare of the family. Are little girls being taught that it is better to

"stay at home?" And does that presage an increasing inequality
in the family toward more male dominance?

The situation is certainly not balanced by other adult
roles portrayed in the text. Men are seen as teachers,
farmers, road repairers, government officials (lots of these!)
school principals, doctors, school guards, policemen, thieves,
coolies, dancers, etc. Women are seen as teachers, sellers in
the market (one tiny picture but no story), and dancers.
Dancer incidentally is not generally considered an occupation,
but because of the emphasis on cultural diversity, there are
many pictures of dancers in costume, and in these there are a
lot of women. The only occupation we really see being
practiced by women is teaching.

Table 2
Percentage of Women Teachers in
Indonesian Schools (All levels)--by Selected Regions[10]

Region	% Female
East Java	35%
Central Java & D.I. Jogja	31%
West Java	31%
D.K. Jakarta	54%
Indonesia	35%

As Table 2 illustrates, women do hold a significant
percentage of positions as teachers; in the capital city over
half. This is reflected in the texts where nearly half of the
references to teachers, where sex is specified, are to female
teachers.

The lack of other female roles is surprising and may
suggest a more limited range of possibilities for girls than is
actually present in Indonesia. This is reminiscent of the
findings of textbook studies in the U.S., Europe, India, and
Israel.[11-14]

Girls and Boys

About forty-five percent of Indonesia's elementary school pupils are female.[15] Generally, the percentage of school-age children in school drops as age rises. Although children are eligible to enter school at age six, most don't enter until age 7 or 8. At age eight 86% of all boys and 75% of all girls are in school, the highest attendance of any age group. By age 12, attendance drops to 64% of boys and 57% of girls and by age 14 only 45% of boys and 33% of girls are still in school.[16] Since a fair number of children get only the first several years of education, what happens in grades 1-3 is crucial to government-influenced socialization. Since fifty-one percent of the population is female, Table 3 indicates the imbalance in the textbook presentation of males and females, in a country where 51% of the population is female. By counting the people identifiable as to sex in the pictures in these PMP books we find:

Table 3
Number and Percentage of Females and
Males in PMP Texts by Grade

Grade	Male N	%	Female N	%	# Pictures with People	Photos
1st grade	33	61%	21	39%	17	2
2nd grade	52	68	25	32	12	2
3rd grade	74	72	29	28	19	2
4th grade	38	78	11	22	14	2
5th grade	11	79	3	21	3	2
6th grade	26	87	4	13	5	2
Total	234	72%	93	28%	70	12

Overall 72% of the people (both adults and children) in pictures are male, with the percentage who are male rising as grade level increases. This is remarkably similar to the male-female ratio in American texts.[17] All photographs are of the President and Vice-President, of course both male. Even in street scenes nearly all identifiable people are male, as though women don't walk on the streets. Many of the pictures are of children and show boys doing active things (playing on the playground, cooking over a camp stove, etc.). Girls are shown to cook, sit in mother's lap, and only occasionally are pictured playing, and then only indoors.

Table 4 presents the activities and characteristics of boys and girls in the PMP texts. Boys are clearly mentioned more than girls and do more active things. They go on trips, see soccer games, and at home they draw water from the well. They do also sweep, an activity girls share. Girls mostly help mother in the kitchen and do household tasks. In terms of characteristics, girls obey, are shy, and study industriously. Boys obey, are good at reading and writing, are not lazy, are dashing, study mathematics, are frightened of traffic, are honest, and are praised for it. Boys clearly seem superior in character to girls. No girl is ever praised by teacher or parent. No girls are mentioned as participating in elections. The class officers are all male.

In short, boys are more prominent than girls; that is, the number of times they are mentioned is considerably more frequent than girls. But they are also dominant: leadership positions are always in their hands. Boys are shown as speaking up in class, but girls are not (the lesson is on how to express differing opinions). Boys are in official positions and we are told in the third grade text that to be class officer one must be "capable, bold, energetic and smart." Of the six pictures where both boys and girls are depicted and there is some position of dominance, boys are always in the leadership role.

What does the pattern mean? What messages do girls and boys pick up from this? The image of the girl staying at home and helping with household chores is likely to reinforce girls' experiences. Girls are more likely to engage in solitary play at home, while little boys are given freedom to play away from home with their friends. The dominance of boys fits in with the ideals of the society, in terms of expectations that public life is the realm of men. But the picture of life in the household is probably atypical, and most boys and girls will experience a disjuncture between the textbook ideal and social reality. Girls do in fact also begin to learn about the economic role of their mothers despite what the school books say. As Geertz notes,

> "Little girls are introduced to the world of buying and selling, soon learn to do the whole family's daily shopping alone, and--if the mother sells in the market--may take over the mother's stand for short periods."[18]

In my own neighborhood in one of the many poor areas of Jakarta, little girls were given significant responsibility in shopping and were generally adept at bargaining. They took care of younger siblings (as did boys). One little girl (about 9) took care of the money for a thriving lottery sales booth near my home.

The range of activities that boys are pictured as engaging in does suggest various economic functions: for example, helping father in the garden or working on broken dikes in the rice fields. The full range of economic activities of little boys is certainly not presented, for little boys sell homemade popsicles (as young as age 5), newspapers, and cigarettes; but these are activities of the poorest people. We can argue indeed that the picture of gender roles is once again classist.

Table 4
Children's Activities and
Characteristics by Sex and Grade

	Females	Males
1st grade	Sits with her mother Obeys (female) teacher Also wakes up early Helps mother in the kitchen (2)* Plays in the yard	Sits with his father Obeys (male) teacher Has a school and a house Draws water from the well Is already good at reading and writing Each day he reads Is never lazy Always obeys school rules Is very dashing (in appearance) Helps his father Goes to city with father Rides a bemo (car/bus) Buys shoes and books for all 3 children
2nd grade	Doesn't play, she is still shy Is not yet known (by children) Has to help mother in kitchen (3)* Has to sweep the yard Arranges the coffee cups Readies her shoes and for school Industriously studies and works Obeys her parents	Goes to school Plays with Edi (another boy) Four schoolboys are like brothers Goes to uncle's house outside the village Draws water and sweeps floor Sets table Readies Dad's shoes Studies math every day Helps his father Cleans his shoes and his bicycle Is somewhat frightened of traffic Only boys make suggestions in class Helps sweep floor

		Late to school because he looks for owner of pencil he found-- Teacher praises him
3rd grade	Boils water and sweeps floor	Sees a soccer game Draws water from well Helps father in the garden Is chosen as class chairperson (2)* Is chosen as class vice-chairperson
4th grade	Cleans the bedroom Helps mother in kitchen Sweeps school yard (assigned)	Rides bus to city with father Draws water from well Sweeps floor Helps father clean garden Helps repair the broken dikes in the rice field
5th grade	None	None
6th grade	None	Boys participate in class election

*Numbers in parenthesis indicate that a statement appears in that grade-level book more than once.

Societal Implications

The ideal family as presented in these texts is headed by a father who gets the most respect. Mother stays home and in the kitchen with her daughters. Sons help fathers in economic activities. Fathers are the family providers. It appears that this "ideal" family may be far from the reality of most families living in Java. In presenting Indonesian society as more "sexist" than it is in reality, we find parallels with gender role descriptions in Western elementary textbooks. The gender role differences are so consistent and repetitive that it would seem appropriate to label them "governmental policy."

But why is it governmental policy in effect to misrepresent the actual and present in state moral education books an ideal so far removed from typical gender roles? What is the intent? Clearly on some matters other than gender roles, the content of the 1975 Curriculum was planned to encourage specific changes in society. Religious tolerance and the equal value of all religions, for instance, were consistently emphasized and eventually challenged by strongly Moslem political leaders who felt governmental policy was anti-Islam. On other matters, the 1975 Curriculum clearly tried to preserve traditional family values of obedience, harmony, cooperation, etc.. How, then, can we explain an outcome that presents the ideal society as more sexist than it is in reality?

This is not simply "author bias" because these textbooks were officially approved for use by a high-level group of bureaucrats in the Ministry of Education. Furthermore the same patterns of gender role images were retained in the series of books which followed these, even though the content in the newer series was different and more sophisticated. For instance, in the new series in the first forty-three pages of the first grade text, there are 211 pictures of males and 79 of females.

A second possibility is that officials in the Ministry of Education do not see the disjuncture between the textbook portrayals and social reality, because they are themselves the group most similar to what is pictured as the ideal. These men do have an office to go to, nice houses, bicycles, etc., like the portrayals in the books. It would seem a plausible explanation for the portrayal of gender roles in the original series of books, analyzed here. Presumably their authorization was only a matter of acceptance or rejection of manuscripts by an official. It would be a somewhat less plausible rationale for the 1981 textbook series, where a group of <u>educational</u> <u>experts</u> were specifically brought together to create new books. It is possible that it is a matter of "stereotypes getting in the way," as U'ren suggested.

However, let us consider the possibility that it is more than an accident. It is possible that such consistent and repetitive descriptions of gender roles appear intentionally, just as the ideal of religious tolerance can be viewed as intentional because it is so different from the norm in the Indonesian society, where Islam is widely accepted as the only true religion.

How might we view such changes of traditional gender roles in the context of Indonesia's national goals under its current political leadership? Indonesian economic policy today encourages quasi-capitalist development complete with massive acceptance and encouragement of foreign capitalist investment. A major theme in written national educational policy is that education must be more relevant to development. Beeby puts it as follows:

> The most constant reference here is to economic growth, productivity, and skilled manpower, but it is insisted that the Government sees development more broadly than this.[19]

An educational policy oriented toward economic growth in an industrializing capitalist economy will aim to produce an appropriately educated workforce in urban areas. Again, Beeby says:

> To get quick results (in economic growth) it would be logical...to seek young workers for the modern sector in the categories that have already made most progress in that direction: in the cities rather than in the countryside, in parts of Java and two or three other advanced provinces, in places where Bahasa Indonesia and European languages are most commonly used, and in the upper socio-economic classes.[20]

Clearly, Indonesian educational policy is not entirely oriented in these directions, but we have seen urban orientations even though the setting is supposedly rural (fathers going to offices, crossing busy intersections, etc.); and various aspects seem oriented to the urban upper classes, such as children owning bicycles or going to soccer matches. Is it then so far fetched to suggest that the portrayal of gender roles is also related to the goal of economic development and that those responsible for textbook production have adopted the model of women found in Western textbooks even though it is far from the typical Indonesian's reality? The role which Indonesian children seem to be prepared for by these books is a patrifocal, male-dominated society, in which women can be prepared to serve as a "reserve labor force" (they are, after all, encouraged to study hard) but in which their primary role is reproduction.

The irony of this is that women have traditionally been the backbone of Indonesia's old trading economy. But the role of women (if these texts are influential) will be far less significant in the new capitalist economy. The new role fosters economic dependency on males. Since Indonesian women have seldom had a major role in public life, the gender role models projected in these texts is not likely in the present circumstances to be the subject of political discussion at the national level.

Martha Logsdon
Central Michigan University

Notes

1. See, for instance, Judith Friedlander's analysis of schools and textbooks in her study, Being Indian in Hueyapan: A Study of Forced Identity in Contemporary Mexico (New York: St. Martin's Press, 1975).

2. C.E. Beeby, Assessment of Indonesian Education: A Guide in Planning (Wellington, New Zealand: New Zealand Council for Educational Research and Oxford University Press, 1979), p. 61.

3. See, for instance the excellent review of this literature in Jeanette Dibrell "A Study of Masculine Generics: How They Are Perceived and Their Effects on Reading Comprehension and Certain Psychological Attitudes Measures." M.S. Thesis, Central Michigan University, 1982.

4. Drs. Abu Ahmadi Pendidikan Moral Pancasila Sekolah Dasar Jilid II (Semarang: C.V. Toha Putra, 1977), p. 19.

5. Ibid., p. 30.

6. Ibid., p. 33 and p. 39.

7. Hildred Geertz, The Javanese Family: A Study of Kinship and Socialization (New York: The Free Press of Glencoe, 1961), p. 122.

8. Stephen A. Douglas, Political Socialization and Student Activism in Indonesia (Illinois: University of Illinois Press, 1970), p. 34.

9. Geertz, op. cit., p. 125.

10. Badan Penelitian dan Pengembangan Pendidikan dan Kebudayaan, Department Pendidikan dan Kebudayaan Statistik Persekolahan Departmen P dan K 1974 Buku 1 (Jakarta, October, 1976). Adapted from Table 18.

11. Women on Words and Images, Dick and Jane as Victims: Sex Stereotyping in Children's Readers (Princeton: Women on Words and Images, 1975).

12. Jane Chetwynd and Oonagh Hartnett, The Sex Role System (London: Routledge and Kegan Paul, 1978). This offers a summary of studies of gender roles in British texts on pp. 54-56. See also Scher et al., "Sex Roles in Israeli Elementary School Readers," Journal of Social Psychology 114:291-92, 1981. In a very interesting study of Indian textbooks by Narendra Nath Kalia, "Images of Men and Women in Indian Textbooks," in Gail P. Kelly and Carolyn M. Elliot, Women's Education in the Third World: Comparative Perspectives (Albany, NY: State University of New York Press, 1982), the author finds a great disparity between the occupations depicted as male and female even though it is official policy that these books should promote gender equality. To quote directly:

> Instead of freeing individuals from conformity to sex roles, the Indian texts fortify a sex-based division of labor in

which men venture into a bustling world of
excitement and decision making while women
remain in the background providing advice
and support. Instead of inspiring each sex
to develop a respectful attitude toward the
other, the texts condone the use of physical
and verbal abuse against women who fail to
comply with archaic sex-role
expectations....What we find in the texts is
not an accurate depiction of the many roles
historically assigned to Indian women, but
what sexist educators and textbooks writers
have selected." (P. 187)

13. Delores Prida and Susan Ribner, "The Portrayal of
Women in Children's Books on Puerto Rican Themes," in We'll Do
it Ourselves: Combatting Sexism in Education (David Rosen,
Steve Weiner, and Barbara Yates, eds.), Student Committee,
Study Commission on Undergraduate Education and the Education
of Teachers, Lincoln, Neb., 1974.

14. Marjorie U'ren, "The Image of Women in Textbooks," in
Gornick and B. K. Moran, eds., Women in Sexist Society:
Studies in Power and Powerlessness (New York: Basic Books,
1971), pp. 318-328.

15. Badan Penelitian dan Pengembangan Pendidikan dan
Kebudayaan, Department Pendidikan dan Kebudayaan, Statistic
Persekolahan Departmen P dan K 1974 Buku 1 (Jakarta, October,
1976). Adapted from Table 15.

16. Beeby, op. cit., p. 335.

17. See, for instance, Jan Jeffrey and Barb Craft, "Report
of the Elementary School Textbooks Task Force" of the Committee
to Study Sex Discrimination in the Kalamazoo Public Schools.
(Kalamazoo, MI: Mimeo, n.d.), p. 4.

18. Geertz, op. cit., p. 116.

19. Beeby, op. cit., p. 265.

20. Ibid., p. 271.

I like to imagine a scene that never happened. The wife of
one of the Peking officials in the late Ching Dynasty leaves
the courtyard where she otherwise spends her whole life to view
the Peking Opera. Carried from her home to a palanquin and
from the palanquin to the theatre, she sits, bound feet hanging
helplessly down, and watches the heroine, a water goddess, lead
her warriors against her brother who is trying to prevent her
marriage to a mortal lover. Imagine the feelings of our wife
watching the resplendent woman fight single-handed against a
troop of men all throwing spears at her which she catches and
flings back, with feet and hands, until her quick-moving figure
is entirely surrounded by flying spears. That the same society
which forced women in real life to undergo the physical and
pyschic tortures of bound feet could have conceived of such an
active and wonderful role for a woman, even in fantasy, simply
forces us to acknowledge the complexity and opacity of human
relationships, especially those between the sexes.

The contradictions inherent in this imaginary scene linger,
in a reduced form, in present-day China, a society where the
feudal past has been so recently replaced, or more exactly,
overlaid by modern values. Walking the streets in Beijing, I
often saw women with tiny feet who, from their apparent age,
must have had their feet bound, certainly, in the 1920s, if not
in the 30s or even the 40s. In fact, one of my students told
me that her mother, a woman in her late 40s who was born in
China, missed having her feet bound only because her father was
away from home when she was at the proper age. At the bottom
of the seemingly endless staircase which finally tops Tai Shan
mountain in Shangtung Province, we met an old woman, coming

down, whose tiny feet seemed unable to bear her weight at all. That night, in Confucius's home town, walking home from dinner, we were called over to a vegetable stand by a bright, open woman, certainly younger than 60, who showed us her bound feet. We listened in the dark stunned as our friend interpreted her simple, pain-filled account of the original binding, of the--most painful of all--periodic unbinding which she still endures, of walking, working, living with that handicap. I realized many times in Beijing how close Chinese women still are to an unthinkable subjugation. Yet often biking, walking, playing with my young women friends I realized how far Chinese women have come in less than one lifetime.

The not-so-distant plight of the Chinese women is something we cannot, I think, appreciate even when we read about it, and those conditions lasted down until liberation, and even after. In fact, remnants are still present. For instance, one of my colleagues, who had spent time at the beginning of the Cultural Revolution living with peasants in Shanxi Province, quoted the following from a woman with whom she lived in the early 60s:

> During the great famine in 1939, I was only 18 and newly married. My parents and parents-in-law all starved to death. People in our village began eating earth after they stripped all the leaves and bark off the trees. My husband and I followed the stream of refugees to Shanxi Province. We begged our way here. People got so hungry that they even resorted to eating each other.... Our baby son died on the way. When we came to this village in Shanxi, we became so weak that we could move no further. My husband lay on the path dying when a man came and talked him into selling me...it was a common practice in the famine. To save both, parents sold their children, and men sold their wives.

Poverty lingers in China, and young girls are still "bought" so that their families can have money to buy wives for their sons. This is one of the main reasons why in China girls have always been considered of less value to a family than boys--girls, simply, will leave the family, thus depriving it of their labor, while sons will bring in new workers in the form of wives. Thus, girls are not considered to be part of the family. A wife's parents are called wai zu-fu, which means outside grandparents--wai is the same character used in wai guo ren--foreigner.

My students, who had spent an average of two years in the countryside, told me that selling wives is still very common there. The practice is wide-spread enough that it was treated in a play which I saw in Beijing during the last year I was there, "The Bright Moon Begins to Shine." This play, written, directed, acted by women, presented in a frank way many problems concerning marriage in current Chinese society. Of course, as in all literature which receives official approval, all problems were solved by the end of the play. The heroine, a middle-aged cadre, goes into the countryside to solve the problems of a young girl who has left the husband she was forced to marry in return for money which her mother needed to give a marriage portion to her brother. The mother is sympathetic to her daughter, but is caught in a situation which she cannot control. Finally, the problem is resolved when it is discovered that the son is in love with the daughter of the heroine. Since her family is well-off, they will not ask for money for their daughter. In reviewing the play, one of my students pointed out the obvious flaw in this solution:

> When Fang makes the final decision, "Give back the money immediately, break up this marriage and begin to arrange Man's marriage with the youth she loves," she solves this conflict by her "new and lofty moral standards." Yet the problem of where Man's mother will now get money for her son's marriage still remains. However in this play her son's lover turns out to be the young daughter of Chairman Fang, whose family is certainly very well off and does not need the money. Therefore, Man can divorce and marry on her own will. Looking deep into this event, we will find the

decisive factor in solving the problem of Man's marriage is not Fang's "new and lofty moral standards," but the solution of the money problem.

The destitution in the backward part of our country is undeniable though many changes have already taken place. There is an old Chinese saying, "A married daughter is the water splashed out." When a poor peasant marries away a daughter, it means he loses a laborer in his family. Labor means money. Therefore, it is justifiable for him to ask for money in return from the relatives by marriage, especially when he has a son. For he has to pay money to get his son a wife. This is what we call a "mercenary marriage." Under such a condition, children cannot be independent in the matter of marriage. The purchasing of true love is simply impossible. No lofty morality can help that without economic problems being first solved. But the author overlooks this very important fact. So she cannot come up with a satisfying solution to the mercenary marriage.[2]

Another realistic look at the problem was given to me in the following paper written by a young woman, about 27, concerning her experience in the countryside in the middle 70s:

Filled with the ambition to wipe out the practice of girls charging their husbands-to-be a large sum of money, I went to a small village to propagate the marriage law and "spiritual love." I exhorted the girls not to degrade females and exploit males by "selling themselves." It seemed my efforts were not in vain, as some of the young girls agreed with me. One day, after hearing that a girl had just got engaged, I went to have a talk with her family. Her parents greeted me warmly when I entered. I could see tattered boys and girls playing on the ground. There was no mat on the kang, which was made of clay. We sat on it and began a pleasant talk. But, when I came to ask them to dispense with the 2000 yuan from the girl's fiance's family, the girl's father said, "I've been doing backbreaking work to bring her up. Now she is grown-up and is going to work for another family while we need help badly. Since I'm old and can't work as hard as before, I will earn less. But her younger brothers and sisters need money to go to school and..."

The girl put in, "In my past 19 years, my parents have never been affluent enough to buy me a decent dress. If I get married and have children, I won't be able to afford to buy clothes myself. The only chance in my life to get a few beautiful clothes is now, from his family. Don't you think it's a wretched life that she is leading if a woman is wrapped in rags all her life?"[3]

This passage shows the persistence of the purchased marriage, but it also gives a slant on it that I had never heard before--the girl involved is obviously now not merely a piece of goods. She feels she also benefits from the arrangement. Thus, though the problem remains, the circumstances of this girl when compared to the Shanxi woman described above show that, even in these desperate situations, women have made some progress.   All of the above simply reinforces my major impression of China: its complexity. China's long and advanced civilization sometimes makes us forget that its repeated insistence that it is allied with the Third World is more than a political ploy. Its problems are those of an emerging nation.

The movement to free women in China started before the turn of the century. The first anti-foot-binding society was founded in 1892 and the first decree outlawing it was issued by the Dowager Empress in 1907.[4] After the Communist Party broke from the Guomindang in 1921, the woman's movement was cut in two, and half of it strangled in the conservative New Life Movement because the Guomindang thought of it as being too disruptive. By its very nature, the women's movement was and is disruptive, but, for the most part, that was an advantage for the Communist Party. The Guomindang was, after about 1911, an in-power party; the Communist Party was from its inception an outside power. This meant two things: first, the Communists required the help of everyone, even the women, as they often expressed frankly and openly. Then, they also required disruption; whereas, the Guomindang, an in-power party, could not afford it. The Communists were, after all, trying to tear the fabric of the society apart. The Guomindang, though it started out with that goal, as an in-power party immediately began to find ways to consolidate, to mollify, to conserve. Thus, the emancipation of women made most progress under the Communists.

In the most up-to-date and complete study on the problem, Elisabeth Croll points out that the uneasy but effective alliance between feminism and socialism has alternated between two explanations of and remedies for female suppression. One is the common Marxist idea that female oppression, like all oppression, is essentially a class phenomenon and can thus be solved best in the context of an over-all class struggle and revolutionary movement. The other is that there are special circumstances, ideological and psychological, over and above the question of class conflict, which must be taken into account in order to deal with the special problems of women.[5] Officially, the Chinese Communist Party has recognized both of these alternatives, but often the second has been submerged in favor of the first. The Cultural Revolution, predictably, was one such period. At that time, there was no separate women's movement, but paradoxically, there was a lot of political action on the part of women, a condition now not so noticeable. Many young women travelled widely taking part in the destructive activities on a more-or-less equal footing in the radical tradition of their earlier sisters who participated actively in the Communist revolution. In China in 1981 there was evidence of no such open political activity on the part of women, but, since the downfall of the Gang of Four, an independent women's organization has again been formed.

Currently, however, this organization takes almost no independent role.

The Communist Party is, after all, now an in-power party, and, especially after the disruptions of the past ten years, is not anxious to push ahead in touchy social areas. Then, too, it is impossible not to recognize the progress made by and for women in China during this century, and especially since liberation. This progress has allowed them to move to a position so much closer to that of men that the sense of equality is very strong in the middle-aged women who have actually witnessed the process. However, especially among the younger women, there is a feeling that things are not all well and a growing attempt to name their current problem. I think that the inequalities now being articulated by these young women are no longer primarily economic, but ideological and psychological and have to do with an ambivalent and confusing sense of themselves which has one leg in the feudal past where a woman's role was circumscribed by the family and the other in the socialist present, where, at least verbally and ideologically, a woman is part of the larger community and is not only entitled, but expected, to play an active role.

The Message of the Media

To return for a moment to our opening scene, the woman warrior, transferred from her sea kingdom into a modern factory or commune, has been a stock figure of Communist Party mythology. Indeed in the early days, some women actually fought alongside the men, and women martyrs have an honorable place in the Party history. During the early struggles for women's liberation, local theatre showing active heroic women was a key weapon. During the Cultural Revolution, all dramatic presentations eschewed feminine roles and showed only revolutionary heroines. I saw a revival of one of the modern Peking Operas produced originally in the 60s. I thought the heroine, a middle-aged proprietor of a wine shop who was an underground member of the Communist Party during the civil war period, was a marvelous character, strong and witty.

In the two years I was in Beijing, I noticed again and again that the woman warrior was still present in the contemporary media, but in a reduced and domesticated form as a middle-aged woman, often a cadre, always a mother, who was usually called upon to make uncomplaining sacrifices both for her family and for her country, to both of which she showed an absolute and unquestioning loyalty. In this muted form the woman warrior is one of the two major favorable media images of women. The other, the young woman, not at all a warrior, has as her main purpose the pursuit of a man, which she does by alternately attracting him with her childish laughter and mourning for him with copious and helpless tears when he is persecuted by minions of the Gang of Four. Generally in the films I saw it was the young man who was persecuted during the Cultural Revolution—a very wide-spread subject for movies now—and the young woman who was forced tearfully to part from him, often by her family. This pattern was basic to three very popular movies, "Sea Lover," "Lu Shan" and "Night Rain on Ba Shan Mountain." This last did have a young heroine, or, maybe more realistically, an anti-heroine, a Red Guard taking a hapless intellectual to prison. She was finally persuaded to help her charge escape largely through the aid of the middle-aged woman warrior figure who throughout the movie comforted everyone, including the ever-present young woman torn from her lover at the beginning of the movie.

During the years of revolution and civil war, and again during the Cultural Revolution, years when political problems or philosophies required the disruption of normal family and social life, non-traditional roles for women were promolgated and stressed both as an embodiment of the revolutionary ideal and as an inducement for support from the women. But now, when the government wants a return to quiet and normality, older, more traditional roles for women are emerging in the media again. Whether this results from governmental policy or is simply a sign that traditional thinking about women still predominates and will surface when political pressure ceases, is not clear. Whatever, these two roles have conventionalized the image of women and brought them very much more into traditional spheres. True, the older women are usually professional workers and their heroism extends into their work, but they are not the fighting heroines of earlier days who defeated national enemies or single-handedly made their communes and factories into models for the whole nation. Their heroism is quiet and motherly and requires the traditional feminine virtues of endurance rather than more active, masculine efforts.

For example, to leave the movies for a while, the heroine of Shen Rong's well known story, "At Middle Age," one of seven chosen for an anthology, Seven Contemporary Chinese Women Writers, published in English for consumption abroad,[6] is a middle-aged eye doctor, a wonderful, truly heroic woman who works herself into a heart attack by her efforts to serve her patients and family. Many of the comments I heard about this story, especially from young women, objected to her self-sacrificing life and labelled her as unrealistic. But all agreed that the accounts of the burdens of her life were accurate and frank--a subject I will return to later. Unrealistic or realistic, however, Dr. Lu's activities in no way involved her in any concerns outside of her immediate work situation or family.

The role described for the young woman not only domesticates her, but usually deprives her of any warrior status at all. The parts for young women in the movies I saw had very little substance, with the possible exception of the young wife in "The Herdsman," who tells her husband, when he must make the choice of staying in China or going abroad with his father, that she at least will remain in her homeland. But even this young woman has no role at all other than wife and mother. I did see one film, a joint Hong Kong-PRC production, "Shao Lin Temple," in which a young woman was, for one scene, a warrior in the old sense (before she was rescued by a young man), and I watched a crew filming a scene in which China's foremost swordswoman was standing off a male opponent. These show that, properly distanced by time or fantasy, young women can be limited warriors, but the usual role for them was passive, helpless, adoring, and the movie posters emphasized that with the women standing, protected by the heroic man, looking childishly into his eyes or dreamily into the middle distance.

The short stories chosen for the English-language collection named above revolve around these domesticated images for women. Of these stories, two have the middle aged mother figure at the center; one, written by a 32-year-old woman, has a male hero; two of the remaining four concern young women deciding on marriage offers, and one tells how a young wife learns again to appreciate her colorless but devoted husband. Only one story, written by a middle-aged woman, has a true modern woman warrior, a young girl who is arrested protesting against the Gang of Four at the famous 1976 demonstration in Tiananmen Square. Significantly this one example is set in the Cultural Revolution.

Socialist Morality

The image of the childish young woman struck me forcefully early in my stay, because it contrasted so sharply with the behavior of my students and colleagues. The girls in the movies were pretty, fashionable, flirtatious, helpless--all the things the young women I saw around me not only were not, but felt constrained not to be. As I got to know some young women better, I began to see they themselves felt confused about traditional images of women and the political and social realities around them. They felt vaguely ill at ease and uncertain about their own relation to marriage, career, family. Their problems were, on the one hand, not political and economic and thus not likely to be addressed by the official world around them, but, on the other hand, were made insurmountable because that same official world reinforced, with social, psychological and even political pressures, restrictive conceptions of women.

The root causes of these problems go back into the feudal past as surely as the economic problems faced by the women in the countryside, and the failure to confront them means that women are still bound by them as their foremothers were by crippled feet, and maybe for some of the same reasons. Though it is possible to posit economic reasons for the practice of foot binding, such an extreme form of subjugation goes beyond economics into the realm of power and dominance. Elisabeth Croll gives the following revealing quotation from a well-to-do Chinese gentleman around the turn of the century who was reacting to the movement to outlaw bound feet:

> Footbinding is the condition of life bringing dignity to man, and contentment to women. Let me make this clear. I am a Chinese fairly typical of my class. I pored too much over classic texts in my youth and dimmed my eyes, narrowed my chest, crooked my back. My memory is not strong and in an old civilization there is a vast deal to learn before you can know anything. Accordingly among scholars I cut a poor figure. I am timid, and my voice plays me false in gatherings of men. But to my footbound wife, confined for life to her house, except when I bear her in my arms to her palanquin, my stride is heroic, my voice is that of a roaring lion, my wisdom is of the sages. To her I am the world; I am life itself.[7]

This statement is frank as only a man can be frank who feels no pressure of shame because he thinks his behavior is in line with the realities, moral and social, of the world, even of the universe. This feeling of needing to dominate someone somewhere is, in China, still reinforced by an excessive obsession with a woman's chastity which now, under the rubric of "socialist morality" makes Mrs. Grundy a political factor in China. The tendency for traditional poets to romanticize the tiny bound feet is well-known, but two old rhymes see below this to the power reality beneath:

> Have you ever learned the reason
> For the binding of your feet?
> "Tis from fear that twill be easy to go out
> upon the street."
> It is not that they are handsome when thus
> like a crooked bow,
> That ten thousand wraps and bindings are
> enswathed around them so.

And:

> Bound feet, bound feet, past the gate can't
> retreat.

These insights are reinforced by the fact that the men's objection to natural feet as well as their later objections to women's free movement beyond the house, were often based on sexual considerations. Hinton found this a powerful factor in Long Bow Village where he lived just before liberation when the land reform movement was bringing peasants into an active participation in their own political and economic life. He found that the peasant men objected to women taking part in the women's organization, or in any public meeting on the ground that they would be free to commit adultery.[9]

The excessive prudery encouraged and enforced by social and political means is still one of the main facts of life for young women in China. The Chinese girl's conception of herself as a sexual being is very limited. For example, one of my colleagues, an American man, found out that two of his young women students had been stopped at the gate of the Friendship Hotel where we lived and questioned in sexual terms about their relationship with him. Talking with one of my female students about this, I asked her why the boys, who often came to see me, were not ever questioned. She replied, "Well, women are not like that are they?" This young woman, in her halting attempts to talk about sex, referred to it as "dirty."

Chinese girls are browbeaten with "socialist morality," in much the same way as American girls were with "Christian morality" in the 50s, and the definition is pretty much the same: "Remain a virgin until you marry." The difference is that girls are not promised, as we were, that sex would be beautiful after marriage. There is not much romanticism concerning sex even though the young people are often romantic in other ways. One of my foreign friends, a man who has lived in China most of the time for the past 20 years, told me that many of his married Chinese women friends had told him that sex with their husbands was very unsatisfactory. Fox Butterfield reports similar experiences.[10] The one Chinese woman who ever admitted to me that she had had sex with a man reported that none of her experiences had been pleasurable. They had been short; the men, from her description, were inept as lovers and had made no effort at all to give her pleasure, not from indifference, but from lack of any conception that it was possible. Most Chinese girls simply would not admit that they had had sex. An American woman I knew had an intimate friendship with a married Chinese woman of about 24 who was exceptionally pretty. The American discovered that her Chinese friend had made contacts with several foreign men and had had repeated sexual relations with them. But the woman would never admit this even though she talked openly and frankly about any other question. I had much the same experience with a young friend who, I knew, was having a relationship with a foreign man.

This reluctance to talk about sexual experience had, I gradually discovered, another strong basis other than feelings of modesty and chastity. The injunctions that the girls receive from parents and leaders about socialist morality can be, and are, backed up with political power. Butterfield tells the story of a forty year-old married woman who was arrested because she <u>discussed</u> her sex life too freely with him.[11] While I was in China, a young woman received international attention when she was "detained" and given a two-year "re-education" sentence for living with a French diplomat. It was not at all uncommon for girls who came to see foreigners to be questioned in explicit sexual terms, even though the foreigners were their teachers. I personally knew of two Chinese girls who were arrested for being with foreign students. No unmarried woman can afford to have her work unit know that she has had sexual relations with a boy before she was married. The consequences can be too serious.

Students, both male and female, were forbidden to have girl friends and boy friends while they were in school, though this was not enforced vigorously. But the concept of open dating simply did not exist. If there were relationships, they were exclusive. I knew of a couple of young men who had the reputation for having had more than one girlfriend, but that would have been unacceptable for a young woman. A young 23-year-old student I knew was constantly under criticism because she was seen associating with various young men. One of the officials at her work unit broke up her chance for marriage to a young man by reporting these rumors to him and saying that he should choose another partner. This official had no reason for saying that as he knew neither of the young people well. He was simply acting out of his sense of socialist morality and his feeling that a young woman who did not abide by its strictures needed to be punished. This same woman was given an undesirable work assignment when she graduated from college, and her unorthodox behavior, her tendency to dress fashionably and her "inability to get along with people," were the main reasons for this. The determination of the future, which every school has, is a powerful weapon for ensuring political and social conformity, and officials never hesitate to use it. Indeed gossip, which spills over into official acts, is a major means for control throughout Chinese society.

The strict emphasis on chastity, along with the emergence of domestic and traditional images for women in the public media, underline for me the fact that women are still not equal and that the problems that define their inequalities are basically ideological as well as economic. Elisabeth Croll gives a list of problems related to women which have not yet been solved.

> The particular and practical aims outlined in the campaign confirm that several problem areas continue to concern the government and the women's movement. These include the insufficient representation of women in political and leadership positions, the problem of equal pay for women in rural areas, the persistence of traditional customs in courtship and marriage and the division of labour within the household.[12]

Even the problem of unequal pay mentioned above has its basis in the widespread and ancient feeling that a woman's work is not as valuable as a man's as much as it does in economic realities. While in China, I saw my comrades, friends and students struggling with these same problems every day. I would like to discuss three of them in some detail, drawing upon my experience that of my friends and upon stories presented in the media to show that in order to make the next movement toward equality, women in China need to become more conscious of the implications for their lives of the image they have of themselves and which men have of them.

Women In Public Life

Take the first problem, that women are under represented in leadership positions. It is obvious to anyone who works in China that the women do not hold up half of the administrative sky. Butterfield has the most recent statistics:

> Women now make up 4.7 million of the 20 million Chinese cadres, 24 percent of the total, it is true. But there is only one woman among the twenty-four regular members of the ruling Politburo, which makes the key decisions, and she is the widow of Zhou Enlai, Deng Yangchao. ... There are no women among the eleven members of the Party Secretariat, the powerful organization that runs the Party on a daily basis. ...none of the first Party secretaries and governors of China's twenty-nine provincial level units are women.[13]

He found no better record on the local level.[14] However, the actual dearth of leadership roles played by women did not disturb me so much—our own record in the United States is not so much better. What did disturb me was the lack of consciousness of the problem on the part of both male and female colleagues of my own age and the growing sense of frustration among my young women friends who felt the situation would not improve.

For example, the school where I taught, The Beijing Foreign Languages Institute was, by general consensus among the foreign experts in Beijing considered to have the most enlightened, progressive, liberal English Department in China. At the time when I arrived, of the over 100 teachers in the department, I could find for sure one woman who held the rank of associate professor (ranks are young teacher, instructor, associate professor, full professor). Recent promotions may have increased this number. No woman was a full professor or anywhere near that. A full professorship is the reward for a life time of service in China, and only men in their 50s attain that. The lack of women in that rank is traceable to the fact that few women received professional training before liberation. But, more tellingly, there were no women in the academic administration of the department. Our department had a Chairman and four Vice Chairmen, all men in their middle to late forties and early fifties. Discussing this, one of my colleagues, a woman about my age, commented that this was not a problem since most women did not want to be bothered with the extra work. However, another of my co-workers, who is, as far as I can recall, the only woman who has been sent out by our department for a Ph.D. abroad, expressed quite another view. The department had a large group of competent, hard-working and loyal middle-aged women. Of these, four are now abroad, three in MA programs. Several times in talking with one of the Vice Chairmen, I mentioned that all the leaders in the department were overworked and that some of the younger people should be brought into leadership positions. Whenever I mentioned any of the middle-age women in this regard, even one whom everyone thought of as totally competent, there was always some demurral. When I would mention men in the regard, the response was always different.

The situation with the young women in the department was even more striking. The students of the 1977 class, the first to enter the universities by examination after the 10 chaotic years, were considered to be the cream of Chinese youth. In our school, one class was specially chosen from the whole 1977 group and given training with the understanding that they would remain in the Institute as teachers. Of these 20 or so students, only two were women. By the time I had been there for a year, many of these students, and of the post graduate students (students selected from earlier classes) had been sent abroad for Ph.D. degrees. I cannot recall that any of these was a woman. The one young woman who was given a Ph.D. fellowship to an American University was refused permission to go because the leaders felt that her relationship with one of her male American teachers was too close. The school leaders told me that this young woman would be allowed to go abroad the next year, but she never was. The last I heard she had received permission to marry an American living in Beijing and will, in all likelihood, leave China permanently. Before I left China she told me that this was the only solution for her since her involvement with the teacher would never be forgotten. The young men who return with Ph.D.'s will undoubtedly be put in power positions. There are no such candidates among the young women--only my one older colleague will be in that category.

The dilemma of young women in regards to schooling abroad is demonstrated by one of my close friends who worked as my assistant in an American Literature class. She was exceptionally able, at least as able as the young man who was my other assistant. He, as it turned out, received the opportunity to go abroad, to Hong Kong, to study for a Ph.D. in Comparative Literature. He sought the opportunity actively and took every examination that came up which would qualify him. I was happy for him when he got his chance. But, his way was smoothed considerably by the fact that he was a man. He was married, and his wife had a baby while I was in China. This did not in any way affect his career. His family had two rooms in the dorm as their living quarters, and with him lived his wife, his child and his mother, who cared for the child since his wife was a doctor. The one room was sleeping quarters for the mother and the child, the other for the young couple. But, whenever Guo was at home, that room was for his exclusive use. He had, as far as I could tell, no responsibilities in the home.

The young woman, on the other hand, decided not to take the examinations which might have led to study abroad, even though the department leaders asked her to in recognition of her achievement. Her problem was a real one, and there was no way to solve it. Her husband had been abroad for a year. If she went abroad it would have to be now. If she turned down these opportunities, others would not likely come again. But, she was now approaching 30. She did not want to be absent from her husband for another year, and the authorities would never give her permission to go abroad with her husband--the obvious solution. She was worried about starting her family because of her age. The differences in her case and Guo's were revealing. He never for a moment had to worry about his family responsibilities; she could never forget hers. He had to make no difficult choices; she did.

One incident at my school gave me insight both into the administration's feelings towards women and into the fact that young women are beginning to realize this at some level and trying to do something about it. It also underlined the fact that there is not much that can now be done. For various reasons--past experience with suppression of intellectuals, low pay, lack of chances to go abroad--teaching positions in high schools are not considered desirable. Thus, many of these positions go to women, especially those who are quiet and unassuming. For example, one of my close friends, a round-faced, pleasant-looking woman whom nobody thought of as outstanding intellectually, was asked to take the most unsought-for position in the 1977 class: teaching in the high school run by the Institute. She was grief stricken, and finally, with a reserve in strength nobody thought she had, she refused. The refusal was bound to be a quixotic gesture. Technically, she had the right to refuse, but really she did not since any other assignment she would be given would have been worse. But, she refused, talking to the party man whose jobs the student assignments were--a man generally feared by the students--arguing and protesting. I talked with her several times and she was never open about her reasons for being upset. Gradually I came to realize that her real objection was not to the assignment (though she was not happy about it), but to the feelings about herself that the choice gave her, and to the image that it revealed she had in other people's eyes. Finally, just after she had given in and decided to take the job, she told me one day, "I showed them. I showed them I wasn't the silly, weak nobody they thought."

Inequality of opportunity begins, however, before the assignment of positions. In our Institute, the major languages school in China, female students have to receive a higher score on entrance exams to be admitted than do the males. I asked several people about this and got several responses. My students told me that it was because women generally did better on exams, so they did this to ensure each class would have at least 50% male. When I asked if, had the situation been reversed, would they have raised the necessary score for boys so that there would be 50% female, they answered of course not. The most surprising response came from a man in my 1979 group. This young man came on many occasions to talk to me because he needed, he said, to talk to someone who would be more open than his friends. In short, he thought of himself as being a radical thinker. He announced one day that he wanted to talk about the women's movement, which we did. When I asked him about China, he replied that there was no such problem here. I asked if he knew that women had to receive a higher score for entrance into the school than men. He did. Didn't he consider that to be discrimination? No, he replied, there was a very good reason for that. I was sure he would give the standard answer about balancing enrollment, so I was not prepared for what came next: "You see, when we graduate the students will be assigned to positions where they will have to travel a lot and even be sent abroad. Such positions are more suitable for men." Holding back my amazement, I asked, "Why?" "Because women can't go abroad; they have to stay home and take care of the kids." I countered, "Why can't the men also do that?" He turned very abruptly to me, his face showing the only anger I ever saw there--he was a master at using a smile to cover his feelings--and replied with the anger in his voice, "Why should men do that?" I replied, almost as angry, "Why should women," but his next reply was a laugh, and I could never get him to open up on that subject again.

One last incident, this time in a more political context, shows again the problem of women trying to assert themselves in a public way. When I first arrived in Beijing, an election campaign was underway for a sort of local city council. The students at Peking University and at my Institute decided to take the election seriously and declared themselves candidates. It was an unprecedented thing to do. Elections had been, for years merely the choosing from a slate presented by the party machinery. My students were serious, almost ecstatic, about this election. The outcome of this experiment--a bad work assignment for one of the students and expulsion from Peking University for others--was extremely disillusioning and, I think, one of the reasons why so many young people I knew decided the following year to turn their backs on political affairs.

But, during the election, feelings ran high. Mass public question and answer meetings were held both at our campus and at Peking University, and the rooms were packed and overflowing. The later punishment of the participants by the officials was revealing of political realities but the punishment of one of the candidates by her fellow candidates and by her fellow students was even more revealing of psychological realities. She, one of the two or three women who had the courage to participate, made the mistake of raising some feminist questions, I'm not sure which or how strongly, since my students were reluctant to discuss this issue. But, I witnessed in one public meeting how this student was humiliated by her fellows. She had attacked the leading candidate personally, obviously a very foolish and unnecessary thing to do, but she was booed from the stage. My student and friend who accompanied me to the meeting, a young girl herself embroiled all the two years I knew her and knew her closely, in questioning what it meant to be a woman in modern China, told me that there were some rather nasty posters put up about this woman's personal life. I saw another female candidate give her spiel at the same meeting. She was properly modest and spoke in an almost apologetic way, and was received unenthusiastically but politely.

Women and Marriage

The second problem mentioned in the quotation from Croll's book, old marriage customs which are detrimental to women is seen in the persistence of buying wives and arranged marriages. Of course, the women I knew, intellectuals and students, would never have been sold. With them, the problem was not so much old marriage customs, though as I will show later, arranged marriages are not unknown among such women, as it was old attitudes toward marriage and toward women's role and place in it. Overall, marriage was a major concern among all the young people I talked to, both male and female. As the interest in politics, just reaching its final peak with the elections I described above, began to fade under the growing realization that the liberalization which had seemed so close in 1978 and 1979, was not a reality, students turned more and more inward and began to find their fulfillment in personal concerns. One of my young male students told me that his dreams of fulfillment in society, both in politics and in his own personal career, were incapable of being realized, so he turned to his future family as the only means left to find happiness. "If that fails," he said, "there will be nothing for me."

The main impressions on this subject which I received from my younger women friends, colleagues and students are hard to define and categorize. "The problem with no name" is still nameless in China. These women felt vaguely discontented, felt trapped. They expressed the same uncertainty about the future, the same doubts, as their male colleagues, but something else was apparent.

In the first place, it is almost unthinkable for a woman not to marry in China. I was always puzzled by the strength of that stricture in the young women's minds. None of my friends could explain beyond saying, "We Chinese women always marry," or citing gossip or social control as the factors. One friend said, "People will think there is something wrong with your body." But most girls didn't understand me when I asked why they felt the need to marry so strongly. They had never asked themselves that question. It was simply part of the way their minds had been put together. Several of my close friends confessed to me that they didn't particularly want to marry, but felt they had no choice. Only one young woman I knew intended not to marry. She told me that she had accepted the hated option of being a teacher in a small institute because she felt there she would get less pressure about marriage than she would have in a governmental agency, but, even so none of her friends believed that she would really carry out her intention. I only ran across one statement questioning this way of thinking. It came at the end of one of the stories published in the English language anthology. The story concerns a young woman who is hesitating before accepting an eligible young man because she remembers her own mother's unhappiness at being married to a man she did not love. Even this statement asks only that women be allowed to wait and choose their own husband, rather than suggesting that a woman should not marry at all, but its implications are strong:

> Who knows? Maybe we should take the
> responsibility for the old ideas handed down
> from the past. Because if someone never
> marries, that is a challenge to these
> ideas. You will be called neurotic, accused
> of having guilty secrets or having made

political mistakes. You may be regarded as
an eccentric who looks down on ordinary
people, not respecting age-old customs--a
heretic. In short they will trump up
endless vulgar and futile charges to ruin
your reputation. Then you have to knuckle
under to those ideas and marry willy-nilly.
But once you put the chains of a loveless
marriage around your neck, you will suffer
for it for the rest of your life.

I long to shout: "Mind your own
business! Let us wait patiently for our
counterparts. Even waiting in vain is
better than willy-nilly marriage. To live
single is not such a fearful disaster. I
believe it may be a sign of a step forward
in culture, education and the quality of
life."[15]

It always surprised me how business-like Chinese could be
about marriage. The young intellectuals I dealt with had
romantic notions about loyalty in love, and, I might add, they
put those ideals into practice. It was not unusual for a man
and woman to remain faithful to each other throughout their
whole college career. But, among those students who did not
have a particular friend, attitudes toward the necessity of
marriage could be practical, and this has led to reinstatement
of a kind of arranged marriage, especially for women who are
now approaching 30. Family, friends, business acquaintances
often introduce a man to a woman, and, if there seems to be
mutual agreement, the couple agrees to be a couple. Once the
agreement is made, it is serious, not broken lightly, and
usually results in marriage. I know of two sad counter cases
which illustrate the principle. One was reported in the
newspapers and recounted to me by a friend. A young woman,
knowing she did not love a man, but feeling obliged to marry
him because he had been introduced by a family friend,
married. The marriage was unhappy, though a child was born
quite soon. The marriage broke up, the husband deserting the
wife. The wife, left alone and desperate, ended up beating her

child to death. My friend expressed only sympathy toward the wife. The second case I heard about first hand. A young woman married a young man though she had known for several months previously that she did not love him, again because the marriage, though not strictly arranged, was promoted and accepted by the families. She divorced him within a few months after the marriage--what she thought she could endure before marriage she found she could not when she had to face it. The young man, a good and kind person, remarried rather quickly. The wife now feels she made a mistake because her chances for remarriage seem almost nil.[16]

All these things affect the women more than the men. First, the compulsion to marry is stronger for women. Second, the matchmaking becomes a test and an ordeal for them. The family always seeks to marry the daughter, and marriages are often arranged not because she is desperate but because her parents are. Butterfield, talking about the power of connections, relates an interesting example of an arranged marriage. A young woman had been sent to Tibet during the Cultural Revolution. Now because she was approaching her thirtieth birthday, her family feared she would be an old maid.

> "So my parents looked around very carefully," the student told me. "They knew that few men would marry a thirty-year old woman. But my father located a very ambitious junior clerk, only twenty-seven, who worked in his office. Then they sounded him out through an intermediary. If he would agree to marry my sister, he could use his Peking household registration certificate to apply to bring my sister back to the city. In return, my father found him a much better job, with a promotion to be a cadre, in one of the hot, new, state import and export corporations that do a lot of business with foreigners."[17]

I became acquainted through foreign friends with an interesting young woman who had spent several years during the Cultural Revolution breaking up rocks, working so hard that even in the coldest winter she could not keep her coat on. One day as we were talking she told me that she had to get married within the next six months. She told me that now, at 29, since she had a good job, was good looking and had a good family, she could still command a good husband, a man who "had a good position and was handsome and educated." But, if she waited until she was 30, at that time only six months hence, she would have to settle for one who maybe had not graduated from college and who would not be so handsome. The whole conversation was matter of fact, as though she were discussing going on a journey for which certain preparations would have to be made in order to avoid certain outcomes.

I talked to her again just before I left and found that the process of being introduced to prospective husbands had already started. She had rejected several. She told me she was fussy, which was probably true, and also true, I am sure, was the fact that she simply did not want to marry someone picked by someone else. She told me another introduction was coming up the next day and that she dreaded it. She felt like she was up for sale.

Clearly, these arranged marriages happen because women must be married, because they are still conceived of mainly as wives and mothers; their real purpose and value to society lie not in the individual contribution which they can make, but in their role in the family, and society cannot rest or feel secure if women are not tucked safely into a family unit. Of course, this is partly the traditional Chinese feeling that any individual finds her true place in a group, but I did not find the same compulsion among the young men, and, in this process, the daughter is seen as the product, the son as the chooser. The most poignant expression of this I have seen comes in a story entitled, "Stereo Interchange." This story gives an exceptionally realistic and hard-headed look at all aspects of life in China. One of the characters, the daughter, has spent her young years in Mongolia where there was no chance for marriage. Now, she returns home and the family sets about finding her a husband, largely, it seems, because the mother wants her to marry someone who can provide comforts for the family. The friend of the oldest brother introduces her to an older man with a good position who, because of political reasons, was not able to find a wife during the Cultural Revolution and who, now past the marrying age, cannot himself hope for the young woman whom he would like, but can still pick and choose among older girls. So, the tryst is held, and it is a failure. The response of her family shows clearly how the outcome is perceived as a disgrace and a failure for the young woman. The brother, who is the first to find out from his friend that his sister has been rejected, tells his mother, in response to her question as to when the couple will meet again:

> There won't be any date. He is not satisfied with Xiao Ying. He complains that Xiao Ying is so ignorant that she even doesn't know where Hong Kong is. Hong Kong is an area contiguous to Guangdong Province, under a British governor, but Xiao Ying thought it was in Taiwan under the Guomindang. This is quite enough for him. He is an editor of literature and wants a wife with common interests. How can be be expected to marry a girl who doesn't have the least sense of geography?

The fact that the sister never had any education because of the Cultural Revolution is not considered. Later, the Mother responds to her daughter:

> Look at the sight of you...No wonder the man doesn't take to you. I'll be damned if he rejected you because of Hong Kong. Your fishy eyes account for everything. Can't you be a bit more lively? How many times have I told you? But you simply remain a dry washboard. Who will ever want a woman like you.

The daughter and her sister-in-law, who has been trying to comfort her, both begin to weep, and the sight makes the mother angry again:

> Xiao Ying, go to work at once! You aren't
> even able to get a husband, but you are so
> extravagant that you will throw away your
> bonus money by being late to work.

Finally, the young woman, driven to despair by her troubles, crawls under the table where she used to play as a small child. There follows a stream-of-consciousness-like passage in which she says:

> I will never go on a date, never, even if
> Big Brother Cai persuades me with fancy
> speeches....Why should one seek for a
> husband? Why should one get married? I'm
> not afraid of a ghost, but I'm afraid of a
> man.[18]

Women and the Home

The third unsolved problem mentioned by Croll, burdensome household responsibilities, is the most tangible ramification in women's lives of their inequality. Again, this condition seems no less widespread in China than it is in the United States, and, of the problems we have discussed here, it has received the most open acknowledgement and discussion. However, not much progress is being made and the general conditions of every day life, even for middle class intellectuals, impose such onerous conditions, that it is a serious problem for women. I once heard a Chinese woman, thinking of her household work, remark that in China women hold up more than half the sky.

The Communist Party has, in the past, taken an active role in trying to solve this problem. Mao Zedong saw this as one of the prerequisites for equality for women. His solution, however, was not to divide the work with men, or even to give the people conveniences in the home, but to socialize housework. To some extent, this has happened and has lifted some of the burden from women. Probably the most wide-spread example of this is the public dining rooms where families can eat or can purchase cooked food to take home. Many Chinese eat at least one of their meals in such places. Further, many middle-class families have maids who help with the children, and there are nurseries, even live-in nurseries, to care for the children. However, Butterfield points out that only 28% of Chinese children are taken care of in this way, as opposed to 53% in the United States.[19] Some of the slack is taken up by grandparents. One often sees on Chinese streets a sight almost unheard of in the U.S.--grandfathers minding their grandchildren, but, very much as in the United States, when the mothers are home from work, the primary responsibility for child care rests on them even though almost all have full-time jobs.

Even with the various kinds of help, the burden of housework, and of daily life in general, is very heavy. Many Chinese must bicycle or ride buses for an hour each way to and from work. Biking is obviously exhausting, but the bus is worse. Buses are crowded, slow, uncomfortable. Then, not many homes have modern conveniences, notably refrigerators, so shopping must be done every day, and most likely this will involve stopping in at least two places. Even within one market, each purchase requires a long queue. Sometimes customers must queue once to pick out a purchase and once to pay for it. Butterfield estimated that people spend two hours a day shopping.[20] Once the food is home, it must be chopped and cooked--there are no convenience foods. Washing clothes is another burden, since it must be done by hand and in cold water. The Chinese are very clean about their persons, so this takes a lot of time also. Finally, Chinese work six days a week and have no weekend to do all these tasks.

Most of the burden of this work still falls on the women. Butterfield reports that when he asked a woman friend why only Chinese men seem to be in restaurants in the evenings, she replied, "The men don't have housework to do."[21] The same colleague who told about the selling of the Shanxi woman reported the following about women's work in the present day:

> I noticed most of the burdens of house drudgery fell on women. As far as field work was concerned, women and men enjoyed equality. But as soon as the wife got home, she would lose no time in doing all sorts of household chores: cooking, sewing, mending, rearing children, feeding pigs, while the man sat in the shade under a tree smoking a pipe. The aunty living next door had five children, and very often she had to make shoes for them until the small hours of the night. But the next day she would rise at five o'clock, cooking breakfast and feeding pigs before she started off for field work. Men were not lazy, but they simply thought rearing children, cooking and sewing conventionally belonged to women.[22]

There is a push now to get men to share housework, and it has produced the expected backlash. One of the common jokes I ran into in many forms was a pun on the Chinese word for bronchitis. It was like the word which meant roughly "hen pecked," so whenever men saw or heard of other men doing housework, they always said they had bronchitis. Just now a lot of men make much of the fact that they are learning to cook, but the only man I ever observed really doing a major share of the cooking was one who had grown up in the United States. True, when I was invited into homes, as I often was, the men would sometimes tell me that they had cooked some particular dish. Many of my male students spoke with pride of their cookery skill, and they always cooked at our parties. But, in the homes, men always sat in the dining room while their wives or mothers cooked in the kitchen.

A very striking, but unconscious, comment on this problem comes in Shen Rong's story mentioned above, "At Middle Age." The middle-aged doctor, thinking of her burdens, recalls the following:

> In the past few years, keeping house had become an increasing burden. During the

"cultural revolution" her husband's
laboratory had been closed down and his
research project scrapped. All he had
needed to do was to show his face in the
office for an hour in the morning and
afternoon. He spent the remainder of his
day and talents on domestic chores, cooking
and learning to sew and knit, lifting the
burden entirely from Lu's shoulders. After
the gang was smashed, scientific research
was resumed and Fu, a capable metallurgist,
was busy again. Most of the housework was
shouldered once more by Lu.[23]

Lu's husband later remarks to a friend:

> I don't want a medal or a citation. I just
> wish your hospital to understand how hard it
> is to be a doctor's husband. As soon as the
> order comes to go out on medical tours or
> relief work, she's up and off, leaving the
> family. She comes back so exhausted from
> the operating theatre, she can't raise a
> finger to cook a meal. That being the case,
> if I don't go into the kitchen, who will?[24]

Still later her husband, because he has lost so much time
during the Cultural Revolution, feels pressed to accomplish
work. So, this already overburdened woman urges him to move to
his unit where he can have a room of his own and not be
disturbed by her or by the children. None of these incidents
is meant as a criticism of the husband--that is clear from the
context. The criticism in the story is not aimed consciously
at women's problems but at poor living conditions, low pay for
intellectuals, arrogance of political leaders. It is simply a
natural part of a Chinese woman's life that she will shoulder
the burdens of her job and of her home. These glaring problems
which women face because they are women are not presented as
problems except in the larger context of society. Indeed, in
one passage, Dr. Lu feels guilt because, in being a good
doctor, she neglects her home and family. No such guilt is
seen on the part of the husband, even when he moves away
leaving her alone, nor does it occur to her that she--a

professional scientist also--might need a place where she could study. Once again, this domesticated woman warrior emphasizes and reinforces traditional roles for women.

Dr. Lu, the middle-aged woman warrior, burdened with her work, her family, her doubts, faithful and nourishing, represents one type of woman in China. Born before liberation, possibly to a bound-foot mother, they have seen real progress made in their lifetime. She, like so many women of her generation, simply accepts and tries to deal as best she can with a reduced and difficult existence. The young women I knew represent another type. Born since liberation, their whole life has been lived under the present regime, and progress is less easy to spot. They suffered the effects of the Cultural Revolution which at once strengthened and disillusioned them. They haven't yet accepted anything as their final reality, though discouragement often lies very close to the surface. Unlike the Dr. Lu's, they tend not to appreciate the progress which has been made--though I think they are not cynical-- instead they see, or are beginning to see, what remains to be done. They don't at all accept the empty image given them in the young women of the movies, but they do not want to look forward to the hopeless battles of the middle aged warrior either. Whether they can in any way transform that role into something more appropriate to the splendor of its ancient type remains to be seen.

LaRene Despain
University of Hawaii

1. Tu Pei, "Women in a Shanxi Village" (Unpublished paper, written for a class at the Beijing Foreign Languages Institute, 1980).

2. Liu Xiao-yun "Success or Failure?" (Unpublished paper, written for a class at Beijing Foreign Languages Institute, 1981).

3. Wang Ke, "Peasants" (Unpublished paper, written for a class at Beijing Foreign Languages Institute, 1980).

4. Elisabeth Croll, Feminism and Socialism in China (London: Rutledge & Kegan Paul, 1980), p. 47, 49.

5. Ibid., passim.

6. Seven Contemporary Chinese Women Writers (Beijing, 1982).

7. Croll, p. 50.

8. Ibid., p. 20.

9. William Hinton, Fanshen (New York, 1966).

10. Fox Butterfield, China, Alive in the Bitter Sea (New York: Times Books, 1982), Chapter 6.

11. Ibid., p. 140.

12. Croll, p. 327.

13. Butterfield, p. 168.

14. Ibid., p. 170.

15. Zhang Kangkang, "The Wasted Years," Seven Contemporary Chinese Women Writers, p. 228.

16. Divorce is another problem for women in China. Though there is now an increase in divorce, it is considered very bad, especially for women. See Butterfield, Chapter 6.

17. Butterfield, p. 96.

18. Liu Xia Wu, "Stereo Bridge" (Publication information not available).

19. Butterfield, p.

20. Ibid., p. 103.

21. Ibid., p. 168.

22. Tu Pei.

23. Shen Rong, "At Middle Age," Seven Contemporary Chinese Women Writers, p. 148.

24. Ibid., p. 155.

INDIAN WOMEN NOVELISTS: NOTES TOWARDS FEMINISM

Consider the following scenario as a paradigm for contemporary feminism in India:

Geeta, a college graduate from Bombay, agrees to her parents' suggestion that she should marry Ajay Singh, a Professor of Science and the only son of a feudal lord in the principality called Udaipur.[1] She assumes that Ajay's "Western" education has liberated him from the outmoded customs still prevailing in the extended families of India and she looks forward to creating a home where freedom, individuality and self-expression--values she has imbibed during her college years in a cosmopolitan town--would be encouraged. Geeta's mother, more realistic about the future, instructs the starry-eyed bride in the observances of a Hindu home, "Keep your head covered, never argue with your elders; respect your mother-in-law and do as she tells you" (p. 14). In the ancestral home of Ajay, where three generations of direct descendents, several cousins and a vast number of family retainers constantly share the activities of an ordinary day, Geeta, the newest member of the hierarchy, is often blessed with the words, "May you always wear red and live to see your great-grandsons" (p. 72). Implicit in this traditional blessing are the fondest hopes of a Hindu bride, that she may not outlive her husband (a widow never wears a red garment) and that she may perpetuate the family through a long line of male descendents. For Geeta, several years go by, punctuated by moments of bewilderment, hours of soul-searching and nights of wakefulness, until she finally understands and accepts the wisdom of the ages taught to her by the older women of the household.

I

The Western educated Indian woman has been influenced by
and attracted towards the concepts of feminism originating in
Europe and the U.S.A. during the decade of the 1970s. Reduced
to very fundamental terms, the Western feminist ideal of
"self-actualization" appears to contradict the traditional
Hindu ideal of "self-effacement" which derives religious
sanction from the legends of Sita and Savitri[2] and which has
been instilled in the practices of the extended family system.
As several generations continually share the responsibilities
of mutual welfare, harmony can only be ensured by invoking an
unassailable code of hierarchy. The domains of male and female
activity are strictly separated. The oldest male member is the
head of the family and responsible for upholding the honorable
reputation of his ancestors. His wife enjoys a corresponding
superior position among the women; she is the supreme authority
for sanctioning even the slightest deviation from the
established religious and social norms.

The Indian feminist has two options. First, she may reject
the burdensome heritage which has designated codes and rituals
for every major activity in life, and may adopt the Western
model of a nuclear family in which individual initiative is
nurtured. In exercising this option, the Indian woman
repudiates her caste-community affiliations and its equipage of
advantages and disadvantages; she creates a unique
micro-structure of a family which is isolated from the social
environment in which it is expected to grow; she hopes to
derive support and encouragement from other like-minded
individuals who are eager to circumvent the tediously slow
process of social change and to express, here and now, a
radical decision.

By a second option, the Indian feminist may choose to
accept the fundamental tenets of the Hindu family and believe
that the wisdom of the ages has perpetuated certain customs to

ensure harmony, mutual trust and useful interdependence amongst the members of an identifiable group. While aware of the need for "self-actualization" she will not repudiate her responsibilities towards the older and younger members of the household but will seek to use her education and "feminist consciousness" to preserve the stability of the Hindu home and to eradicate the social malpractices which have insidiously crept in. Her view of "change" is not a radical dissociation with the past, but the gradual assimilation of feminist principles within the traditional commitments of an extended family. No spectacular results are to be expected immediately; however in the long run, such a direction to feminism in India may ensure that the traditional support system is maintained instead of being replaced by nuclear and single-parent homes which are, at best, poor imitations of the Western patterns and which, in India, are too alienated from tradition to ever receive social sanction or practical support from the community.[3]

This paper will examine these controversial dialectics of feminism in India in the novels of three women writers--Rama Mehta, Anita Desai and Ruth Jhabvala--by focusing upon the attempted reconciliation between ancient customs and contemporary expectations. The novels were written directly in English by women who were familiar with both Western and Oriental concepts of womanhood, hence written from a point of vantage permitting an author to consider the diverse components of feminism in an effort to create workable models for the women of her own country. One surmises from the novels that modern feminist consciousness in India, while deriving its impetus from the West, has evolved in a manner particularly relevant to its own cultural milieu. Since the dominant feature of the sociological scene is the extended family, and women are the custodians of unwritten, traditional values, Indian notions of feminism must be initially expressed within the hierarchical domestic structure. Social change must come literally from within, from "inside the haveli" as it were, from those busy interiors surrounded by impenetrable walls where women and girl children learn venerable customs and occasionally catch glimpses of newer modes of behavior.

The novelists I have mentioned address themselves to this unique aspect of Indian feminism, the relationship of woman to woman within the hierarchical structure--mother-in-law to daughter-in-law, grandmother to grand-daughter, sister to sister, mother to daughter--because any young woman who wishes to experiment with an "alternative life-style" would first seek the approval of the dominant mother figure in the household. Rama Mehta, a sociologist who studied at the Radcliffe Institute of Harvard University, based the novel Inside the Haveli (1977) on her own experiences as a bride in an aristocratic Udaipur family. Anita Desai, winner of the Sahitya Akademi award and a contender for the 1980 Booker Prize, portrays the complex demands made on an urban housewife in Fire on the Mountain (1977); Ruth Jhabvala, Polish by birth, educated at London University and married to an Indian, writes Heat and Dust (1975) as an observation of social manners to which she is both an "outsider" and an "insider." What I wish to emphasize through my selection of novelists and their novels is that the fiction bears faithful witness to the uncertainties and hopes of feminism in India. On the political front, the Government of India's Sixth Plan document outlines the appropriate strategy for women's liberation as a "three-fold" thrust towards "education, employment and health."[4] While there is such a national concept of "feminism" available to the contemporary Indian woman the workable design must be wrought from the resources within her tradition. Otherwise, one is in the danger of erecting a mere facade.

II

Rama Mehta's <u>Inside the Haveli</u> depicts the most traditional kind of Hindu extended family. Bhagwat Singhji, the father-in-law of Geeta, is the head of a household which proudly preserves the social etiquette and domestic ethics established in the ancient court of the Maharana of Udaipur. The house (<u>haveli</u>) reflects the pattern of life as it has emerged in the three hundred years of the family's existence:

> The courtyards divide the haveli into various sections. The separation of self-contained units was necessary because the women of Udaipur kept <u>purdah</u>. Their activities were conducted <u>within</u> their apartments. The courtyards connected their section with that of the men. The etiquette established through the years permitted only close male relatives to enter the women's apartment. Even so no man entered the courtyard without being properly announced (pp. 3-4).

Into this community where elaborate formality governs the interpersonal relationships amongst men and women and amongst the women themselves in the <u>zananah mahal</u> (women's residence), comes a bride with a city education and a graduate degree and is told of her primary task: "to make [her] reputation as a good daughter-in-law."

One might envisage here the seeds of conflict between extreme traditionalism and modernity but Rama Mehta develops the story along more subtle lines. The protagonist figure, Geeta, has Western education but not entirely Western values. She had chosen to marry a man she had hardly known, and although her expectations of setting up a nuclear family are early shown to be futile, she never challenges the Hindu sacrament of marriage as expressed in the concept of "<u>Pativrata</u>": "the complete devotion of woman to her husband, alive or dead, seeing in him her god and her ultimate salvation."[5] Once it is obvious to Geeta that Ajay's status as Bhagwat Singhji's only son endows him with a responsibility towards the continuance of the ancient family traditions, she tries to comprehend the elaborate courtliness and conduct of the haveli residents. Her intelligent and realistic evaluations lead her to perceive that as an educated "outsider" her actions will always arouse suspicion, but if she became one of the trusted members of the household, she may have an opportunity to introduce attitudinal changes within the haveli, arouse the women into re-assessing the traditions they have inherited. This strategy proves eminently successful as a few details of the novel will reveal.

One realizes that the primary relationship is between Geeta and her mother-in-law. At first the mother-in-law seems an awesome figure embodying the rigid traditions of the haveli. Geeta observes:

> Her mother-in-law's personality was such that it is difficult to contradict her or even express a different point of view. She had her own way of prevailing over others, a blend of craft and tenacity. She never lost her temper, she was always seemingly considerate and gentle. She never raised her voice; she was patient and prepared to listen....There was something in this way of life that frightened and fascinated [Geeta] at the same time (p. 27).

Geeta dons the purdah (veil) in deference to custom. Through the protective cover of the diaphanous fabric, she curiously observes haveli events, participates in conversations, and launches her own proposal for reform without arousing too much contradiction. She must start a school in the haveli for she anticipates that once the young girls are introduced to the rudiments of learning, a process of social change will have been inaugurated.

Yet, to run a school in the premises of an ancient home where women have always been denied education would be a radical enterprise and only possible if approved by the head of the family and his wife. As an indulgence to an educated daughter-in-law's "whim," permission is granted; soon one child, then another, their mothers and the younger servant women arrive at Geeta's door to listen to stories, to look intently at alphabets and laboriously copy them out. In deciphering the meaning of a printed word lies the promise of discovering the self and its relation to the environment around it. This is Geeta's gift to the haveli women.

Her mother-in-law's gesture of "indulgence" is soon strengthened into statements of definite approval for what Geeta has undertaken. When the village folk express their anger against educated women by citing how husbands were eating cold meals and young men were breaking off engagements to educated "defiant" girls, it is the old lady who opposes the detractors: "You know as well as I do that havelis can no longer give employment to servants' children. Times have changed. It is our duty to prepare them for the future" (p. 92). All dissent is silenced--even Geeta's anxious self-questioning--by the authoritative statement, "Once your father-in-law gives his approval to something then I am not afraid of what the world says" (p. 139).

Thus an old-fashioned justification for an experiment in social reform becomes the appropriate strategy for initiating change. Through the emblem of Geeta's school, novelist Rama Mehta reveals how Hindu traditions are not as inflexible as they are often made out to be.[6] In fact the support system inherent in the hierarchical family structure can be advantageously used to persuade the larger community to accept an innovation.

Such a process of change is, undoubtedly, a slow one; and the initiator, if a sensitive woman of Geeta's temperament, must be prepared to undergo a personal transformation. Her acceptance of the codes of the haveli--the veil, the respectful silence before elders, the deference to a mother-in-law--is an expedient measure at first but soon an expression of identification with the life of the haveli: "I don't want to leave Udaipur now. The haveli has made me a willing prisoner within its walls. How stupid I was not to see all that it holds. Where else in the world would I get this kind of love and concern? The children must grow up here. They must learn to love and respect this ancient house" (p. 137).

Geeta's story illustrates a way of introducing feminist ideas in orthodox communities, it enacts a strategy proposed by contemporary sociologists:

> The process of emancipation of women is quickened when there is caste-community support and the position of women is strengthened not only by legal rights but by her having confidence that in the exercise of her rights, she has the understanding and the support of the family and the caste-community.[7]

III

Anita Desai's Fire on the Mountain takes the reader into another kind of Indian family, into the homes of people who have absorbed several western social modes along with their western education. There the caste-community affiliations are weak, the women are educated and do not observe purdah, men and women meet as equals at social gatherings. The family pattern may be designated as "nuclear" with the important modification that a close connection between direct descendents is maintained although the adult members do not share a common home.

The protagonist figure in Fire on the Mountain is an elderly woman, Nanda Kaul, the widowed wife of a University Vice-Chancellor. Details of her busy life, as she recalls them in old age, evoke a lively scene:

> There had been too many servants in the long low row of whitewashed huts behind the kitchen....There had been too many guests coming and going....The many rooms of the house had always been full, extra beds would have had to be made up....Too many trays of tea would have to be made and carried to her

husband's study, to her mother-in-law's
bedroom, to the verandah that was the
gathering-place for all, at all times of the
day. Too many meals, too many dishes on the
table, too much to wash up after.

They had had so many children, they had
gone to so many different schools and
colleges at different times of the
day....(pp. 29-30).[8]

Nanda Kaul had suffered from the "nimiety, the disorder, the
fluctuating and unpredictable excess" (p. 30) and yet she had
suffered silently, never voicing her desire for privacy. Only
after the death of her husband had she been able to withdraw
from the several roles of wife, daughter-in-law, mother,
hostess, to begin "life" anew in a remote hill cottage bearing
the romantic name "Carignano." Tucked away among the pine
trees and bushes of blue hydrangeas, Nanda Kaul admitted to
herself the dissatisfaction with numerous years passed in
mundane domesticity and expressed her determination to add
nothing "to her own pared, reduced and radiantly single life"
(p. 31). Whoever came here or whatever happened at Carignano
"would be an unwelcome intrusion and distraction" (p. 3).

Nanda Kaul thus voices the feminist desire to create a life
patterned to suit her personal needs and to reject all
traditional demands made by society upon women. However, the
retrospective passages in the novel indicate that the
indignation against domestic drudgery had been hypothetical and
never put into action through the slightest gesture of
rebellion. The retreat to Carignano and the desire for an
uninterrupted life are similarly hypothetical, for when her
family makes a further demand, she cannot repudiate her
"responsibility."

The unexpected "intrusion" in Nanda Kaul's life is a
great-grand-daughter. A letter brings the news that Raka, a
child from a broken home, will stay at Carignano until her
parents have reached an amicable settlement. Raka is coming

305

uninvited; the decision for her "well-being" has been taken by elders who have definite ideas about the nurturing role of the traditional grandmother and who believe that the "lonely" old lady and the impetuous child will mutually profit by each other's company. Nanda Kaul bitterly resents this imposition on her privacy but does not refuse to admit the child, thus showing her desire for actualizing a self-contained life to be theoretical merely. She has always fulfilled her traditional obligations and at her age, she cannot express a radical option. She takes what she thinks will be a last silent stroll through an empty house soon to be filled with "those wails and bawls" (p. 19) which shatter adult peace.

Raka turns out to be a shy, secretive child. "She looked like one of those dark crickets that leap up in fright but do not sing, or a mosquito, minute and fine, on their precarious legs" (p. 39). The child seems resentful about her mandatory stay in Carignano and unwilling to make any gestures of affection towards her hostess. So two people linked by blood, separated in age by three generations, remains anxious to maintain their simple, separate selves. Instead of a warm greeting "both moved a step closer to each other and embraced because they felt they must" (p. 40).

Circumstance has thrown these like-minded persons together where companionship was not sought, where it was least expected and grudgingly conceded. Nanda Kaul and Raka discover a camaraderie of spirit. While each holds a sacred notion of "freedom" the old woman and the child assert their needs for self-actualization in very different ways. The novelist, Anita Desai, clarifies the roles in which she places the figures:

> If Nanda Kaul was a recluse out of vengeance for a long life of duty and obligation, her great grand-daughter was a recluse by nature, by instinct. She had not arrived at this condition by a long route of rejection and sacrifice--she was born to it, simply (p. 48).

Nanda Kaul, recognizing her alter ego in the independent minded child, never places the traditional restraints by which she brought up her own children. Indeed, she lives vicariously through Raka, imagining the many adventures the child might have as she clambers over the garden wall and slides down the hillside in search of wild birds and snakes, or disappears into the semi-darkness to peer into the club, or treads over brambles to select her pine cones. The two women are unafraid of the dangers of the forest, for the assertion of freedom must engender its own consequences just as a protective upbringing will condition the mind along predetermined patterns.[9]

That the dangers of the forest are real is made obvious in the story of the third character in the novel, Ila Das, a spinster of Nanda Kaul's age and a social worker among the villagers of Kasauli. To the intellectually conceived, hypothetical feminist notions of Nanda, and the spontaneous, nascent feminism of Raka, Ila Das adds a third feminist possibility.

Ila Das had been born in a "Europe-oriented" Indian home where the need for educating children was accepted. Characteristically, the sons went to universities in England, the girls were educated at home by governesses. The method of education, borrowed from Victorian homes, had served no purpose other than to create futile ambitions in the young girls, thus making them social misfits in their own cultural milieu. "Isn't it absurd" says Ila in her older years, "how helpless our upbringing made us, Nanda. We thought we were being equipped with the very best--French lessons, piano lessons, English governesses--my, all that only to find it left us helpless, positively handicapped" (p. 127).

Just how hopelessly impractical the pseudo-Western education has made Ila becomes obvious in the final chapters of the novel. Ila has inadvertently aroused hatred in the village folk by insisting upon radical social changes. In particular, she has been actively resisting the marriage of a seven year old girl to a rich widower who has six children (p. 130). The parents of the child-bride, their community, the village priest, see nothing socially or morally wrong about enacting a ritual which, though illegal, has the blessing of tradition; and they bitterly resent the interference of the Indian memsahib who threatens to bring the law against them. The villagers know only one solution to the problem--the ancient one of taking justice into their own hands and "punishing" Ila Das as only a woman can be punished. On a dark evening, Ila is attacked by Preet Singh (the father of the child bride), strangled and raped and cast away among the pine trees and blue hydrangeas of the Kasauli hills.

Anita Desai's novel portrays the harsh truth about feminist notions derived from the west; they cannot bring rapid social change in a community which does not recognize even the basic tenets of feminism. The notion of self-actualization can be expressed as a personal goal by the single woman in special circumstances. Nanda Kaul, after meeting her traditional commitments throughout the active periods of her life has, oddly enough, retained a theory about the sanctity of the self and is prepared to begin afresh in old age. The arrival of Raka, viewed first as an "intrusion," turns out to be an opportunity to exercise her theory; and because Raka is by instinct and parental neglect "free" of traditional constraints, Nanda can easily play the supportive role of granting independence to a member of the extended family. However, at this stage, Nanda's family is severely restricted to two members isolated from society. One recalls that Nanda's ideas had never been expressed in the real "home" over which she had presided. Such feminism has a mild beginning and a milder end. However, when Ila's western education and beliefs pose a threat to a community entirely different from herself, the resulting violence raises disturbing questions about the gulf between the East and the West.

IV

Summarizing briefly at this point, let me recall that the essential difference between the Western and Oriental concepts of womanhood rests upon the interpretation of the word "self-actualization." Traditions in India view a woman's roles as wife, mother, mother-in-law as modes of self-actualization; the Western traditions tend to perceive self-actualization as an individual goal. Feminist consciousness of the last decade has led to a blurring of conventions even in India but more and more feminist thinkers are arriving at the conclusion that the universal objectives of the women's movement are to be specially defined within a specific sociological context and that desirable social change has to be strategically introduced within the system. The slowness of the process is preferable to the instant rejection often activated by an obvious infiltration of new ideas.

In terms of the literature portraying these sociological truths, one sees in Rama Mehta's novel how an elementary school has tremendous potential as an instrument of social change. By contrast the feminism depicted in Nanda Kaul (Fire on the Mountain) is a desire for personal change, at best it supports the already liberated sensibilities of a girl-child in the family hierarchy. Ila Das's militant feminism has no appropriate place in India.

Turning now to a third novel, Ruth Jhabvala's Heat and Dust, one may observe the different expectations society has from Indian and "foreign" women, making quite evident that society is aware of feminist options but will not allow certain manifestations of "modern" behavior in their own women.

The narrator of the story is a young English woman who is visiting India to reconstruct the scandalous history of her

English grandmother, Olivia, who had married a British colonial administrator and then eloped with an Indian Nawab. The novel continually shifts between Olivia's story, set in 1923, and the narrator's own experience in contemporary India. For the purpose of understanding feminist issues, the sections about the young English narrator highlight features of Indian domestic life which are most puzzling to foreigners. The English woman rents a room in the house of Inder Lal who lives with his wife, three children and his mother. Because of the proximity of the dwelling units and the "openness" of a lower middle-class Hindu home, the English woman is a constant observer of the complex and (to her) perplexing relationships in the family.

Clearly, Inder Lal's mother plays the dominant role. She had "selected" her son's wife, Ritu, as is the practice in arranged marriages and "she had not wanted him to marry a very educated girl; she said there was nothing but trouble to be expected from such a quarter. Ritu had been chosen for her fair complexion and her suitable family background" (p. 49).[10] Having found a "suitable" bride who, by all reckoning, would be willing to play a subordinate role in the joint family, the mother-in-law goes about further consolidating her power at home and enhancing her prestige in the community.

Ruth Jhabvala's sketch of Inder Lal's mother emphasizes the worst features of an Indian joint family. The woman continues to be the nurturing parent even when her son marries: "it was she, not Ritu, who does everything for him like serving his food and laying his clothes out" (p. 53). The uneducated and timid daughter-in-law is reduced to the position of a household drudge constantly slaving for others. When an important visitor arrives, such as the English tenant, Ritu scuttles about the room clearing the mess left by her children while the mother-in-law makes the appropriate gestures of welcome and gives orders to Ritu "in a practised hiss aside" for refreshments to be served.

Never a word of protest escapes Ritu, and although she is a generation younger than her mother-in-law, it is the older woman who has a striking personality at home and a busy life outside the home in the company of friends. Her own lack of education has not hindered her assertion of freedom (within the Hindu framework) at all and she can be openly cynical about marriage. The narrator reports, "I have the impression that, although she is a widow, the best part of her life is now. She does not seem to have a high opinion of married life. She has told me that the first years are always difficult...it is difficult to get used to the new family and to the rule of the mother-in-law" (p. 53). Nevertheless, she plays the domineering mother-in-law so effectively in her own turn that Ritu develops a psychotic illness. For this again, the diagnosis is traditional--an evil spirit has entered her body--and the prescribed treatment requires exorcism by "applying a red hot iron to various parts of her body, such as her arms or the soles of her feet" (p. 81).

One may validly enquire at this point what role the young woman's husband has to play in the tyrannical rule of his mother. Unfortunately, he assents to all the proceedings, not out of "belief" or lack of knowledge about psychotic illness but because "mother wanted it" and "all her friends had advised it" (p. 82).

The same dominant mother and passive son are perfectly willing to accept an entirely different code of behavior in their English tenant. She roams freely amongst the people of the town pursued by urchins who ridicule her "strangeness." After a while everybody accepts her presence; she is a white woman in Indian clothes who speaks a few words of Hindi. Inder Lal's mother invites her to join in her outings, introduces her proudly to friends, bullies the vegetable venders into giving her a fair deal (pp. 53-55) and takes her sight-seeing to religious places around town. Inder Lal follows the cue and offers to help the English visitor to find the old landmarks of grandmother Olivia's life. This entails several day-long excursions in buses to somewhat remote and secluded spots but nobody seems to think ill of the time Inder Lal is devoting to the foreign visitor instead of staying home with his family. In fact, the arrangement seems convenient to everybody.

The separate expectations of behavior in Indian and foreign women become disturbingly evident when Inder Lal and the Englishwoman develop a sexual relationship. It begins surreptitiously on one of their expeditions to a deserted tomb and the initiative is taken by the woman:

> ...at that moment I did have a desire, and a strong one: to get close to him. And since this seemed impossible to do in words, I land my hand on his...He did not know what to do next, nor what I was going to do next. I could see...it was ludicrous!...how everything he had heard about Western women rushed in his head....Although the next few moves were up to me, once I had made them he was not slow to respond (p. 127).

The later meetings are not so surreptitious. Inder Lal visits his tenant, now lover, every night. His mother, wife and children are away on pilgrimage to "cure" Ritu's ailment. "For the sake of the neighbours, he makes a pretence of going to sleep downstairs but when it is dark he comes creeping up. I'm sure everyone knows, but it doesn't matter. They don't mind" (p. 140). The Englishwoman becomes pregnant, midwives come to her door to offer their services, everybody knows and still nobody minds. Before the child is born, she leaves the town for the mountains to make a separate home. Grandmother Olivia had met much the same fate in India.[11]

What do these vignettes from novels about contemporary India reveal about the status of women and the future of feminism? Clearly, the extended family system, perpetuated by several hundreds of years of tradition cannot be eradicated by a feminist call for individual "self-actualization" nor is it desirable that tradition be so radically erased. The Western concept of "self-actualization" has somehow to be related to the Indian ideal of "self-effacement" which carries the formidable weight of religious sanction and social custom. To see "self-realization" and "self-effacement" as irreconcilable opposites, Western and Oriental, is to lose the game even before it has started. The categories are not mutually exclusive if studied in some detail, and the appropriate strategy for arousing women to an awareness of their potential is to make them understand, not reject, the social environment in which they function. No tradition is so rigid that it will not admit a small change, no custom is so unassailable that it will not add a new ritual. Woven into the patterns of tradition are several customs which women can turn to their advantage to create a brighter future for themselves and their progeny.

The women novelists have brought to their books this rich texture of Indian society and suggested through their portrayals of life-like characters and situations, ways of introducing social change. Inside the Haveli portrays the most orthodox form of the Hindu joint family, yet it admits the light of learning for women and girl children who might have remained unlettered. In Desai's Fire on the Mountain, one sees the futility of reaching for short term, self-centred feminist goals. The Western educated Indian woman belongs to a small minority, her manner of expressing "freedom" is appreciated only within her group and has little relevance to the larger social scene. Ruth Jhabvala brings a "liberated" Englishwoman into a conservative Hindu home to expose the different norms by which Western and Indian versions of "femininity" are adjudged.

Considered together, the novels show how concepts of feminism in India have to be formulated within the hierarchical pattern of the extended family irrespective of the caste or class to which the initiator of feminist sentiments belongs. Her appropriate strategy is to understand the intricacies of the system and to introduce such changes within it which will be acceptable to the women of the community. By winning the support of the group which is the custodian of tradition and the primary influence on domestic ethic, a social revolution may have a slow but sure beginning.

Malashri Lal
Jesus and Mary College
University of Delhi

Notes

1. The scenario is based on Rama Mehta's prize-winning novel, Inside the Haveli (New Delhi: Arnold Heineman, 1977). Page numbers in parentheses refer to this edition. The haveli denotes a home in Rajasthan. For more information on the structure of Indian joint families and their resistence to change, see M.N. Srinivas, India: Social Structure (Delhi: Hindustan Publishing Corporation, 1982); Maria Mies, Indian Women and Patriarchy (New Delhi: Concept Publishing Company, 1980), examines the dilemma of students and working women in particular.

2. Sita, the wife of Rama, was abducted by the demon king Ravana. She was rescued by Rama but later exiled by him when his people expressed doubts about her "purity." Nevertheless, Sita affirmed her fidelity to Rama and spent her exiled years praying for his well-being. Savitri's fasting and praying for her dead husband Satyavana compelled Yama, the God of Death, to restore him to life. The present continuity of the mythological image of women is supported by studies such as Doranne Jacobsen and Susan S. Wadley, Women in India: Two Perspectives (New Delhi: Manohar, 1977).

3. For details, the following books may be consulted: Rhoda Lois Blumberg and Leela Devaraki, India's Educated Women (Delhi: Hindustan Publication Corporation 1980); Devaki Jain (ed.), Indian Women (New Delhi: Ministry of Information and Broadcasting, 1975); Rama Mehta, The Western Educated Hindu Woman (Bombay: Asia Publishing House, 1970); B.R. Nanda (ed.), Indian Women: From Purdah to Modernity (New Delhi: Vikas, 1976); Barbara Ward (ed.), Women in the New Asia (Paris: UNESCO, 1963).

4. "Women and Development," Sixth Five-Year Plan Document (Government of India Publication, 1980), p. 1063.

5. The Western Educated Hindu Woman, p. 19.

6. For a data-based analysis of social change in Udaipur see Indian Women: From Purdah to Modernity, pp. 113-128. According to a reliable source, "A random sampling of working women in India who have done well in their careers, reveals that they could reach the upper rung only if the household ethos was congenial"; Urmila Phadnis and Indira Malani (eds.), Women of the World; Illusion and Reality (New Delhi: Vikas, 1978), p. 15.

7. B.R. Nanda, ed., p. 128. A very useful annotated bibliography was sponsored by the YWCA, India; Kalpana Dasgupta (ed.), Woman on the Indian Scene (New Delhi: Abhinav Publications, 1976).

8. Page numbers in parentheses refer to Fire on the Mountain (Bombay: Allied Publishers, 1977).

9. Anita Desai's novels have been studied through her symbols and images; See Madhusudan Prasad, Anita Desai: The Novelist (Allahabad: New Horizon, 1981).

10. Page numbers in parentheses refer to Heat and Dust (London: John Murray, 1975). While reading this novel, and other narratives which describe women from different social segments in India, it may be useful to remember that the educated urban women's problems are rather different from those of the women belonging to the semi-educated or illiterate "labour" class. For comparisons, see The Educated Woman in Indian Society Today, A study carried out by YWCA of India (Bombay: Tata McGraw-Hill, 1971); and Devaki Jain (ed.), Women's Quest for Power: Five Indian Case Studies (New Delhi: Vikas, 1980).

11. See also R.S. Singh, Indian Novel in English (New Delhi: Arnold-Heinemann, 1977), pp. 149-163.

The revival of feminism in the sixties sparked one of the truly remarkable social developments of fundamental importance in contemporary times. The past two decades have produced an enormous amount of documentary material on the changing status and aspirations of women in both Western and non-Western societies over time. Centuries-old institutions and traditions inspired by beliefs in male dominance and female inferiority are increasingly being challenged by the new wave of feminism. Foremost among these institutions that are being subjected to singular scrutiny particularly by Western feminists is the patriarchal system, which is identified as the basic source of women's oppression. This is an awesome task since the patriarchal model has endured over time and continues to be legitimated by four sets of factors, which Iglitzin characterizes as biological, cultural and anthropological, religious, and the shift from communal to private property.[1] As impossible as this task seems to be, the fact that the feminist critique has taken it on represents one of the most significant changes of our time. Everywhere there is a greater stirring and awareness on women's issues than, say, thirty or forty years ago.

This inquiry has been motivated by the "internationalization" of feminist concerns, due largely to such recent developments as the U.N. declaration of the seventies as the "Decade for Women." We live in a rapidly changing global community and the new feminist awareness has spread beyond the Western scene. The developing countries themselves are undergoing rapid change in nearly all aspects of national life--politics, technology, education, employment, morality, customs, etc. Western values have had a dramatic impact on certain sectors in these countries and Western women are often perceived as highly independent, mobile, educated, and free. There are advocates of "women's liberation" in many of these countries.

Yet, there is a great ambivalence, if not reluctance, shown by women in the Third World in dealing with the tenets of Western feminism. In her seminal essay on feminism in Southeast Asia, the late Indian feminist Usha Mahajani remarked that the image of Western feminism is not appealing to Asian women. "The kind of shrill, iconoclastic, radically militant 'women's lib' of America has no counterpart in Asia. Feminists in Thailand, Laos, Malaysia, and Singapore are not against religion nor out to destroy traditional culture. They frown upon what they perceive to be an anti-male, aggressive Western feminism and have no admiration for the high priestesses of American women's lib. Many have not even heard of Gloria Steinham (sic.)"[2]

Observations like this naturally make us curious about the character and quality of feminism in societies outside of the United States. Like their counterparts in the United States, feminists in the non-Western world are committed to full equality for women in social, political, and economic life. Both groups face formidable barriers posed by sexist institutions in their search for equality. Finally, women all over the world are still a long way off from substantive equality with men, even with the gains made in recent years on women's issues. "Women in every country, Western and non-Western, industrialized and rural, modern and pre-modern, are underutilized in terms of their numbers, denied access to positions of prestige and power, and expected to find their primary fulfillment as mothers and wives."[3]

But no matter how similar are the situations in which women now find themselves, their historical experiences and responses to change vary widely across cultures. Each country's experience on the changing role of women in society is unique and must be judged on its own terms. The main purpose of this essay is to try to look closely at some of these cultures and to find what is truly unique as far as the emergence of feminism is concerned.

For comparative purposes and using mostly secondary sources, the American and Southeast Asian examples will be explored and analyzed with no intention of making value judgments. The Southeast Asian examples are drawn from historical and current experiences in feminist struggles in Vietnam, Indonesia, and the Philippines.

Feminism in America: Alive and Well

Despite the defeat of the Equal Rights Amendment (ERA) at the United States Congress in 1982, feminism is very much alive in contemporary American society. The largest feminist organization, the National Organization for Women (NOW), has once again begun to mobilize support for the reintroduction of ERA in Congress. It has also become more directly political in its strategy by campaigning at the grassroots to elect legislators who are supportive of women's issues and defeat those who are not. Millions of women are involved in this struggle and are linked to the movement through various organizational networks. It seems that the ERA setback has only served to increase the momentum of the women's movement in its continuing struggle for full sexual equality. It also seems that the ERA debacle has provided an opportunity for the movement to reflect on its previous mistakes and devise alternative strategies.

There is reason for renewed feminist activity in the United States. In a report released by the National Academy of Sciences in 1981, persistent discrimination and not free market forces was found to be the major cause for the wage differentials between men and women, i.e., women of all races who worked full-time in 1978 earned only 55.3% of what white men made in comparable jobs.[4] The concept of "comparable worth" was the main issue in a nine-day public employee strike in San Jose, California in July 1981, which ended in a victory for the women workers whose wages were raised to put them at par with the men.

This legal battle to end sexual discrimination in employment has been a major issue in American feminism since World War II with the entry of millions of women in the labor force. A uniform pay scale was proposed as early as September 1942 when the National War Labor Board adopted the equal pay principle "for female employees who in comparable jobs produce work of the same quantity and quality as that performed by men."[5] The fact that the pay equity issue has not been resolved and women continue to earn substantially less than men in the workplace after forty years is living proof of the tenacity of institutional discrimination. Feminist leaders think that ERA would have been a major step in resolving the sex discrimination in employment issue, by providing a nationwide, rather than piecemeal, framework to combat discriminatory practices and policies.

It is not possible to detail the long history and complexity of American feminism, but one issue, the unnecessary shrillness that Mahajani deplored, probably deserves comment here. There has always been a tradition of militancy in the American feminist movement, and this would probably be true in other countries as well. This militancy peaked during the heady days of women's liberation in the late '60s and early '70s. American feminists, whatever their ideological persuasion, have been highly visible, articulate, and uncompromising in their respective positions on "the woman question." Current feminist theory in America divides along three major ideological groupings, i.e., radical feminist,

Marxist, and socialist feminist. Shulamith Firestone started this ideological dialogue in 1970 with the publication of her pioneering work on radical feminism called The Dialectic of Sex.

It is possible that it is the strident dimension of the women's movement that is readily perceived by non-Western feminists, who consequently label it as anti-male, offensive, hostile, etc. There was only one large demonstration in Atlantic City on September 7, 1968 to protest the Miss America contest in which the feminists enjoined women to "bring old bras, girdles, high-heeled shoes, women's magazines, curlers, and other instruments of torture to women" to be discarded in a symbolic trashcan.[6] But not one bra was in fact burned, and so this myth of "bra-burning" which is used to trivialize feminism is a misrepresentation essentially created by the media.

In Asia, feminism has a much longer history and women's movements there, while basically addressing the main issues of oppression and exploitation, have not developed as autonomously as in the West. As will be seen in the following examples, feminism flourished in that region, at a time of revolutions and national upheavals.

Women in Southeast Asia

There is probably no other area of the world, comments anthropologist Cora Du Bois, so richly endowed with diverse cultural strains and so prepared to view the world tolerantly as Southeast Asia.[7] Indeed, this tremendous diversity arising from the mixture of indigenous, Hindu, Buddhist, Islamic, Christian, Chinese, European, and other cultures makes it difficult to generalize about Southeast Asia. Any generalizations made here therefore should be interpreted with caution and seen only as tentative or partial simplifications of reality.

Unlike in Western industrial societies where the majority of people have more or less gravitated to the urban centers, populations in Southeast Asia are still highly concentrated in the rural areas. The vast majority of women in Southeast Asia live in villages or towns with limited or no access to educational, health, social and other facilities or resources. Urbanization has not touched, or is just beginning to touch, their lives. The middle and upper-class women, who are far fewer in number, live in much more modern environments in the cities and bigger towns. They are products of, or have been exposed to, Western influences. Class differences exist to a pronounced degree and elite women are a world apart from the great majority of peasant or village women in Southeast Asian societies. There is not only a great deal of variation among women across cultures, but within them.

As a whole, however, women in Southeast Asia generally have had greater mobility and higher status than their counterparts in South and East Asia and the Middle East. Traditional Southeast Asian cultures did not have the very rigid clan systems that severely restricted women's freedom in places like ancient India and China. They also did not observe such customs as purdah, suttee, footbinding, child marriage, and other restrictive practices that reduced women to virtual prisoners, slaves, or properties owned and controlled by men. The status of women was high in pre-colonial Southeast Asia and in fact matrilineal societies existed in the region.

The growing literature on Southeast Asian women document instances of the dynamic and active role of women in various societies before the coming of Western imperialism and organized religions, which summarily imposed their own codes of morality on these cultures. Women in pre-contact times served as ruling queens, priestesses, warriors, and patrons of art. Women in the non-ruling classes worked in the fields, sold their produce in the markets, and engaged in various forms of trading activity.

Malay women, for instance, "especially those from Negri Sembilan and parts of Malacca, often draw attention to their matriarchal social organization in the past as indication of their high position in days gone by."[8] Women owned land which was traditionally passed on through the female line. Malay women were also traditionally active in small-scale trading in villages and towns. Women in pre-Spanish Philippines could assume the headship of the barangay* and Filipino folklore speaks glowingly of figures like Princess Urduja.[9] In Indonesia, various examples, such as the Minangkabau and Ambonese, show the high traditional status of women. "All evidence supports the conclusion that the woman's position in traditional Indonesian community has always been very elevated."[10] In Burma, the biological family is called a "mitha-su," meaning "a mother-child group." A well-known anthropologist hypothesizes that the stock's founding female "contributes more than its founding male to its common kinship."[11] He cautions, however, that this is a tentative proposition and more research needs to be done on the role and status of women in traditional Burmese society. One reason that is usually given to explain the greater status and mobility of Southeast Asian women is the existence of a bilateral kinship system, which means tracing one's descent from both parents rather than from a single patriarchal or matriarchal ancestry. Every individual therefore is equally related to the relatives of both parents, although in practice, some relatives are regarded more important than others. This

*A settlement composed of anywhere from thirty to a hundred families, which served as the main social, economic and political unit in the Philippines before the Spanish conquest in the 16th century.

has consequences that affect the status of women. For example, they are "never removed from the support of their kinsmen and that partial self-selection of mates exists for both males and females."[12] Bilateralism also means that inherited property is divided equally among all children regardless of sex, although again this may not always be true in practice. But at least, female children can hope or expect to acquire property. Thus they have some access to decision-making authority and do make "many of the families' investment decisions including the establishment of business in which women performed all the marketing functions, purchased the land, directed agricultural production, and determine which children would receive education and for how long."[13] It is also observed that in a bilateral kinship system, women are likely to develop a strong sense of self-esteem, "in part because as children, little girls are given a great deal of responsibility whereas little boys are not."[14] This seems to be true in Philippine society where, as Filipina sociologist Mary Hollnsteiner says, survey data indicate that Filipino men expect women to be better than they are.[15] The general attitude seems to be "boys will be boys" but girls are expected to be morally superior and to do better. Boys expect to be forgiven their excesses or even failures for the simple reason that they are boys, but girls are expected to be disciplined and responsible. However, this double standard can put a disproportionate burden of duties and responsibilities on women, and can have negative consequences, according to Hollnsteiner, "if it keeps a woman apart and prevents her from participating as fully as she wants in the life of the community."[16]

Thus, in Southeast Asian countries like Burma, Thailand, Indonesia and the Philippines, the traditional social structure, the division of labor between the sexes, and the acquisition and management of property and business by women have contributed to their relatively greater status and mobility. "Members of small, simple (or 'nuclear') two-generation family households usually with near relatives living close at hand, these Southeast Asian women have been subjected neither to the overriding rule of mother-in-law as in India or China, nor to the overriding demands of domesticity, as in the West."[17]

There was, we may conclude, a strong strain of indigenous feminism in Southeast Asia, which was undermined but not completely wiped out, by the subsequent incursions of Buddhism, Islam, Christianity, Western colonialism, and other external influences into the region. The following section will analyze the impact of Western colonial rule on the role and status of women in Southeast Asia.

The Coming of The West

The Western impact on women in the colonized societies is something of a paradox. On the one hand, it is seen as having given women a "modern" personality and education. Women became teachers, lawyers, doctors, engineers, nurses, chemists, even politicians, under the aegis of Westernization. Opportunities were opened up for the acquisition of new skills and training for employment, health care, nutrition and other areas. Improved communication and transportation facilities enabled several women to expand their activities and goals in life. Only the privileged women from the upper classes however, benefited from these new opportunities. Peasant and lower-class women were never brought into the mainstream of colonial rule.

On the other hand, as Ester Boserup has argued, women suffered a loss of status under European rule, particularly in the agricultural systems of the colonized countries. She points out that European settlers, colonial administrators and technical advisers are responsible for this loss of status by neglecting the female agricultural labor force when "they helped to introduce modern commercial agriculture to the overseas world and promoted the productivity of male labour."[18] Virtually all Europeans, she adds, believed that men were superior to women in the art of farming and therefore the latter were discouraged or excluded from participating in agriculture. Men were taught modern methods of cultivation and the spread of education saw many more males than females going to school for agricultural training and scientific research. Women were left to do the menial jobs such as weeding and carrying loads on their heads while the men used the bicycles or trucks. "In short men represent modern farming in the village, women represent the old drudgery."[19] Under European administration, land rights were also transferred from women to men. In the Negri Sembilan example mentioned earlier, in which land was owned by women, the British changed this practice by allowing only land under cultivation to pass through the female line. This had the effect of making women lose their rights over forest land--a "significant loss when the men began to plant rubber trees in the forest areas."[20]

The position of Vietnamese peasant women also declined under the French whose policies and monopolies virtually destroyed the traditional crafts and occupations of women and made them dependent on men for their survival.[21] Several Vietnamese accounts during the French colonial period document stories of women being mistreated and committing suicide.[22]

Another negative effect of Westernization on Southeast Asian women was the curtailment of the mobility and freedom they enjoyed in traditional times. Of course, this is not to be entirely attributed to Western colonial rule since the introduction of non-Western organized religions like Islam also led to the seclusion and subjugation of women. But in most cases, the coming of the West brought with it an alien cultural and religious system as well, which would relegate women to an inferior status vis-a-vis men. Nowhere was this transformation to the "colonized woman" more dramatic than in the case of the Philippines, which underwent nearly four hundred years of Spanish and American rule. The imposition of Spanish Catholicism carried with it a puritanical and subservient Victorian model for Filipino women, i.e, Maria Clara. She was the shy, protected, melancholy, and tragic heroine of the novels of Jose Rizal, the Filipino national hero who was executed by the Spaniards in 1896. Modelled after Rizal's real-life sweetheart, Maria Clara was intended to symbolize the Philippines as a country oppressed by Spanish colonialism. But for some reason, Maria Clara became the paragon of Filipino female virtue. An outspoken feminist in the Philippines calls this the greatest misfortune that has befallen Filipino women in the last one hundred years. In a very real sense, Carmen Guerrero-Nakpil argues, millions of Filipino women trying to live up to the Maria Clara mystique became other than their real selves. Elaborating on this characterization, which particularly refers to bourgeois women, Nakpil adds, "They forced their persons into the narrow mold of Maria Clara's maidenly charms and became effete and exceedingly genteel caricatures. They affected modesty to an absurd degree and became martyrs to duty and familial love. They tried to disguise their native industry and energy with put-on airs of languidity. And because Maria Clara was ill so often, and so elaborately sad and tragic, it became vulgar to be healthy and almost un-Filipina to be happy."[23] Thus, the Spanish period set up a false symbol for Filipino women that emphasized obedience to and dependence on male authority, sentimentalism, gentleness, sacrifice, and especially proper behavior. This may have started the whole sexist character of Philippine society, which frowns upon open, aggressive, and independent female behavior. Parents socialized their daughters to be feminine, patient, understanding, considerate, forgiving, and "not to argue." Defiant female behavior is chided but for boys, it is "natural." Fortunately, the cult of Maria Clara has largely disappeared and she is nothing more than a caricature of a bygone age in present-day Philippine society.

American colonial policy in Philippines did not significantly reverse this conservative feminine trend, although it introduced universal education and opened up new social opportunities for Filipino women. Compared to the Spanish, American policy was much more enlightened, but judged on its own, it did not actively encourage the full expression of female equality and independence. It was Filipino feminists like Encarnacion Alzona and Carmen Planas, among others, who worked feverishly for the passage of women's suffrage in the 1930s. American feminists at the time, like Carrie Chapman Catt, supported the incipient women's movement in the Philippines. Catt visited the Philippines and gave speeches on equal rights for women similar to those she had delivered in various places in the United States. Many Filipino feminists also came to America to pursue graduate education. Alzona, mentioned earlier, was the first Filipino and probably the first Asian woman to become a Barbour scholar at the University of Michigan in the 1930s.

The other major outgrowth of Western imperialism in Southeast Asia was the development of a nationalist consciousness, which brought women into the mainstream of national independence or liberation struggles against the colonial powers. The women did not wage these struggles on their own. They became part of a bigger revolution to regain national sovereignty from the Western rulers. History books underplay or hardly mention the role of women in Southeast Asian nationalist movements, but more and more research on Asian women is being done and we now have fuller accounts of their activities in the past.

Revolutionary Feminism in Southeast Asia: The Vietnamese Example

The most militant form of feminism in Southeast Asia is exemplified by Vietnamese women, who have a long tradition and history of struggle against feudal and colonial oppression. The legendary Trung sisters led the first national insurrection against Chinese invaders in 40 A.D. One sister, Trung Trac, was the strategist who won the confidence of her people by killing a tiger and using the tiger skin to write a proclamation urging the Vietnamese to resist the Chinese. The other sister was a fearless warrior. "They issued a call to all people to share responsibility for leading the insurrection. From those who came forward, they chose 36 women, including their mother. They trained these women to be generals."[24] After their victory, Trung Trac was renamed by her followers "Trung Vuong," meaning, "She-king Trung." However, the Chinese were militarily superior and kept coming back to defeat the Vietnamese. Rather than capitulate, the sisters maintained their Vietnamese pride and dignity, and committed suicide.

Subsequent historical developments in Vietnam brought a long and violent colonial rule under the French and an equally violent period of American intervention. As early as 1905 and 1906, women resisted the French colonialists in order to survive, and engaged in sabotage activities in the countryside. One woman innkeeper was known to have poisoned 200 French soldiers occupying her district.[25] A Women's Labor-Study Association was founded which enjoined women to reject the moral code prescribed by the "Three Obediences," i.e., as a child, a daughter unconditionally obeyed her father; as a married woman, her obedience extended to her husband; and as a widow, she was bound to obey her eldest son. This was described as patriarchy in its purest form, which was observed more in the elite classes in Vietnamese society.

The continuing resistance of women, which included thousands of factory workers, led to the birth of the Women's Union in 1930. The Indochinese Communist Party (ICP) incorporated the women's twin struggle against patriarchal feudalism and French colonialism. It sought to defend the rights and interests of women and their revolutionary consciousness. Ho Chi Minh enthusiastically supported the women's struggle by repeatedly saying women made up half of society and if they were not liberated, society would not be free. The women organized mutual aid societies for weddings, funerals, and other social events and recruited new members to the Union on these occasions. Village life and a tradition of resistance in Vietnamese culture strengthened solidarity among the women. They increasingly became political and in 1938, 500 of them attended a mass rally in Hanoi in which they voiced their demands for democratic rights and grievances against forced marriages. Subsequently the Union organized the Women's Association for National Salvation for guerrilla activity. They became part of the Vietminh and participated in armed operations against the French and Japanese. "Some women... formed collectives to purchase arms and transport weapons. They opened inns and restaurants to finance the movement. They served as liaison, protected other revolutionaries, agitated among the enemy soldiers and served as spies."[26]

Even if the Communist Party subsumed the smaller women's struggle, the leadership encouraged the women activists in 1959 to intensify their own movement for emancipation. Le Duan, one of the top leaders of the Democratic Republic of Vietnam "echoed Ho Chi Minh" when he said, "...women should not merely take part in a general movement but also build a revolutionary movement of their own."[27]

This commitment to women's liberation, the high degree of political unity among the women, and their organizing skills were once more put to a test by the arrival of the Americans after the defeat of the French. Jayne Werner has documented the dramatic increases in women's economic and political roles during the second resistance war (1965-1973).[28] She argues that during this period, sexual equality and women's liberation became a special focus of Party policy. "New policies and decrees were formulated to increase women's productive capacity and political participation. Party initiatives in promoting the fuller participation of women clustered around the years 1960 to 1967. They were tied to efforts to increase economic production as a result of the escalating war against the United States."[29] One of the major campaigns involving women was the "Three Responsibilities" movement, so-called because it entailed: 1) fighting to defend the country; 2) replacing the men who had gone to the battlefront and taking charge of the household; and 3) preparing husbands and sons to build a socialist Vietnamese society. In the South, women played an equally crucial role, not only by taking up jobs that the men left behind. Women were more involved in day-to-day fighting and frequently had the responsibility of "liberating certain villages and of setting up new governments in border areas."[30]

In a spirit of solidarity with the American women's movement, Le Thi Xuyen of the Vietnam Women's Union wrote on May 17, 1972:

> ...This great victory is inseparable from your militant solidarity, assistance and support as well as that of all women and peace- and justice-loving people in the world. We always remember your beautiful deeds and lofty activities that find full expression in rallies, demonstrations, petitions, leaflets, cables, letters in protest against the U.S. aggressive war in Vietnam in the past years...We think that our victory is also yours..."[31]

Although Vietnamese women have made great strides in women's liberation mainly through revolutionary feminism, this does not mean that full sexual equality has been achieved. Werner notes that the Party's commitment to women's equality appears to have waned after the war and that the sexual division of labor, the nature of the socialist economy, the household structure, and the cultural expressions of these factors pose continuing obstacles to full equality.[32] Nevertheless, in Southeast Asia, the Vietnamese provide the best example of militant feminism that probably surpasses the experience of the West in comparable times.

Indonesian Women And The Nationalist Movement

Very few accounts exist on the role of women in Southeast Asian nationalist movements, which led the struggles for independence from colonial rule in various countries. Nationalism is usually equated with a charismatic leader or "father figure," such as Sukarno, Ho Chi Minh, Sihanouk, Aung San, Tunku Abdul Rahman, Rizal, etc. Yet, as the Vietnamese case discussed above shows, women and women leaders were very much part of the movements in their societies.

Another example worth mentioning here is the role of Indonesian women in the nationalist struggle against the Dutch. Indonesian feminism usually evokes the name of Raden Adjeng Kartini, the Javanese princess whose letters in the early 1900s became part of "the early drive for female emancipation which led to the intellectual and social coming of age of the Indonesian woman, in the sense that she achieved a new kind of freedom of action and at the same time equal rights."[33] Kartini's views rebelled against traditional patterns of Javanese behavior predominant at the time. Raise the Javanese woman, she once wrote, "educate her heart and her understanding. Teach her a trade, so that she will no longer be powerless when her guardians command her to contract a marriage which will inevitably plunge her and whatever children she may have into misery. The only escape from such conditions is for the girl to learn to be independent."[34] Unfortunately, Kartini's early death at age 25 prevented her from seeing some of the gains made in later years on the political and legal emancipation of women in Indonesian society.

In 1928, when the first Indonesian Women's Congress was held, women had become an important part of the nationalist movement. The most significant result of the Congress was the founding of a women's federation, the <u>Perikatan Perempuan Indonesia</u> (PPI), which advocated more rights and an improved social position for women in Indonesian society.[35] Like their Vietnamese counterparts, the Indonesian women had to reckon with a double struggle: in the latter case, against Dutch colonialism and the restrictions imposed by Islamic law.

When the 1945 Revolution against the Dutch was launched, several women's associations were drawn into the movement and performed a variety of tasks that included anything from cooking to espionage. "They rallied in large numbers to help the guerrillas behind the fighting line...the women organized themselves into teams of nurses and liaison officers; they operated soup kitchens and mobile clinics."[36] During this period, the best-known women's organization to emerge was the PERWANI (Union of Indonesian Women), which initiated the first congress after the proclamation of Indonesian sovereignty in December 1945. In this meeting, PERWANI and other women's associations united into yet another bigger organization called PERWARI (Union of the Women of the Indonesian Republic), whose immediate goal was "to form the rear-guard in defense of the country's liberty." Finally, as the revolution against the Dutch continued, the women formed a permanent federation called <u>Badan Kongress Wanita Indonesia</u>, or KOWANI, which presided over the second postwar congress of Indonesian women in East Java in June 1946. Several KOWANI congresses were held subsequently, and in the fourth one, held in August 1948, the association adopted the <u>Pantjasila</u> program laid down by Sukarno in 1945, which emphasized five basic principles, namely, belief in God, respect for human values, nationalism, democracy, and social justice. These yearly congresses were important not only in reinforcing the women's commitment to the achievement of national sovereignty, but also in ironing out political dissension among the various women's groups. "Such conferences had not been held nearly so frequently in the past, but this was a [revolutionary] period during which there was a continuing need, both for mobilization of as much of the population as possible and for repeated expression of the intense public commitment to nationalism."[37]

In sum, the revolution crystallized and consolidated the women's movement in Indonesia, which has long roots in the history and cultural traditions of the country. The end of colonial rule found the women more organized and forceful in demanding "more governmental attention to such problems as employment opportunities for females, marriage legislation, growing threats to public morals, and the like."[38]

Both the Vietnamese and Indonesian cases are historical examples of feminist activity inspired and propelled by revolutions in an atmosphere of colonial rule. Today, the colonial masters are gone but many nationalist or liberation groups, which include large numbers of mostly young women, are still very much around. This time they are fighting against their own governments or ruling elites, which they see as neo-colonial and repressive. It is instructive at this point to examine one contemporary example of Southeast Asian feminism in a country that underwent two prolonged colonial experiences.

The Philippines: Bourgeois and Radical Feminism

To some observers, the achievements of Filipino women are cited as the most striking examples of rapid advance for women on all fronts in Asia.[39] They have made tremendous contributions to education, government, labor, business, the professions, and have substantially affected the political process as well. They are the equals of men, remarks anthropologist Robert Fox, and the relationships between Filipino men and women are "remarkably equalitarian."[40] This is a highly positive view of Filipino women, which occasionally leads to such facetious remarks as, perhaps it is the Filipino males who need liberating.

These observations pertain more to articulate, highly-educated, and, in many cases, wealthy Filipino bourgeois women, who have indeed excelled in their respective callings. Most existing accounts highlight the accomplishments of this particular group of women in such fields as politics, law, labor, business, social welfare, education, and various areas of "national development." One such group is the Concerned Women of the Philippines (CWP), which counts among its ranks Cecilia Munoz Palma, retired Supreme Court justice who was the first Filipino woman to be named to the high court. Her colleagues include women who are prominent in elite circles such as Paz Policarpio Mendez (university dean), Mita Pardo de Tavera (physician), Mary Concepcion Bautista (lawyer), Teresa Nieva (executive director), and Eulalia Hidalgo Lim (business executive). The CWP has waged several battles with giant corporations like the Meralco (Manila Electric Company) and even with the government itself. It has represented workers against oppressive employers, helped political detainees, advocated freedom of the press, established health services, and organized other women around community issues. It has gone further than these and has protested military abuses in the current regime and has collaborated with the Third World Movement Against Exploitation of Women to denounce the degradation of Filipino women through sex tours encouraged in some government circles. It has also supported the efforts of the Nuclear-Free Philippines Coalition in opposing the establishment of nuclear plants. The major goals of CWP are:

> ...the promotion of human dignity; the restoration and protection of civil liberties and human rights through peaceful

and legal means; the equitable distribution
of the country's wealth and resources; the
defense of the poor, the exploited, and the
victims of injustice; the preservation of
the patrimony of the nation; the assurance
of a legacy of justice and freedom to our
children.[41]

These are fairly liberal and progressive ends compared to
earlier traditional women's organizations such as the Catholic
Women's League, which emphasized social graces, domestic bliss,
and other conservative goals. The presence of Palma in the
group is bound to have some "radicalizing" effect. As a
Supreme Court justice, she had opposed many of Marcos' decrees
and fought fiercely for civil liberties and individual rights.
Concerning her role in CWP, she says women should not only be
concerned with helping flood victims and giving scholarships.
She thinks these are all right but "we should not forget that
we are citizens of this country so we should be involved in
issues. Just like during this critical period [the Marcos
regime]. I think this is a period of testing for our women.
Many women's groups are too limited to traditional concerns.
They shy away from political issues...It's rather
disappointing."[42]

While Palma's observation is true for many existing women's
organizations, it does not apply to at least one group that has
opted to go underground and promote revolutionary struggle
against the system. Radical feminism in the Philippines today
is associated with the activities of young, educated, and
committed women who have either joined or are supporting the
New People's Army (NPA) and other radical organizations. It is
not known exactly how many women there are in the underground
but they are certainly not few. An indication of their numbers
can be seen from the ranks of political prisoners who are now
in the various detention centers maintained by the regime.
Many of them are young, articulate women who are picked up by

the military for "subversive" work like organizing community groups or suspected links with the NPA.

The NPA is a growing mass movement in the Philippines which advocates national liberation through armed resistance. It was formed in 1969 with no more than 60 members as the military arm of the re-established Communist Party of the Philippines. Today it is reported to have between 5,000 to 7,000 regulars and is active in such places as North and Northeastern Luzon, Central Luzon, Bicol, Panay, Samar, and Mindanao. The NPA is seen as the only thriving people's movement in Southeast Asia and the Marcos regime has expended enormous amounts of military and governmental resources trying to contain it.

Why have young women abandoned the comfort of their homes and joined this underground movement at the risk of their lives and safety? The answer to this question is best provided by a well-known woman cadre, Clarita Roja (not her real name), who is also a poet. Coming from a middle-class background, she joined the incipient movement in 1970 after attending the University of the Philippines, convinced that active participation in the "national democratic revolution" was the only way women would gain the knowledge they have been deprived of for centuries. In a letter dated July 1973, Roja details some of the major gains made by women as they operate in the countryside away from the mainstream of Philippine society:

> An underground house is first and foremost a productive unit in the most general sense of the term. Even in posts where unit members do not "produce" in the material sense of the term, all are enjoined to conduct political work, if not among the masses, among themselves...A woman's part in the struggle for production and the class struggle therefore becomes for her very real, very felt. The leap in her consciousness becomes tremendous. In addition, since she performs ideological, political and organizational tasks as heavy as the men's, adjustments are made so that she alone is not tied down to the kitchen,

housework and children. Toward this end, household chores are rotated, assignments going to men and women alike.[43]

The beginnings of the current militant orientation of the women in the underground may be traced to 1970 with the founding of Malayang Kilusan ng Bagong Kababaihan (Free Movement of the New Women), or MAKIBAKA, for short. This was the first women's liberation organization in the country formed during the height of the radical student movement two years before the declaration of martial law in 1972. Its founder, Maria Lorena Barros, was a student activist at the University of the Philippines, where she eventually obtained her B.A. in Anthropology. She led the first MAKIBAKA mass action, which was to picket the Miss Philippines beauty pageant on April 18, 1970. "The picket attacked the commercialization of sex, the degradation of women as objects of pleasure, and the irrelevance of beauty contests in a poverty-stricken country."[44] MAKIBAKA activists later gravitated outside of Manila to do political work among women in factories and in the barrios. When President Marcos suspended the writ of habeas corpus in August 1971, Barros and other activists went underground and continued organizing among the people. She was arrested in October 1973 and tortured in prison, but escaped in 1974 with four other detainees. She headed up a squad of the NPA and operated in the Bicol region. In addition to her revolutionary duties, she became a wife and a mother. She also wrote poems, stories, and essays. In March 1976, she was captured by the Philippine military and killed in front of her hut in a village in Quezon province. She was only 26 years old. MAKIBAKA was short-lived but it started a new wave of militant feminism that young women cadres have taken up as part of their revolutionary struggle. Some of these women's lives are presented as case histories in a recent book which was fictionalized to protect their identities.[45]

No less militant are the activities of a growing number of Filipino nuns, sometimes referred to as "the religious radicals." They are not working on strictly feminist concerns but on a wide array of social issues. The violations of human rights under martial law saw the emergence of a politicized clergy which began to espouse the "theology of liberation," i.e., that their duties as religious should also include fighting against injustice and oppression. Nuns work among workers, squatters and slumdwellers, families of political detainees, and community groups, teaching them to organize and become more aware of their rights. This consciousness-raising process is known in Philippine religious circles as "conscientization." The most well-known of these activist nuns is Sister Mariani Dimaranan of the Franciscan order. She was the first woman religious figure to be arrested in October 1973 and detained in a military camp for 47 days for being a "subversive." When she was released, she organized the Task Force of Detainees (TFD) of the Association of Major Religious Superiors of the Philippines to look after the needs of political prisoners and their families. She takes long trips to the provinces checking out reported cases of human rights violations by military or para-military elements of the regime. Under her direction, TFD has published various documents on such violations and helped the victims by providing legal and financial assistance, much of which is raised by Sister Mariani herself during her trips in the Philippines and abroad.

Another activist nun, Sister Christine Tan, is involved in the campaign to withdraw the American bases from Philippine soil and in anti-nuclear issues. Coming from bourgeois origins, Sister Christine now lives among the urban poor in Manila along with four other Good Shepherd nuns. "Conventional religious life cannot respond to the screams of the people," she claims. "We have to live like the 80 per cent who are poor. Otherwise we will be a living lie to the people we serve."[46]   Like Sister Mariani, Sister Christine was also arrested in 1980 for her political activism.

There are other feminist causes in the Philippines that are too numerous to discuss in detail in this essay. One of these, the Third World Movement Against Exploitation of Women, is alarmed at the rise of the so-called "hospitality industry," a euphemism for prostitution in Philippine society, and has issued several indictments against those promoting it. In a very direct way, the government has exacerbated this problem by aggressively promoting tourism, a dollar-earning industry. The week-end "sex tours" in Manila are widely publicized, along with such exploitative promotional campaigns as the "mail-order bride" business. The Center for Women Resources (CWR), which was set up to counter these trends, has delivered this message:

> The gallery of women's problems will be an increasing concern among policymakers. But the roots of their problem can only be unearthed and destroyed if women (prostitutes included) as a collective force become conscious, mobilize huge numbers to build a national movement....We shall put our house in order.[47]

Since very early in its history, feminism has always been a lively and vital force in Philippine culture, existing or dividing along bourgeois, moderate, or radical streams. Historical developments in Philippine society have seen the emergence of diverse feminist models and philosophies: from the militant tradition of the first woman general, Gabriela Silang, to the more laid-back posture of such elite female leaders as Librada Avelino, Sofia de Veyra, Jacinta Zaera de Cailles, Maria Ylagan Orosa, etc. Like their counterparts in Asia and other countries, Filipino women today, in general terms, have not achieved the conditions for full equality with men. The broader goal, that of women's liberation, is appealing to certain sectors of society, particularly among young, articulate and politically aware women, and among those who feel trapped and restless in a society that perpetuates traditional male dominance and repressive measures like the lack of divorce. However, women's liberation will probably not develop along the strong ideological and independent lines of Western feminism, as we will see.

Feminism in Different Cultural Contexts

The above examples of feminist activity in Southeast Asia demonstrate the meaning of historical experience and cultural traditions for women's roles and positions in society. This can probably be better appreciated if we point out some of its salient differences or similarities with American feminist philosophy and practice.

American feminism stresses sexual equality, which some scholars have conceptualized as an androgynous model.[48] Basic to this model is the freedom for both men and women to choose their roles and behaviors. Options available to males should be open to females as well. Oppression results from reinforcing the roles of women as wives and mothers and discouraging them from seeking new or alternative roles. This "sex-role stereotyping," which is perpetuated by the family and other social institutions has relegated women to subordinate and inferior positions. The American feminist critique challenges some of the most fundamental assumptions about the nature of men and women in society, and advocates radical change in its major institutions. "Each major branch of the women's movement--women's rights and women's liberation--from its own perspective is working toward the elimination of the sex-role system: by external reform of social institutions and internal raising of consciousness, respectively."[49] The twin institutions of patriarchy and capitalism are seen as the major factors that systematically devalue the roles of women and exclude them from positions of power and importance in society.

In Southeast Asian cultures, the tendency is not as strong as in the West to confront the traditional social structure and fault the family or male authority for injustice to women. The female self-concept is less individualistic and is defined by a more complex set of institutions that do not necessarily emphasize abstract notions of self-help, equality, independence, justice, and control over one's life. Instead, such values as solidarity, reciprocity, cooperation, harmony, and unity are stressed. One's family or kin group is paramount, and is seen as an institution to be preserved and strengthened rather than questioned. Of course, it is also being eroded gradually by the demands of modernization. But for the most part in contemporary Southeast Asia, family solidarity is still very much the norm.

The family-oriented socialization one goes through is hierarchical and generally marked by the sex-role "oppression" that American feminists deplore. But women in Southeast Asia, even those who would call themselves "feminists," think of their families first and do not lament the heavier domestic burdens that they end up having even if they, like their husbands, hold down full-time careers. There is a strong inclination among Filipino women, which could be true elsewhere in Southeast Asia, to act more as partners or supporters, rather than as equals of men. They value complementary or compensatory roles rather than separate ones. There is still much of that nurturing quality that women are noted for. But Nakpil, Filipino feminist mentioned earlier, takes issue with this. "We have spoiled the men," she says. "Not only have we spoiled them, but the majority of women do not like the idea of talking about their rights."[50] She adds that women think these rights may turn into duty, and therefore the price for independence is high. In true feminist fashion, she urges "an internal revolution in every woman" and "to make up her mind to become a person first." This is similar to what Kate Millett

or Shulamith Firestone would say, which indicates that the
liberation concept is appealing to a particular class of women
in Asia. Nakpil, however, hastens to add, "There is no
confrontation. We don't consider man an enemy, to be exploited
and to be outwitted."[51] This response seems to be typical of
the ambivalence with which feminists in Southeast Asia deal
with such issues as rights and equality. Equal rights can be
achieved without upsetting the traditional male role or
cultural values. They do not see this as a contradiction. Or
perhaps they do, but they could live with it. This is an
empirical question and much more research needs to be done on
the nature and roots of this ambivalence. Are women really
facing a conflict between desires for independence and equality
and the demands of traditional culture?

Inequality is the other side of the issue and here, the
American and Southeast Asian examples appear to be divergent.
As noted earlier, redressing sexual inequality is the major
agenda of most feminist groups in America. In Southeast Asia,
where as high as 80% of the populations of certain countries
live under conditions of poverty, class inequality is a much
more pervasive phenomenon than sexual inequality. And women in
such societies are subject to the double-bind of class and male
oppression. It is argued that it is this vast majority of men
and women in the lower class strata in the factories, slums,
and depressed rural areas that need to be liberated from
poverty, illiteracy, disease, and economic deprivation.
Revolution is advocated in many of these countries as the
ultimate liberation of the underprivileged classes in society.
Other groups see education as the basic means to reduce class
disparities. As an Indian feminist has argued, "The
Constitution of India guarantees equal rights to women, but how
can illiterate women exercise their rights?"[52] The
Constitutions of other Asian countries also enshrine the goal
of equality and women's rights, but profound class differences

between elites and masses and widespread socio-economic inequality make that an irrelevant and meaningless, if not an unattainable, condition.

Thus, class, rather than sex, is the more significant variable in analyzing the role and status of women in Third World countries. This is not to say that sexual inequality is unimportant. But as an Asian woman church leader notes, there are differences which go beyond sex and culture. "We must make a special effort to realize the differences between generations and economic classes. If we can understand and respect differences, and unify in our struggle, radical feminism will be a powerful force in the liberation of our people."[53]

In American feminist circles, there is some concern about the rights of lower-class and minority women living in ghettos and depressed neighborhoods, whose basic needs are adequate housing, employment, day-care, and other social services. But the main thrust of the women's movement is still oriented to resolving questions on the basis of sex. Now, there is apparently a second stage in the American sexual revolution which is being called "men's liberation." Feminist high priestess Betty Friedan comments that "American men are on the edge of a tidal wave of change--a change in their very identity as men."[54] In short, the traditional male image of masculinity and aggressiveness is "softening" towards the personal, emotional qualities that are normally associated with women.

Sexual liberation is not unknown in Southeast Asia and a few observers would comment that it is already happening in the major cosmopolitan centers of the region. As to whether it will become a major issue deserving of serious policy consideration in government and professional circles is another matter. Historical traditions, cultural conditioning, religious norms and conservative political ideas inhibit the kind of openness on sexuality that we see in America.

Consequently, sex-related issues like sex education in the schools, abortion legislation, gay rights, etc., are not likely to become popular in Southeast Asian societies, such as the Philippines, where even milder measures like divorce are not legal. Feminist efforts will probably remain conservative for some time and revolve around areas such as law, education, employment, social services, and other programs of national development. Many of these countries are still suffering from the backwash effects of Western or internal colonialism, and major priorities will concentrate on economic development, however that is defined.

Another significant difference between the Americans and Southeast Asian perspective lies in the concept of liberation itself. As has been said earlier, American women's liberation tends to devalue the family unit and the sexual division of labor. Women are asked to alter their consciousness and elevate the "personal" to the "political." Women whose beliefs were shaped by "the feminine mystique" began to see the need for self-fulfillment and self-identity. They broke out of the confines of domesticity to work in the civil rights and New Left movements in the sixties. Finding that they were only pouring coffee and providing companionship for the male leaders in these movements, the women became politicized and launched their own cause, based on a critique of family and personal life. They needed space to develop within and among themselves in an environment away from male or patriarchal dominance. Within a few years, the women's liberation movement had spread to various sectors of American society. This is one of the remarkable developments in contemporary America. The increasing numbers of women "going it alone" in American society in a sense testify to the acceptance of the feminist ethic.

Southeast Asian women were also washing the dishes, typing, pouring the coffee, making the soup, and taking orders from the men. And they still do. But the degree of alienation or resentment that American women liberationists felt while working with male "politicos" was not as bothersome to the Vietnamese, Indonesian, and Filipino women as they went about their tasks. This is essentially because the women who joined the nationalist movements were aware that there was a broader social and political revolution that was more urgent. Discipline required them to subordinate their personal desires and anxieties to the movement. There was no need to form a separate movement since, as in the Vietnamese case, the Communist Party leadership encouraged independent women's activities.

From the Western point of view, this could be interpreted as patronizing and sexist because the prevailing attitude seems to be, that women have to earn their equality, instead of being entitled to it. This argument would say that women have to prove themselves within the context and standards of male supremacy. This is therefore anti-feminist. But from the Southeast Asian view, these situations are not seen as threatening power relationships, which reinforce male prerogatives and demean women's dignity. Delia Aguilar notes that there are two dominant tendencies in Western feminist theory that fail to appreciate the role of women in national liberation struggles in other countries. These are, "the removal of women's issues" from the general social context and, not unrelated, the view that ideology is primary and autonomous of the national conditions of society."[55] There is merit in this argument if one examines the Southeast Asian experience in feminism, as presented above with these concrete examples. Women's issues and participation were integral parts of a larger socialist revolution or nationalist movement. It was not a male conspiracy to mystify and obfuscate feminist goals. As to the view that Western feminist ideology is not sufficiently materialist, it is instructive to remember Zillah

Eisenstein's suggestion of "beginning where most women are." Marxist and radical feminists have debated this issue for years, and the controversy has taken on a patriarchy versus capitalism aura. Eisenstein says that most women in the West, at least those who are involved in the movement, are "liberal feminist in their consciousness."[56] This essentially means their feminism springs from an ideology of individual freedom and choice.

The majority of women in the Third World are in the lowest classes of society, who cannot possibly see in their lifetimes things like affirmative action or equal opportunity before the law. Conditions in which they live are much more authoritarian and repressive, socially, economically, and politically. Any movement, therefore, that seeks to grant equality to women must be rooted in an understanding of the objective conditions of their reality. Hence, it is not entirely appropriate to apply the autonomous liberation ideology developed in the West to the conditions and struggles of women in other parts of the world. They have a different history and consequently, a different story.

Conclusion

Whatever the differences are between the feminist movements in America and Southeast Asia, each is unique on its own terms, and reflects increasing women's consciousness, if not strength, in facing up to formidable age-old barriers of reaction and oppression. The role of women and their contributions to history are just now beginning to be studied in a systematic and scholarly fashion. Comparative studies are truly valuable for as Alva Mydral comments, "the destiny of women is obviously conditioned to a large extent by the cultural climate in the different countries of the world."[57] She suggests that to be most meaningful, such comparative studies should concentrate on the profound changes that have occurred in the status of women.

I have attempted to show in this essay some of the major patterns of feminist thought and behavior in the American and Southeast Asian scene. Much more research needs to be done on the conditions, status, and role of women in various settings. As we do this, we will be able to expand, or even reformulate current feminist theories, which have evolved mostly out of the Western experience, and which necessarily have to change as we find new material on women across cultures and over time.

Belinda A. Aquino
University of Hawaii

Notes

1. See Lynne B. Iglitzin, "The Patriarchal Heritage," in Lynne B. Iglitzin and Ruth Ross, eds., Women in the World: A Comparative Study (Santa Barbara and Oxford: Clio Books, 1976), pp. 7-24.

2. Usha Mahajani, "Feminism in Southeast Asia," The Asian Student 25 (October 1975), p. 6.

3. Lynne B. Iglitzin, op. cit., p. 7.

4. See Donald J. Treiman and Heidi I. Hartman, eds., Women, Work, and Wages: Equal Pay for Jobs of Equal Value (Washington, D.C.: National Academy Press, 1981), Chapter 2.

5. Hoyt Gimlin, The Women's Movement - Agenda for the '80s (Washington, D.C.: Congressional Quarterly Inc., 1981), p. 12.

6. Judith Hole and Ellen Levine, eds., Rebirth of Feminism (New York: Quadrangle Books, 1971), p. 123.

7. Cora DuBois, Social Forces in Southeast Asia (Minneapolis: University of Minnesota Press, 1949), p. 27.

8. Betty Jamie Chung and Ng Shui Meng, The Status of Women in Law - A Comparison of Four Asian Countries (Singapore: Institute of Southeast Asian Studies, Occasional Paper No. 49, October 1977), p. 3.

9. See Teresita B. Infante, The Women in Early Philippines and Among the Cultural Minorities (Manila: University of Santo Tomas, 1969), for accounts of pre-colonial Filipino women.

10. Cora Vreede-De Stuers, The Indonesian Woman - Struggles and Achievements (The Hague: Mouton Land Co., 1960), p. 44.

11. Melford E. Spiro, Kinship and Marriage in Burma (Berkeley: University of California Press, 1977), p. 47.

12. Sylvia A. Chipp and Justin Green, eds., Asian Women in Transition (University Park and London: Pennsylvania State University, 1980), p. 105.

13. Ibid.

14. Ibid.

15. Mary Racelis Hollnsteiner, "Men Expect Women to be Better," Archipelago (Manila: Ministry of Public Information), II (1975), p. 18.

16. Ibid.

17. Barbara E. Ward, "Men, Women and Change: An Essay in Understanding Social Roles in South and South-East Asia," in Barbara E. Ward, ed., Women in the New Asia (Paris: UNESCO, 1963), p. 64.

18. Ester Boserup, Woman's Role in Economic Development (New York: St. Martin's Press, 1970), p. 54.

19. Ibid., p. 56.

20. Ibid., quoting Michael Swift, "Men and Women in Malay Society," in Barbara E. Ward, ed., Women in the New Asia (Paris: UNESCO, 1963), pp. 276-277.

349

21. See Ngo Ving Long et. al., Vietnamese Women in Society and Revolution I: The French Colonial Period (Cambridge, Mass.: Vietnam Resource Center, 1974), p. 35.

22. Ibid.

23. Carmen Guerrero-Nakpil, Woman Enough and Other Essays (Quezon City, Philippines: Vibal Publishing Co., 1963), p. 29.

24. Arlene Eisen Bergman, Women of Vietnam, rev. ed. (San Francisco: People's Press, 1975), p. 30.

25. "The Women Inn-Keeper at the Southern Gate," South Vietnam in Struggle 232 (January 20, 1974), p. 6, as quoted in Bergman, op. cit., p. 48.

26. Bergman, op. cit., p. 55.

27. Le Duan, "We Must View the Women's Question from a Class Standpoint," in On the Socialist Revolution in Vietnam 3 (Hanoi: Foreign Languages Publishing House, 1967), p. 114, as quoted in Bergman, op. cit., p. 206. Emphasis in the Vietnamese edition.

28. See Jayne Werner, "Women, Socialism, and the Economy of Wartime North Vietnam, 1960-1975," Studies in Comparative Communism XIV, 2-3 (Summer-Autumn 1981), pp. 165-190.

29. Ibid., p. 175.

30. Charlotte Bunch-weeks, "Asian Women in Revolution," Liberation Now! Writings from the Women's Liberation Movement (New York: Dell Publishing Co., Inc., 1971), p. 343.

31. Bergman, op. cit., p. 251. Letter was addressed to Bergman herself.

32. Werner, op. cit., p. 87.

33. Sartono Kartodirjo, Introduction to Letters of a Javanese Princess - Raden Adjeng Kartini, trans. by Agnes Louise Symmers (Kuala Lumpur: Oxford University Press, 1976), p. vii.

34. Ibid., pp. 118-119.

35. See Cora Vreede-De Stuers, op. cit., pp. 89-90.

36. Ibid., p. 114.

37. Stephen A. Douglas, "Women in Indonesian Politics," in Chip and Green, op. cit., p. 162.

38. Ibid., p. 163.

39. Barbara E. Ward, "Men, Women and Change: An Essay in Understanding Social Roles in South and South-East Asia," in Barbara E. Ward, ed., op. cit., p. 72.

40. Robert B. Fox, "Men and Women in the Philippines," in Barbara Ward, ed., ibid., p. 364.

41. Lorna Kalaw-Tirol, "The Concerned Women: Tomorrow May Be Too Late," Philippine Panorama, May 29, 1983, p. 3.

42. Ibid., p. 10.

43. "Letter to Mrs. D..." by Clarita Roja, July 1973, obtained through author's personal communication.

44. Leon Fortaleza, "Daughter of the People," Philippine Resistance III (1982), p. 12.

45. See Alison Wynne, No Time for Crying (Hong Kong: Resource Centre for Philippine Concerns, 1980).

46. Ma. Ceres P. Doyo, "The Sisters Have Come a Long Way," *Philippine Panorama*, May 29, 1983, p. 20.

47. Ma. Ceres P. Doyo, "The Prostitution Problem Must Be Viewed from a National, Even Global, Perspective," *Philippine Panorama*, May 29, 1983, p. 58.

48. See, for instance, Carolyn Heilbrun, *Toward a Recognition of Androgyny* (New York: Alfred A. Knopf, 1973).

49. Judith Hole and Ellen Levine, eds., *op. cit.*, p. 398.

50. Carmen Guerrero-Nakpil, "Work is Part Life," *Archipelago* (Manila: Ministry of Information) III, A-31 (1976), p. 15.

51. *Ibid.*, p. 17.

52. Agness Loyall, "Asian Women: A New Image," in Kiran Daniel and Lee Soo eds., *Asian Women Confront Challenge, Change* (Singapore: Christian Conference, n.d.), p. 8.

53. Rayann Ma, "Asian Women and the Peace Programme," in Daniel and Jin, eds., *op. cit.*, p. 12.

54. Betty Friedan, "Their Turn: How Men Are Changing," *Redbook*, May 1980, p. 23.

55. Delia Aguilar, "Feminism and the National Liberation Struggle in the Philippines," *Women's Studies International Forum* V, 3-4 (1982), p. 253.

56. Zillah Eisenstein, "Reform and/or Revolution: Towards a Unified Movement," in Lydia Sargent, ed., *Women and Revolution* (Boston: South End Press, 1981), p. 343.

57. Alva Mydral, "Afterward: New Research Directions," in Lynne B. Iglitzin and Ruth Ross, eds., *op. cit.*, p. 405.